THIS VAST BOOK OF NATURE

D1363665

AMERICAN LAND AND LIFE SERIES

Wayne Franklin, series editor

PAVEL CENKL

WRITING THE LANDSCAPE OF

This Vast Book

NEW HAMPSHIRE'S WHITE MOUNTAINS,

# of Nature

1784–1911

FOREWORD BY WAYNE FRANKLIN

UNIVERSITY OF IOWA PRESS

IOWA CITY

University of Iowa Press, Iowa City 52242

Copyright © 2006 by the University of Iowa Press

http://www.uiowa.edu/uiowapress

All rights reserved

Printed in the United States of America

Design by April Leidig-Higgins

The University of Iowa Press is a member of Green Press Initiative
and is committed to preserving natural resources.

Printed on acid-free paper

Library of Congress Cataloging-in-Publication Data

Cenkl, Pavel, 1971 – .

This vast book of nature: writing the landscape of New
Hampshire's White Mountains, 1784 – 1911 / by Pavel Cenkl;
foreword by Wayne Franklin.

p.   cm. — (American land and life series)

Includes bibliographical references and index.

ISBN 1-58729-498-2 (cloth)

1. White Mountains (N.H. and Me.) — Historiography.
2. Landscape — White Mountains (N.H. and Me.) —
Historiography.   3. Natural history — White Mountains (N.H.
and Me.) — Historiography.   4. White Mountains (N.H. and
Me.) — Environmental conditions — Historiography.   5. Landscape
in literature.   6. White Mountains (N.H. and Me.) — Description
and travel.   7. Tourism — White Mountains (N.H. and
Me.) — History.   I. Title.   II. Series.

F41.3C46 2006   974.2'203072 — dc22

2006044504

06 07 08 09 10 C 5 4 3 2 1

TO MY FATHER,

FOR SHOWING ME THE WAY

CONTENTS

Foreword by Wayne Franklin ix

Acknowledgments xiii

Introduction: The White Mountains from
Northern Frontier to Tourist Resort
xv

CHAPTER ONE
Texts and Terrain: Jeremy Belknap and
Eighteenth-Century Landscape Ideology
1

CHAPTER TWO
Economic Topographies: Unsettling the
History of Early Tourism in New Hampshire's
White Mountains
25

CHAPTER THREE
The Sublime and the Sumptuous: The Currency
of Scenery and White Mountain Tourism
59

CHAPTER FOUR
Alone with Scribe and Staff: Rewriting the
White Mountains, 1870–1900
103

Epilogue:
Reading and Teaching Region
143

Notes 149

Bibliography 159

Index 173

Wayne Franklin

WITH APOLOGIES TO Alfred North Whitehead's *Science and the Modern World*, one might argue that anything or anyone exists as such (that is, has *value*) only because it occupies *the most concrete actual someplace*. Location, in other words, is not incidental but constitutive. I am who I am because always I am someplace: I am the particular sensibility occupying a particular spot at any given moment, and the lines organizing the universe lead from and return to that spot. To be sure, place as we commonly define it seems to be an absolute. But it is no more permanent or less apparent than most other categories by means of which we sort and try to understand our experience.

Take a landscape view. One looks out across a middle distance of abandoned pasture, thickening now with mullein heads and goldenrod and a few saplings, its old stonewall boundaries partly tumbled as a result of gravity, weather, neglect; just past where an old dairy barn is exfoliating into dust, the grade shifts as flat graduates to upland; farther back yet, hill amplifies into mountain, rounded and grey but, with granite insistence, both ancient and obviously present. Above everything visible in the whole scene, a smear of deep blue, mottled by cloud and lined with shots of light, weighs down on earth like the thickest of Van Gogh's skies, so that its mass seems to keep things in their places. All of this seems so real that one turns away and, having other places to go, leaves it in the full belief that it remains right *there*.

Only of course it does not. What gave shape to all of the things making up that view was not the enduring, absolute interrelation of all the points in space that it includes, but rather the single point the viewer occupied. The interrelation does not cease to be when the eye is withdrawn, and indeed there are many kinds of interrelation the eye never took in (for I am talking here of the "classical" landscape, landscape at a human scale), but the view as such was nothing other than a temporary assemblage of impressions. It was incident to the viewer's occupation of the point that organized it for the moment of its apprehension.

Take the viewer away and the view collapses — nay, ceases to exist at all. Even just move the viewer along a bit and the whole thing changes with surprising ease. Perspective, we need to remember, is an amalgam of the points seen and the viewer's stance. This was the lesson discovered with fresh intensity during the mechanization of travel. As Wolfgang Schivelbusch has shown in *The Railway Journey*, trains challenged the eye in ways it had never been challenged before. Varying speed, the confinement of the traveler to a mostly lateral view, even the corporate corridor of the right-of-way — all were factors in re-forming popular perception. With the shift away from the railway and toward the automobile, some of these factors remained the same (a highway is the new corporate corridor, both allowing movement and confining it along a set axis), while others (such as the frontal assault of motion on the driver) were deeply altered. In either instance, however, what allowed place to make sense was its organization through the definitely *placed* observer. On the train, place became a sequence of variably blurred sidewise panels — moving very fast right at hand, more slowly in the middle distance, and hardly at all (or seemingly in reverse) at the back of the whole. In the automobile, the drivers suddenly took over the engineer's seat. Place now roars directly at the eye, relentlessly strung on a line of sight. There is no escaping it as long as one keeps on keeping on. Seemingly, there is always more of it.

Place is far more complex than we assume when, pulling off the highway in response to a sign announcing "View Point Ahead," we cease our motion and take on a socially programmed passivity in expectation that we, too, will see the prescribed thing. Even so, the highway department sign can be taken to indicate all the means by which the phenomenon of the mere spatial glimpse — the fleeting apprehension indicated above — becomes a passable commodity in the trade of ideas and images and values we call culture. Place endures not so much as topography — rather, as *topos*, as the human, verbal commonplace that allows for its circulation. Pavel Cenkl's core sample of writing about the White Mountains demonstrates the profound persistence of cultural *topoi*. With a rare combination of place savvy and historical scholarship, he shows how particular places endure through a kind of diachronic dialogue, a handing on of terms and tales. The world, he might offer, is a conversation we navigate by means of verbal maps. What are the White Mountains? To what precisely does that topographic label refer? In the gazetteer, they are "Mountains of the Appalachian range, in Northern New Hampshire." But that sort of definition, useful enough for some purposes (for instance, it distinguishes *these* White Mountains from those on the border of California and Nevada), will not take us very far. The White Mountains in Cenkl's sense of things become the long verbal line, continually refreshed by new infusions, that ties that particular gazetteer entry to *us*. Cultural landscape is the chatter that constitutes our world.

Not that this chatter is always one "line," as I have called it, or always the same. To the contrary, with admirable attention to historical context, Cenkl shows us how the conversation evolves and shifts — and what forces direct and deflect it as the *topoi* are passed on. It is in fact remarkable that we can recognize the White Mountains as persisting amid all this change from the time of seventeenth-century explorer John Josselyn to that of nineteenth-century figures such as novelist and traveler Nathaniel Hawthorne or tourist operator and local historian Lucy Crawford, let alone that of early environmental activist Frank Bolles. As *This Vast Book of Nature* points out, the shift from a focus on the economic worth of the mountains to the view that they had worth aside from the economic was enormous. "Views," Cenkl stresses, involve more than the literal perspectives people occupy. Ideology also shapes place, both in a material and an intellectual sense: where, indeed, one might ask, do we stand on the environment? On that topic, Cenkl is particularly insightful.

The White Mountains have been, above all else, a collection of itineraries and pauses. This book reminds us of how crucial to the collective endeavor writing that place has been. In the process, it offers a tour of one historical landscape that will inform how we look at any other.

ACKNOWLEDGMENTS

I COULD NOT EVEN have begun a project of this scope without the help of many others who share my love for the history of the White Mountain region. I would like to thank the following organizations, institutions, and individuals for their guidance and assistance: the New Hampshire Historical Society, Concord; Dartmouth University Rauner Library, Hanover; the University of New Hampshire Milne Special Collections, Durham; the Brick Store Museum, Kennebunk; the Appalachian Mountain Club, Boston and Gorham; Bob Cottrell and the Remmick Farm Museum, Tamworth; the Frost Place, Franconia; Alan Phenix; the Johnson Family; Plymouth State University, Plymouth; and the White Mountain School, Bethlehem.

The support and advice of my teachers, colleagues, and students were also essential throughout my work, from the initial idea to the final product. I wish to extend my gratitude in particular to Wayne Franklin, Guy Rotella, Mary Loeffelholz, and Lorianne DiSabato. This project would have been impossible without the support and love of my family. My parents, Gina and Mila Cenkl, have encouraged me throughout the process, and my wife, Jen, who has patiently walked beside me since I took my first steps on this path, has supported me in more ways than she will ever know.

The White Mountains from Northern Frontier to Tourist Resort

REFLECTING ON HIS 1832 visit to the Notch of the White Mountains in northern New Hampshire, Nathaniel Hawthorne describes the moment at which he entered the narrow "romantic defile" at the height of the Notch and was suddenly overtaken by a rapidly moving stagecoach. When he later spent the evening with the stage's occupants at the Notch's Crawford House, he was drawn to observe the variety of roles they played in the changing Northern Forest landscape:

> One was a mineralogist, a scientific, green-spectacled figure in black, bearing a heavy hammer, with which he did great damage to the precipices, and put the fragments in his pocket. Another was a well-dressed young man, who carried an opera glass set in gold, and seemed to be making a quotation from some of Byron's rhapsodies on mountain scenery. There was also a trader, returning from Portland to the upper part of Vermont; and a fair young girl, with a very faint bloom like one of those pale and delicate flowers which sometimes occur among alpine cliffs. (*Sketches* 29)

Hawthorne's description of this encounter in the heart of the White Mountains offers not only a neat typology of nineteenth-century visitors to the region but also a map of their differing responses to the landscape through which they traveled. Through a number of physical and literary uses of the mountains, travelers like these represent a change in both the mountain landscape and its inhabitants in the early nineteenth century. The trader in Hawthorne's sketch views the bleak environment of the Notch as a place to move through rather than visit. The traveling mineralogist's focus on resource extraction illustrates early nineteenth-century expansionist ideology — his presence in the Notch of the White Mountains defining an early tourism of a particular sort, with which Hawthorne shows his unease. The clearly out-of-place young man shows the growing use of the mountains for an exploitation (and inhabitation) different from that of the mineralogist and trader. In his choice of Byron's rhapsodies, the young man repositions the White Mountains in the context of an imported aesthetic rhetoric. Much like his literal framing of the mountain vista in his opera glass, by adopting such an aesthetic, the young man attempts to situate the northern New England landscape within the framework of a European iconology. Finally, the sketch's young girl represents perhaps all that is in jeopardy in the mountain landscape at the hands of these three men; her ephemeral, "delicate" beauty gives her an immature, fragile, and as yet untrammeled wildness.

After the first decades of the nineteenth century, the natural and cultural landscapes of the White Mountain region of New Hampshire were in the midst of a transformation built on the foundations of an expansionist national rhetoric, whose cornerstone had been laid in the last years of the eighteenth century. The imperialist agenda of the early eighteen hundreds was institutionalized in a 1785 congressional mandate to "improve" American public lands, a mandate that often associated discordant notions of ideology and place. Such rhetoric is apparent in northern New Hampshire as early as 1803, when Yale president and travel writer Timothy Dwight identified in Eleazer Rosebrook, grandfather of Ethan Allen Crawford and one of the area's first entrepreneurs, a "spirit of enterprise and industry, and perseverance, which has surmounted obstacles, demanding more patience and firmness, than are in many instances required for the acquisition of empire" (*Travels* 96). This imperial ideology, also seen in the Jeffersonian attempt to standardize federal lands, serves as an appropriate starting point for an engagement of the dialogue between abstract political and ideological principles and the realities of specific places, what Lawrence Buell identifies as the blurred boundary between "map knowledge and place sense" (*Imagination* 278). These tensions between social and political constructions of landscape born in the forests of early nineteenth-century New Hampshire remain today implicit in the residents' relationships to the particularities of a place. As a reading of nineteenth-century northern New Hampshire literatures suggests, the crossing of political, economic, cultural, and natural influences in the region helped define a landscape that is, even today, divided into a variety of townships, grants, purchases, and locations that often bear little connection with the topography of the landscape they circumscribe or the lives passed upon them.

The image of the White Mountains was steadily transformed by writers like Dwight, the New Hampshire historian Jeremy Belknap, and travel writer Edward Kendall from an inhospitable northern frontier to a destination popular among tourists during the first decades of the nineteenth century. The region began attracting writers and artists who sought to re-present (in effect to advertise) the region to audiences in distant urban centers. Among these early travel writers, Edward Kendall, Nathaniel Willis, and Basil Hall suggested that the mountain landscape was empty of character and value because its peaks did not resound with echoes of either prominent literary figures, significant historical events, or aristocratic landowners. Many writers and artists drawn to the White Mountains in the 1830s and 1840s, however, including Thomas Cole, Albert Bierstadt, William Henry Bartlett, Nathaniel Hawthorne, and Henry David Thoreau, began to create these associations themselves. Others (including guidebook writers Thomas Starr King, Julius Ward, John Spaulding, and Moses Sweetser) drew on local histories and the work of other established writers to create a context for the mountain landscape. In their paintings, fiction, and guidebooks, these writers and artists often looked to local tragedies and other significant events to invest the landscape with associative value. This book traces the development of the mountain region as a place that, as Robert McGrath observes, existed as a culturally constructed "idea before [it was] a reality" ("Real and Ideal" 59). When tourism became a profitable commercial enterprise in the White Mountains, the landscape itself — the vistas, scenic bridle paths, lakes, rivers, peaks, even the weather — was packaged for consumption and interwoven with the voices of popular writers and with regional histories.

If the beginning of a foray into the White Mountains might be prompted by an explicit (if uncomfortable) *arrangement* of space for economic and political purposes, its close can be marked by an *identification* of that space as having value beyond the economic. Public concern about the increasing exploitation of the mountains by the lumber industry, as well as a growing realization that the White Mountains' popularity among tourists would soon have a noticeable impact on the regional environment, led to the need for legislation to preserve the White Mountains as a shared environmental resource. The passing of the Weeks Act in 1911, which allowed for the initial designation of more than 70,000 acres of the White Mountains as National Forest (a federally managed area that would eventually expand to encompass more than 700,000 acres), signified a national realization that "urban" demarcations of territory do not always effectively describe rural or wild places. The Weeks Act merged issues of conservation, inhabitation, tourism, and varieties of land use. It was the fruit of many seeds planted by White Mountain writers who expressed an incipient environmentalism over the course of the nineteenth century.

Although the framing moments of this period, 1785 and 1911, are overtly political, within this larger frame lies a complex dialogue about how writers from a variety of perspectives define place. Pondering the intricate relationships among time, place, and culture, Laguna Pueblo writer Leslie Marmon Silko notes that "time is an ocean" in its simultaneous embrace of contemporary and historical events, underscoring the inseparability of even temporally distant events from contemporary experience (*Yellow Woman* 33). Silko's oceanic metaphor illustrates that time cannot effectively be thought of only as a continual, linear current. This is, as John Hanson Mitchell points out in *Ceremonial Time*, particularly significant with respect to a specific landscape. Much as forestry and inhabitation practices leave their indelible traces on the landscape more than a hundred years after their passing, the literature of the Northern Forest also illustrates these same imprints of land use. The edge of the woods where fir and spruce give way to the hardwoods like black birch and pin cherry create what is described as an ecotone, a marginal forest community on the edge of a more established forest. These edges pervade the White Mountain forest still today, often evidence of logging more than a century ago, and illustrate how cultural and economic histories can be read in the landscape itself and can affect our perceptions of "nature." The voices of the mountain region similarly overlap one another, creating ecotones through which we can read a similar history of the landscape.

As this study is rooted more deeply in a specific place than a particular moment, I explore a breadth of perspectives on the mountains and investigate how often competing visions of landscape work to transform the White Mountains both in writing and by changing the topography of the region itself. It is this transformation of the landscape, distinctly pointed to in Hawthorne's mineralogist, that is my principal concern. A variety of cultural documents from the period, including histories, guidebooks, magazine articles, essays, journals, and works of fiction and poetry, as well as pictorial representations of the mountains and their hotels, overlap with one another to create an elaborate picture of northern New Hampshire as a used landscape. At the same time, the physical transformation of the mountains themselves, through settlement, development, farming, logging, tourism, and other regional industries, illustrates a similar dialogue among a variety of competing interests. Reified today by the National Forest Service in its philosophy of "multiple use," this variety of demands placed on a single, relatively compact region often creates dissensus among the region's residents and reveals a landscape in a state of cultural, social, and ecological flux.

In his introduction to *Writing Culture*, James Clifford asserts that "there is no longer any place of overview (mountain top) from which to map human ways of life. . . . Mountains are in constant motion" (22). Clifford's discussion focuses on what has become a familiar rhetorical move in cultural analysis; he echoes contemporary cultural critics who argue the inability of the critic to present an objective framework. A recent move to reground American studies to focus on the specific *place* of the critic as one that "informs . . . identity" (5), as Wayne Franklin and Michael Steiner suggest, identifies an appropriate starting point for an examination of the rewriting of culture and landscape apparent in the documents at the center of a regional transformation in the Northeast. Much as the critic's cultural and spatial context underlies his or her interpretation of a text (or indeed a landscape), northern New England, too, is constructed by a variety of perceptions. An attentive reading of texts from the mountain region reveals a layering of voices and perspectives that, through their multiple re-presentations of the region, in effect work to compose the White Mountain landscape. The region's inhabitants, writing in local histories and journals, define the landscape in very particular ways, whereas a growing tourist class often considers the mountains entirely differently. It is the implicit dialogue between local history and outside perspective that begins, in the second half of the nineteenth century, to blur boundaries between the commercial interests of a distinctly tourist perspective on landscape and a more rural, local one. Though the sentiments of these groups may often conflict, and their views of the potential of landscape may differ, they inhabit the same region. By looking comparatively at a variety of texts, we can consider how perspectives on landscape work to construct the White Mountains in multiple, often overlapping ways: as an inhospitable wilderness, as a landscape to be preserved or to be inhabited, or as a product for commercial consumption.

Much as White Mountain texts involve a crossing of discourses and representations of place, there is a similar crossing evident in theoretical discussions of place and literature. An engagement of contemporary theoretical perspectives on the multiple conceptions of place as it intersects with cultural and class issues illustrates that place and text are not mutually exclusive critical terrains. Much of the book explores the White Mountains as a place sustaining a diversity of critical, historical, and social identities. By drawing on a variety of cultural texts, including guidebooks, histories, newspapers, and advertisements, as well as regional literature, it is possible to see the landscape as situated within a multiplicity of economic and cultural interests. Such an inquiry into the effects of class on landscape perception highlights the ways that the economy is frequently an implicit influence on land representation. I focus not only on the differences that social class implies, but also on the overlapping voices presented in mid-nineteenth-century guidebooks, local narratives, and regional histories. A reading of both tourist and local reflections on the mountains makes it clear that although visitors and residents view the landscape often through very different lenses, their texts reveal a similar engagement of land use issues. This study considers, then, how the multifarious, often conflicting representations of the Northern Forest blur as well as reflect the boundaries between inhabitant and tourist, culture and nature, and wilderness and civilization.

Much recent critical work on the crossing of landscape and literature focuses on the effect of social and cultural changes on the landscape as a product of human occupation and order. By foregrounding the interpenetration of the social and the ecological, I seek, rather, to offer a revision of the anthropocentrism that underlies many of these perspectives. The literal text of the animate world, contends David Abram, "shot through with suggestive scrawls and traces, from the sinuous calligraphy of rivers winding across the land" to the "swooping flight of birds" (95), was at once revealed and occluded by White Mountains writers as they attempted to rewrite the mountains as wilderness, as objet d'art, and as tourist commodity. A comparative study of texts such as Charles Hitchcock's 1874 *Geology of New Hampshire*, Lucy Crawford's 1846 *History of the White Mountains*, and Thomas Starr King's 1859 *White Hills* reveals not only the development of landscape writing in northern New Hampshire, but also the ways these voices are interwoven with issues of land use. These three texts, however, like the stage passengers in Hawthorne's sketch, do not exist entirely independently from one another or from the mountains themselves. They are, in a very real sense, fellow travelers. Hitchcock, echoing much of the sentiment of King's earlier guidebook, asserts, "those who would thoroughly understand the features of [White Mountain] scenery are invited to peruse [its] various geological details" (589). By interweaving the appreciation of scenery with an understanding of its underlying nature, Hitchcock ties together the discourses of science and of "scenography" much as King himself does in his guidebook. Both texts deny a simple reading and suggest that, although both exist to entice tourists (or industry), they also appeal to the readers' understanding of the White Mountains as a particular place and not merely something to be consumed. The interaction between people and the landscape is not a simple one, but often involves competing voices and agendas, which continue to define northern New Hampshire.

This book traces these voices as they begin to develop regional environmental perspectives through writing, and also as they shape the mountain environment itself. The often implicit interweaving of human voices with human action in the White Mountains foregrounds a tension between land use and landscape perceptions. As writers, artists, travelers, scientists, and journalists traced the changes in the mountain landscape over the course of the nineteenth century, they often illustrated a transformation that resulted from the public's preconceptions about the region's landscape. Jeremy Belknap's expedition to Mount Washington in 1784 marked an interweaving of imported notions of a sublime landscape with the realities of the White Mountains' intricate ecosystem. Belknap's narratives of his expedition underscore how the explorer's gaze began to turn inward to consider the language of the intimate landscape, rather than the broad, expansive viewscapes desired by many early nineteenth-century tourists.

To accommodate the influx of tourists, wealthy proprietors built dozens of lavish resort hotels throughout the region, and guidebook writers offered explicitly detailed descriptions of not only what one should look at and during what time of day, but even what response one should have to a particular mountain vista. Thomas Starr King, for instance, writing in 1859, focused on the "view" of the landscape rather than its "interior," suggesting that in accord with his law of focal distance, the mountain vistas were being presented as paintings for consumption (7–8). Lucy Crawford's *History* spans fifty years of tourist expansion and illustrates early attempts to transform the landscape into an accessible destination for urban visitors. Later in the century, members of the Appalachian Mountain Club recorded their explorations of the mountains' interior wildness in hiking journals and letters of the period. These texts foreground an apparent conflict between an emerging industry of tourism and the appreciation and preservation of the mountains. By engaging the relationships between the region's seasonal and year-round residents and the land itself, I argue that the cultural transformation of the White Mountains through a variety of texts both re-creates the marginal space of a Turnerian "frontier" and interweaves inhabitant, visitor, and landscape in an increasingly complicated construction of place.

As early as 1848, George Perkins Marsh addressed the growing imbalance between land use and abuse among New England farmers. Thoreau's sentiments in *The Maine Woods* and *Cape Cod* similarly promote preservation of the landscape "for inspiration and our own true recreation" (Thoreau 712). This biophilic sentiment, permeating environmental writing through the middle and late nineteenth century, frequently created discord between local inhabitants' perspectives on landscape as utilitarian and tourists' visions of the mountains as romantic. Even before the explosion of White Mountain tourism at midcentury, articles in publications like the *Farmer's Monthly* began to reflect on the inevitability of development and on the likelihood that the forests would eventually succumb to the pressures of the logging industry. In the last quarter of the century, tourist newspapers, including the *White Mountain Echo* and *Among the Clouds*, added their voices to a campaign to stop over-developing the forests. Though proponents of preservation for very different reasons, these texts illustrate a change in sentiment toward the landscape, away from exploitation and toward the preservationism of Henry David Thoreau and the conservationist ethic promoted by George Perkins Marsh. Explicit in environmental documents and media representations of landscape, this rift between preservation and resource use is also apparent in both regional fiction and later environmental essays. In their indictment of a growing tourist class, essays by Frank Bolles and Bradford Torrey illustrate a concern with the land-scape that parallels the preservationist sentiment expressed by the more active engagement of the environment by Appalachian Mountain Club members in the 1880s. These early mountain climbers, including Charles Fay, Marian and Lucia Pychowska, and Isabella Stone, marked a change in the type of tourist coming to the region; more content to reside on the periphery of the grand resort hotel culture and explore seldom-visited mountains, these late-century tourists helped to lay the foundations for public sentiment that would lead to the conservation-minded legislation in the early twentieth century. The roots of nineteenth-century conservationism, finding fertile ground in the disclimax of the northern New England environment, also found themselves implicated in a complex negotiation between place and identity in the writing of the White Mountain landscape.

Using contemporary critical discourse as a framework for discussing the merging of ecological, economic, and cultural issues, this book engages the literature that both produces and is produced by the landscape. In the context of both specific regional perceptions of place and broader visions of landscape, I will look to works by regional New England poets and writers as well as a variety of cultural documents including guidebooks, journals, and newspapers, which often illustrate an implicit crossing of landscape and culture. The intersections of place, culture, and class in fictional re-visions of landscape, apparent in the stories of Hawthorne and Annie Trumbull Slosson and the poetry of Lucy Larcom, John Greenleaf Whittier, and Thomas Parsons, for instance, underscore the effects of topography on the demographic reformation of the region. These issues are evident not only in works of fiction and poetry, but also in a variety of cultural documents, including exceptionally popular mid- to late nineteenth-century tourist guides by John Spaulding, Thomas Starr King, Benjamin Willey, Moses Foster Sweetser, and William Oakes, among others, which reconstrued the White Mountains for their visitors as a commercial, usable place.

By looking variously at intersections of culture and landscape in regional texts and at crossings of ecological and literary concerns, I revise traditional interpretations of the White Mountains as a unified subject. Through a reading of class and place, it is possible to revise that definition of northern New Hampshire to show it as a region that foregrounds different perceptions of the landscape and the synchronicity of the multiple perspectives from which the landscape is written. As constructed in American discourse, the late nineteenth-century White Mountain landscape presents an intersection of spatial and cultural ideologies. This active intersection between a landscape constructed by tourist perspectives and one written by local communities acts to continuously revise the White Mountains and present a layering of commerce, text, ecology, and ideology that even today continues to reshape the landscape of northern New Hampshire.

In chapter 1, I trace the origins of tourism in the White Mountains to the Belknap-Cutler expedition to the region's highest peak (not yet called Mount Washington) in 1784. Whereas the aim of the expedition was to both climb to the high point and to circumambulate all the higher summits of the region, it is in Belknap's own solitary descent of the mountain as he turned back from the climb early on that a new perception of the intimacies of the landscape is apparent. Belknap's thoughtful reflection on the interconnectedness of the natural world beneath the forest canopy represents a departure from the emotional response to a sublime vista and an admission that the mountains' complex topography demands a closer look. Like contemporary responses to landscape in Thomas Jefferson's *Notes on the State of Virginia* and William Bartram's *Travels*, Belknap's accounts of his expedition are situated between pre-Revolutionary era exploration narratives and the proliferation of histories, guidebooks, and literary sketches in the nineteenth century. By straddling these divergent discourses, rather than drawing exclusively on either the rhetoric of the sublime or that of mere commercial potential, Belknap's intimate mountain landscape sketches the rough outline for a new, American environmental discourse.

Chapter 2 looks closely at writing by the White Mountain region's early settlers. The chapter focuses principally on Ethan Allen and Lucy Crawford, whose grandfather Eleazer Rosebrook opened the first overnight house in the White Mountain Notch in 1803. The story of the Crawfords and of early tourism and development in the region is recorded by Lucy both in her 1846 *History of the White Mountains* and in her 1860 revision of the same text. By comparing the two versions of her text, it becomes possible to trace transformations in tourist and resident relationships to the mountain landscape. During the decades of the Crawfords' expanding entrepreneurialism, the wilderness that John Josselyn had called "daunting terrible" (*Josselyn* 4) in the 1670s was transformed into a destination for tourists seeking to place the experience of the wilderness into the framework of a sublime aesthetic. Such a change in perception, however, also drove settlements like the Crawfords' to a peripheral existence. The *History*'s interwoven narratives of inhabitation, environmentalism, and tourism reveal the Crawfords as participants in an often strident debate between settlement and a developing speculative, entrepreneurial economy as the region's first settlers were displaced by the largely unchecked growth of the tourist economy.

Chapter 3 considers the veritable deluge of publications that followed Crawford's *History*. The many volumes of White Mountain material printed between 1850 and 1875 preclude an exhaustive survey of all the era's histories and guidebooks. I focus instead on particularly popular guidebooks and specific events that serve to ground tourism's virtually unbridled growth during this period. In the midst of a burgeoning tourist industry that colonized the White Mountain landscape with outposts of upper-class urban luxury, popular guidebooks like Thomas Starr King's *White Hills*, Benjamin Willey's *Incidents in the White Mountains*, and Samuel Drake's *Heart of the White Mountains*, effectively balanced the role of the guidebook with a conscientious engagement of the nonhuman world. Despite the contradiction inherent in simultaneously emphasizing the White Mountains' complex ecosystem and promoting a tourist economy that would only further marginalize the wild by importing the civilized into the very heart of the mountains, these writers planted the seeds of an incipient environmentalism that would eventually lead to the reshaping of tourism and the preservation of the mountains in the early twentieth century.

The reaction to the combined impact of the competing resource-based industries of tourism and logging in the last decades of the nineteenth century helped to concretize issues of preservation in the popular consciousness. By the end of the century, the White Mountains were mediated by often conflicting rhetorical and economic discourses of commercialism, industry, inhabitation, and preservation. Chapter 4 examines the writings of this new generation of explorers, including mountain climbers such as Marian Pychowska and Isabella Stone of the newly founded Appalachian Mountain Club, and their contemporaries Frank Bolles and Bradford Torrey, whose popular nature essays bolstered public interest in preserving the White Mountains as a natural resource. In the voices of these writers we see a clear movement toward a consciousness of the ecosystemic relationship among White Mountain industries and the nonhuman environment that parallels a larger, American environmental sensibility. Although still rooted in the discourse and apparatus of tourism, these fin-de-siècle writers cultivated environmental concern sown earlier in the century, effectively integrating a sense of sustainability into the White Mountains' contested terrain.

THIS VAST BOOK OF NATURE

CHAPTER ONE

Texts and Terrain

Jeremy Belknap and Eighteenth-Century
Landscape Ideology

ON THE AFTERNOON OF 24 July 1784, Rev. Manasseh Cutler looked out from the summit of New England's highest
mountain, more than a hundred miles north of his home
on the coast of Massachusetts, and saw not the "daunting
terrible" land the explorer John Josselyn described a century
before, but rather a landscape that "suggested immediately
the idea of viewing an extensive marsh from an eminence far above it, with
numerous stacks and cocks of hay settled down and extending over a broad
base" (*Life* 104). Before either Cutler or the eight men who stood with him on
the summit could offer other comparative views, the weather changed, as it
typically does above treeline in New Hampshire, to a "thick fog . . . as cold as
November" (*Life* 105 – 7), requiring a difficult and dangerous retreat from the
exposed peak. After spending a night in the relative safety of a ravine below
treeline, the men returned to their camp at the base of the mountain, having effected what was at that date the most prolifically documented ascent of
the peak.

New England's highest peak, called Agiocochook by the Abenaki, and later
named Mount Washington by Reverend Cutler and the New Hampshire historian Jeremy Belknap, saw its first and second recorded ascents in 1642. These
initial explorations were performed by Darby Field, who had become an Indian
interpreter shortly after his arrival in Boston in 1636. Governor John Winthrop
recorded Field's expeditions in his journal, noting that "the report he brought
of shining stones, etc., caused divers others to travel thither, but they found
nothing worth their pains" (417). Nevertheless, Field, traveling to the mountains with the help of Native American guides, returned with a report of the
region's agricultural and industrial prospects, finding near the Abenaki village
of "Pegwagget" (Pequawket) "upon the Saco River . . . many thousand acres of
rich meadow" and, below the summit of the mountain sheets of mica "40 feet

long and 7 or 8 broad," "stones which they supposed had been diamonds" (394) and the springs of "four great rivers, each of them so much water, at the first issue, as would drive a mill" (418). Among the earliest of colonial explorers to visit northern New England, Field offered a vision of an inhabited landscape promising untold riches, which was largely at odds with the contemporary rhetoric regarding uncultivated forests, in which Governor Winthrop saw only a "wilderness, where are nothing but wild beasts and beastlike men" (416).

Field's hyperbole over the landscape's potential for settlement and its topography was nonetheless repeated, and embellished, by his contemporaries. Thomas Gorges, deputy governor of the Province of Maine, wrote to his cousin, Sir Ferdinando Gorges, of a "ledge of rocks which [Field] conceaved to be 12 miles high, very steep" and of the "many rattle snakes" (115 – 16) that Field said he had encountered above treeline. Thomas was informed by Field's report and accompanied him on his second trip to the White Mountains. He was apparently disappointed at not encountering many of Field's spectacles, however, and he wrote to his father simply "I have bin at the White Hills. The fear of the Indians. The next year I hope to see you" (121).

Two decades after this initial flurry of activity in the White Mountains, John Josselyn, sailing from London at the dawn of the Restoration in 1663, reported on the region to the Royal Society in his book *New England Rarities Discovered* (1672). The society's reception of both *New England Rarities* and Josselyn's 1674 *Two Voyages to New England* was less than enthusiastic, mainly as a result of the accounts' inclusion of regional myths and a narrative describing the New World in hyperbolic, Edenic terms rather than with a strict, scientific empiricism. In textually fashioning from the New World an earthly paradise, Josselyn participates in the rhetorical salesmanship that abounds in the works of his contemporaries and predecessors. Though he draws substantially from accounts by John Smith and William Wood, among others, Josselyn's descriptions of "ample rich and pregnant valleys . . . grass man-high unmowed . . . spacious lakes or ponds well stored with Fish . . . . mountains and Rocky Hills . . . richly furnished with mines" (43 – 44) so permeate *Two Voyages to New England* that he feels obligated to defend his text from detractors. Toward the conclusion of his narrative of the second voyage (1663 – 1671), he counters "sceptick Readers muttering out of their scuttle mouths": "Our tongues are our own, who shall controll us. I have done what I can to please you, I have piped and you will not dance. I have told you as strange things as ever you or your Fathers have heard" (149 – 50).

Despite the newly founded Royal Society's emphasis on scientific inquiry,

Josselyn's report is shaped more as a narrative than is Field's enumerative, substantive report to Governor Winthrop. In *New England Rarities Discovered*, Josselyn provides only a very brief overview of the journey to the northern mountains: quite remarkably, although the first page of the narrative is his departure from London, Josselyn describes his climb in the White Mountains just five short paragraphs later. Josselyn is also careful to include the reader in his account, noting, for instance, the convenient handholds in the ravines among the mountains (without which he asserts the peaks would be unclimbable): "*Saven* Bushes [dwarf spruce], which being taken hold of are a good help to the climbing Discoverer" (3). Later, he remarks how, when ascending Mount Washington's summit cone, "called the Sugar-loaf, to outward appearances a rude heap of massie stones piled one upon another . . . you may as you ascend step from one stone to another, as if you were going up a pair of stairs, but winding still about the Hill till you come to the top" (4). In juxtaposing this ease of ascent with a landscape that remains "full of rocky Hills . . . [and] cloathed with infinite thick woods" (4), Josselyn struggles as he attempts to reposition the White Mountains as accessible, despite their inherent connection with the land described by William Bradford as a "hideous and desolate wilderness, full of beasts and wild men" (70). Although the highest summits appear to lie at the very edge of the colonial frontier, and Josselyn notes that "the Country beyond these Hills Northward is daunting terrible" (4), by situating the reader in the landscape, he not merely presents his observations but also invites those of future visitors. Indeed, the lack of detail and superficiality of his description *necessitate* further exploration.

Its poor reception by the Royal Society notwithstanding, Josselyn's narrative was positioned within an existing political discourse of appropriation. The very verb *to discover*, as Bruce Greenfield notes, "implies anticipation, and later knowledge, of an object that has already been defined or allowed for in the contemporary discourse" (20). Such foreknowledge suggests the import of a traveler's preconceptions about a specific place. As a hopeful future member of the Royal Society (a position he would never be offered), then, Josselyn's attempt to integrate his observations with the canon of existing New World writing reveals a politics of landscape that will inhere in New England exploration and discovery narratives throughout the eighteenth and nineteenth centuries.[1]

THE YEARS BETWEEN the end of the French and Indian Wars and the American Revolution saw renewed interest in climbing among the White Mountains. In 1772 a company including New Hampshire governor John Wentworth climbed what he later believed to be "the second [mountain] in height and magnitude" (Belknap Papers 6, 3:64). The White Hills' highest summit was climbed at least three times in the summer and fall of 1774. It was ascended on 6 and 19 June by parties under the direction of Captain John Evans, whose company was building a road through what is now Pinkham Notch, just to the east of Mount Washington. In October of that year, Nicholas Austin ascended the same peak climbed by Governor Wentworth two years earlier (most likely one of the peaks of the lower, southern range), but, "discovering a large mountain E.N.E. from this he travelled about eight miles to the bottom" (*Belknap Papers* 6, 3:64) and subsequently *rediscovered* what he believed to be the highest of the White Mountains. The 1784 expedition led by Belknap and Cutler was the first to try to bring scientific methods, including regular temperature readings and barometric measurements to ascertain elevation, to the White Mountains. The timing of the expedition, at the onset of a period of national expansionism, positions it to uniquely negotiate between the rhetoric of occupation (and potential exploitation) illustrated by Josselyn and Field and an incipient focus on the importance of the terrain underfoot that would prevail in later nineteenth-century travel narratives about the region.[2]

Seeing in the forests of spruce and fir that covered the White Mountain landscape the "stacks and cocks of hay" of the sea coast, Manasseh Cutler reads the landscape in the language of his native Ipswich, Massachusetts, ascribing to the northern forests of spruce and fir the quasi-domestic fecundity of coastal salt marshes. Cutler's re-vision of the wilderness before him as a familiar domestic landscape draws attention to a number of significant issues. As an explorer charting the northern frontier in America's first decade of independence, Cutler looks to the mountains as a potential resource, seeing in the region areas for future settlement and agricultural abundance. At the same time, as an amateur scientist, Cutler resists the exuberant rhetoric of Burkean sublimity, tempering his remarks to heed the caveat later written by the expedition's leader, Jeremy Belknap: "when amazement is excited by the grandeur and sublimity of the scenes presented to view, it is necessary to curb the imagination, and exercise judgment with mathematical precision; or the temptation to romance will be invincible" (*History* 3:32). Curbing an aesthetics of rapture and "astonishment . . . of the soul, in which all its motions are suspended, with some degree of terror" (Burke 57) by evoking an agricultural scene, Cutler seconds Belknap's own fear that the unchecked emotion afforded by sublime rhetoric might work against scientific objectivity. Whereas Pamela Regis argues that the sublime and the scientific gaze of late eighteenth-century explorers, notably of William Bartram, "complement each other" (41), in the narratives produced by the Belknap expedition, the two discourses are often in conflict. The tableau of the sublime vista and the static, removed scenes it represents are antithetical to Belknap's agenda of looking past the superficial and to the mountains' details with "mathematical precision." While sections of Belknap's narratives might suggest that he returned from the mountains "filled with astonishment at the romantic sublimity of the peaks" (Lawson, *Passaconaway* xii), his ability to tread between the rhetoric of scientific and that of sublime observation points to the challenges of accurately representing the details of the mountains' terrain. As much as the sublime was to become central to the tourist experience in the White Mountains in the nineteenth century (though often more as a textual than as an experiential enterprise), Cutler and Belknap do their best to temper Burke's imported rhetoric in the name of both scientific empiricism and an incipient nationalism.

Cutler's reduction of the "strange to the ordinary" (Franklin 108) at the apex of his journey to the White Mountains situates him, like other members of the 1784 Belknap expedition, at the beginning of an era that interwove scientific inquiry, imperialist expansion, and tourism. Less than a year after the Belknap expedition, on 20 May 1785, the United States Congress adopted the "Ordinance for Ascertaining the Mode of Disposing Lands in the Western Territory," a version of Thomas Jefferson's vision for dividing the public domain into distinct rectilinear units, without regard for the underlying terrain or the residents' cultural identity. This arbitrary construction of what Philip Fisher calls "democratic social space" (Fisher 60) pushed an ideological framework onto a landscape in which, particularly in regions like the White Mountains, it collided with an existing intricate topography. The Belknap expedition was a watershed event in White Mountain exploration *and* tourism, as numerous accounts of the "tour" were published and found a wide audience among the traveling elite at the turn of the century. Belknap, infamous for his penchant for revision (his allegorical novel, *The Foresters*, for instance, underwent several distinct permutations), rewrote his account of the expedition in a number of publications. By the publication of the third volume of his *History of New Hampshire* in 1792, Belknap was able to both confect the reports of his companions and more fully realize the narrative's role as a re-vision of the White Mountains.[3]

Yale president Timothy Dwight was one of the first writers to tour the mountains after Belknap's expedition. Traveling in 1803 along a route similar to Belknap's, Dwight rode north through the Notch of the White Mountains (now known as Crawford Notch) and stayed in the region's first overnight house, operated principally for traders en route from the mountains to Portland and Portsmouth. In his *Travels in New England and New York*, Dwight wrote admiringly of the inn's proprietor, Eleazer Rosebrook, saying that he exemplified "a spirit of enterprise and industry, and perseverance, which has surmounted obstacles, demanding more patience and firmness, than are in many instances required for the acquisition of empire" (96). Dwight's expansionist rhetoric is not only a reaffirmation of the progress of the 1785 congressionally mandated "improvement" of the landscape that created the nation's "spatial physiognomy" (Buell, *Environmental* 269) but also the beginnings of a transformation that would shape social perception of the mountain landscape for a century to follow. Acting as one of the White Mountains' earliest tourists only two decades after Belknap's circumambulation of Mount Washington, in his praise of Tocqueville's "poetic ideas" of American expansion (75) Dwight portends the re-vision of the landscape from "an absolute wilderness" to a productive settled region and, eventually, to a tourist resort.

Echoing the sentiments of Jeffersonian agrarianism, the narratives of the Belknap expedition written by Belknap, Cutler, and Reverend Daniel Little of Kennebunk, Maine, variously extol the richness of the region's natural resources. Depictions of springs, with "water sufficient within a mile of their source to carry a Sawmill" (Little 4), or "freshets which bring down the soil to the intervals below, and form a fine mould, producing corn, grain and herbage in the most luxuriant plenty" all conspire to entice New England farmers northward (Belknap, "Description" 49). These specifics of the expedition are framed in the larger context of Belknap's own views of the newly independent nation. In his exhaustive *History of New Hampshire* Belknap, as Stephen Haycox has said, advocated treating the country "not as a resource awaiting exploitation" but rather as a place in which to build a permanent home (Haycox 48). Belknap shares with his contemporary chroniclers of American identity (among them Hector St. John de Crèvecoeur) the notion of a "hospitable geography," what Leo Marx called the *middle landscape*, perched between city and wilderness and serving as an "inherent hospice to settlers" (Tichi 100).

Although in a number of ways the descriptions of the Belknap expedition retain the wonder previously expressed by Josselyn and Field, the Cutler, Belknap, and Little narratives resound with a sense of "the wonder of discovery fading off into an anticipation of use and profit" (Franklin 83). Belknap was certainly not the first Euroamerican explorer to visit the mountains, and he was well aware of the fact. Prior explorers of the White Mountains, as I note above, intent on enticing further exploration and settlement, often returned with a bounty of overstatements concerning the region's potential. Belknap addresses these earlier descriptions in his own account by asserting that they have

> differed so widely from each other, and their accounts have been embellished by so many marvellous circumstances, and on the whole have been so unsatisfactory, that I have long wished for an opportunity to visit these mountains in company with some gentlemen of a philosophical turn, furnished with proper instruments and materials for a full exploration of the phenomena that might occur. . . . I flatter myself that what follows will prove more satisfactory than any which has yet been published or reported. (*History* 3:43)

Setting his description apart from those of his predecessors, Belknap points to examples of inaccuracy in earlier texts, criticizing their claims of rare gemstones and other riches, as well as the very appearance of the mountains themselves. In his 1784 expedition that in fact comprised "some gentlemen of a philosophical turn, furnished with proper instruments and materials," Belknap was acting as a representative of an incipient national emphasis on scientific inquiry. He set out less to *discover* the White Mountains, as that had already been accomplished centuries earlier, than to *re*discover or reframe them in the discourse of a new era. Belknap's own experience in the mountains did not offer the possibility of revising many of the prior claims he held to be untrue, since he was one of only two members of the expedition who did not venture above treeline to the mountain's summit. The expedition (particularly for Belknap) was principally a tour *around* the White Mountains' highest peaks, and the penetration of the interior was limited to the ascent of their highest point by ten of his party's twelve men. Belknap, too, understands the limitations of his trip and apologizes that the "ridge . . . extends north-east and south-west to an unknown length . . . [and] the number of summits within this area cannot be ascertained at present, the country around them being a thick wilderness" (*History* 3:43). Belknap's best intentions often confront the realities of the region's topography. Despite the apparent contradictions it creates in his narratives, the very distinction between intention (or perception) and reality lies at the heart of Belknap's refashioning of the White Mountain landscape.

Belknap initially paints for his readers a distant view of Mount Washington, detailing the different colors the mountain range presents at different distances and at different times of the year. In his *History of New Hampshire*, he includes a brief table of the mountain's colors as seen from about sixty miles to the south in Rochester, New Hampshire, from September to November 1784.[4]

Belknap's lengthy dissertation on color takes pains to disprove any persistent myths about gems or crystals responsible for the mountains' perpetual white hue, as he asserts with some finality that "it may with certainty be concluded, that the whiteness of them is wholly caused by the snow and no other white substance, for in fact, there is none" (*History* 3:37). As an explorer, Belknap struggles here against preconceptions of the mountains as he attempts to re-frame the White Mountains and look at the landscape more closely by elimi-nating the distance.

Despite Belknap's plan to focus on the details of the mountain landscape — prefiguring his preoccupation with ecological minutiae — which I discuss later — what is perhaps more significant about his treatise for my concerns here is its very positioning of the mountains at a distance. The distance at which Belknap places the mountains prior to his visit, when he hires an informant to observe their changing color, can be seen as an example of empirical observa-tion, but it also anticipates pictorial representations of Mount Washington by nineteenth-century artists like Benjamin Champney, John Frederick Kensett, George Inness, Thomas Cole, and Sylvester Hodgdon.[5] Belknap's telescoping perspective, whereby with close scrutiny white "streaks" on the mountainside can be "plainly discerned to be the edges or the sides of the long deep gul-lies, enlightened by the sun" (*History* 3:37), at first creates of Agiocochook a placid, two-dimensional tableau, lacking depth or engagement. Belknap, how-ever, seeks to complicate the mountain's status as a distant, unwavering, white beacon. The whiteness of the peaks is not uniform, nor does the color remain constant as one travels toward the peak from a great distance. Belknap's re-porter in Rochester reveals that change comes not only as a result of distance, but of weather and certainly season. He is thus able to reinvent the mountains as a living, dynamic landscape, rather than the one John Josselyn described as a range "known by the name of the White Mountains, upon which lieth Snow all the year," making them "a Land-mark twenty miles off at Sea" (*New England* 3). Belknap's agenda of demystifying assumptions about the White Mountains, then, begins to question the image of the mountains as a static, idealized tableau.

Edward Augustus Kendall, who toured the region in November 1807, quotes at length from Belknap's *History of New Hampshire* in his 1809 *Travels through-out the Northern Parts of the United States* and argues that by citing observa-tions only of local residents, "Dr. Belknap places his reliance on the statements of persons very incompetent to make such as are to the purpose" (3:179). It is interesting that Kendall himself confers with a local authority, Abel Crawford, the patriarch of Crawford Notch, and concludes that "the whiteness of the summits, when devoid of snow, is an unquestionable fact" and, at the same time, that "the substance of the summits, when viewed under the feet, is not white" (181). It is in the distinction between the distant view, in which the mountains indeed appear white, and the more intimate perspective of the mountain climber (like Belknap and his party), or resident (like Abel Crawford), that we can read the beginnings of a disparity between the mountains as a landscape merely seen from the distance and as one experienced up close. The topographical division between a distanced and intimate experience grew to almost satiric proportions in the decades following Kendall's tour through the region. Thirty years after Kendall's visit, Nathaniel Hawthorne parodied this very preoccupation with distanced perception in his story "The Great Carbuncle." The story's eight characters are drawn to the White Mountains to seek a "wondrous gem" whose light caused "mists to roll back before its power" (*Great* 56). The stone that is eventually discovered proves to be similar to what disappointed early explorers like Field and Gorges themselves found: "only an opaque stone, with particles of mica glittering on its surface" (*Great* 60).

This focus on the intimate landscape — at odds with the early tourist's penchant for the grand viewscape — would find voice in the work of Ralph Waldo Emerson and Henry David Thoreau in the decades that followed. Emerson was able to read nature in the minutiae of the landscape, perceiving in "the whirling bubble on the surface of a brook" and in "every shell on the beach" keys to understanding nature's larger interrelationships (547). Thoreau, whose own sojourns in the White Mountains are well documented (and who relied on Belknap's *History of New Hampshire* as a guidebook), also echoes Belknap's sentiments in his concern with a landscape's details. In his attempts to read what Yi-Fu Tuan might call a landscape of "visual chaos" (*Space* 34), however, Belknap continues to attempt to categorize the heterogeneity of the White Mountain landscape within the framework of an existing discourse. The resulting slippage between generality and detail, between static and dynamic landscapes, creates a fertile idea that will become central in the representational refashioning of the White Mountain region over the course of the nineteenth century.

Belknap creates a complex and often contradictory rhetoric of exploration as he attempts to mediate between preexisting landscape ideology and aesthetics and a developing interaction with the terrain underfoot, which is forced in part by the dynamic topography of the White Mountains themselves. Belknap's struggle with surfaces becomes even more apparent if we consider his own map of the expedition. For Belknap, who was in poor physical condition at the time of the expedition and could not climb to Mount Washington's summit, the expedition was indeed a "tour" (as he titles his narrative) — a circling of the mountain's base. The reports of his companions who did reach the summit, however, enrich Belknap's description of the mountains' interior. Belknap's letter to Ebenezer Hazzard dated 16 August 1784, less than a month after the expedition's return, includes a sketch map of the tour drawn in Belknap's own hand, though based largely on an existing map rather than on his own observation (fig. 1). The map traces the group's circuitous route around the highest of the White Mountains. Sharing conventions with traditional sketch maps by including, as the geographer Yi-Fu Tuan enumerates them, settlements, rivers, lakes, and paths that indicate the direction of travel (77), Belknap's sketch map nonetheless leaves the interior vacant. Belknap identifies the interior by writing on his sketch, "High Lands from which is an interrupted ascent to the top of the White Mountains & which is reckoned to be part of them." This blank "Area of the White Mountains" is framed on the east and northwest by profiles of the summits as they appear from below. Also absent is any indication of what lies outside the party's circuit, save for a line tracing the group's journey through Conway and half a dozen scattered summits. Michel de Certeau (121) reads maps as static, "totalizing" products, whose "tour describers have disappeared." In the case of Belknap's cartographic representation of his "tour," the narrative that formed the map, though partially extant on the map itself, creates tension with the map that it created; "what the map cuts up, the story cuts across" (de Certeau 129). Belknap's sketch map, much like the narrative itself, limits the hundreds of summits in the White Mountains to the relatively limited region known today as the Presidential Range. The profiles he includes on the map, and the absence of an interior, stress a preoccupation with distant, visual perception rather than focus on the interior. The circular nature of his expedition sought to contain and understand by circumscribing rather than penetrating the region. Indeed, the "fashionable tour" of the late nineteenth century would follow virtually the same course as Belknap's scientific tour, in a circular pattern that kept tourists gazing at a landscape that was itself "being shaped by the needs of its new consumers" (Brown 62).

It is perhaps more meaningful, as Lawrence Buell suggests, to see maps like Belknap's not merely as inscriptions of cultural imperialism, but rather as sites of negotiation and as spaces which "provok[e] . . . environmental consciousness on account of the oscillation in the mind between 'mental maps' and scientific maps" (*Environmental Imagination* 270). Belknap's map, not unlike his narra-

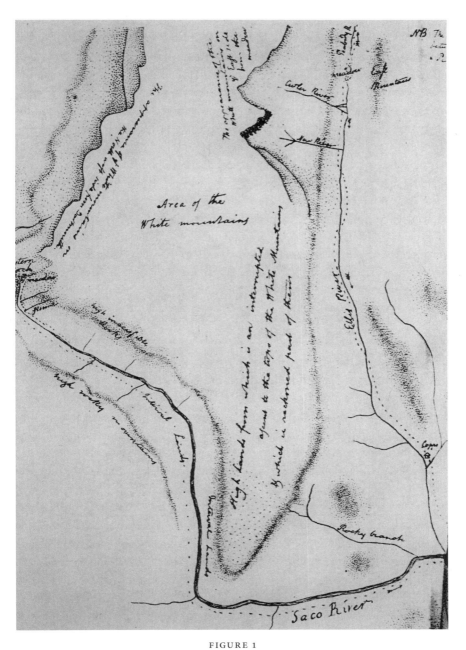

FIGURE 1

Jeremy Belknap, *Sketch Map of the White Mountains of New Hampshire*, 1784, detail.
Included in a letter to Ebenezer Hazard dated 19 August 1784. *Belknap Papers*,
Massachusetts Historical Society.

tives of the expedition, is a text that engages its boundaries—both physical, in the shape of "high inaccessible rocks," and perceptual, in its mediation of narrative and cartography. The tension between the mountains' surface and an intimate knowledge of place is apparent in Belknap's construction of the map from both existing cartographic information and his own perceptions. Belknap's general knowledge of the region was indeed limited; the expedition party hired several local guides and "axe-men" and depended on their services for the entire ascent and tour around the mountains' base. Owing to his lack of an overview of the area, Belknap based his own "plan" on one developed by Colonel Joseph Whipple, an expedition member with whom the party stayed in what is now Jefferson, New Hampshire. In a letter to Hazard, Belknap laments that Whipple's map "extended no further N[orth], so that the northern part of our circuit . . . [is] not comprehended in it." Despite having traveled through the region, Belknap is unable to extend the map northward based on his own experience. Using Whipple's map as a guide, however, Belknap writes that he "added the sketches of the appearance of the Mountains on the E[ast] and the N[orth] W[est], and marked their area as nearly as I could" (Papers 5, 3:189). Taking what was apparently a rough outline of the extent of the White Mountains' highest range, Belknap, focusing on his experience in the forest, tried to fill in some of the voids on Whipple's map. Despite his best efforts, however, this endeavor fails in its earliest attempts, since Belknap himself never penetrated into the interior of the mountains. In the third volume of his *History*, published in 1791, Belknap is able to represent the mountains' topography more completely (if not more accurately) on a map of the entire State of New Hampshire that accompanies his text.

As much as Belknap declines to write a complete landscape on his map, the expedition does write its presence on some of the landscape's significant features. The group names the river whose course they followed up the mountain's eastern slope for Reverend Cutler and, what is most significant, shortly after the expedition's return, the White Mountains' highest peak is named Mount Washington.[6] By naming the summit, in effect rewriting the landscape in explicitly politicized terms, the expedition members asserted on the mountains a "strange toponymy that is detached from actual places" (de Certeau 104). Although the peak's Abenaki name Agiocochook was never used by early colonial explorers, nor by Belknap, the renaming of the peak (believed at the time to be the fourth highest summit in the world) is an overt appropriation of the mountain to appeal to a political and ideological hubris. At the same time, the popular decision to rechristen the summit Mount Washington removed it from its somewhat ambiguous past and situated it within the evolving discourse of a new nation.

In addition to naming the peak, the expedition members participated in a tradition of writing on the landscape itself, both by leaving behind a lead sheet engraved with their names and the date and by carving their initials into rocks on the mountain's summit. Even this they found comparatively difficult, since, as they summitted, their view was abruptly obscured and the "diversity of scenery closed in a thick fog, and as cold as November" (Little 2). Daniel Little began to carve the letters NH in the highest rock but was unable to finish and "was forced *to give up the chizzel to Mr. Whipple, who finished the H*" (Belknap Papers 5, 3:176). The party's inability even to inscribe their presence on the summit rocks underscores the struggle the party members had with the adverse climate above treeline as well as the difficult and foreign landscape they tried to place in a familiar context. As much as Belknap, Cutler, and Little, as the chroniclers of the expedition, essayed to do the work of nation building on the mountain, by suppressing the imported rhetoric of the sublime, by naming the mountain after the new nation's patriarch after their return, and by physically chiseling the initials of the state into the summit rocks, their attempts to overwrite the mountain with nationalist fervor were frustrated by the mountain itself. This was not terrain that could simply be overwritten by text; the undulating topography of its countless ledges and scree slopes proved a challenge not only to the climbers' physical ability but also to their descriptive lexicon.

With the erroneous readings of elevation, the loss of instruments, the clouding over of the view from the summit, and Belknap's own inability to complete the ascent (a fact that he regretted for several years as he continued to plan a never-realized return trip with Manasseh Cutler), the Belknap-Cutler expedition to Mount Washington might seem to a large degree a failure.[7] What saves it from failure, however, are the pains that Belknap took to promote the trip and the region through his letters, his articles, and his expansive three-volume *History of New Hampshire*. Though the trip was billed as the first scientific expedition to the peak, Belknap's subsequent descriptive and narrative texts present it in the framework of a "Tour of the White Mountains," and indeed Belknap's party can be said to fulfill multiple roles—among them scientist, explorer, and tourist. Belknap's initial narrative of the expedition, which appeared only months after the 1784 expedition, was published in the same ten-year period as such seminal American works of environment and ideology as Thomas Jefferson's *Notes on the State of Virginia* and William Bartram's *Travels*. Like those texts, Belknap's narrative is bordered by the works of seventeenth-century New England explorers like John Josselyn and Darby Field on one side and, on the other, by the proliferation of texts by travel and guidebook writers that would begin to appear shortly after the beginning of the nineteenth century.

Where Cutler's moment in the sun atop what was purported to be the new nation's highest peak enabled him to "be a solar Eye" and redefine the mountainscape before him in more familiar environmental and economic terms, Belknap's own slow descent of the mountain dissolves the abstract *space* of the expansive view into a closer relationship with the *place* of the mountain.[8] It is Belknap's narrative (and that it is a *narrative* is significant, as we will see below) that enables him to create a closer relationship with the particulars of the forest. The dialogue precipitated by the different accounts of the Belknap expedition foregrounds what Laurence Buell sees as the "interplay of map knowledge and place sense" (*Environmental Imagination* 278). The "alterity" or "betweenness" created by the slippage between place and space during the 1784 climb in the White Mountains engenders a politicized space. Belknap's eventual naming of the peak in the third volume of his *History of New Hampshire* (1791) finally, and grandly, enfolds the White Mountains into the political landscape of the early republic. Belknap, who was particularly enamored of General Washington during the War for Independence, sent him a copy of the first volume of his *History* and met him during the new president's trip to Boston and Portsmouth in October 1789. Finally naming the mountain after Washington in 1791, Belknap echoes popular sentiment by carving out of Josselyn's "daunting terrible" wilderness a monument to the hero of the new nation. Cutler's projection of his local topography onto his view from the mountaintop, juxtaposed with Belknap's intimate relationship with the mountain as *place*, underscores the complexity of this expedition's narratives, as they unsuccessfully attempt to define the heterogeneity of the mountains in a unified, static narrative. It is when Belknap, and later Cutler as well, look to the intricacies of the mountainside that the narrative of the climb begins to distinguish between the mountains as a discrete, fixed *space* and as a knowable *place*.[9]

Whereas his focus on the White Mountains' exterior is apparent in his general descriptions, Belknap's experience during the expedition, as it can be reconstructed from his narrative in the *History of New Hampshire* along with a number of earlier letters and published articles, follows a different storyline. Belknap, whom Daniel Little describes as "very corpolant" (1) at the time of the expedition, accompanied the others only to just below treeline, where he opted to return to base camp on his own. Belknap states that he "had the pleasure of seeing what none of the rest did" (*History* 3:174). The rest of the party was intent upon reaching the summit, and indeed had time to look at little else; Cutler, for example, notes that the party wished to explore a cascade they saw a short distance up the mountainside, and they "fully determined to explore the river thoroughly, and measure the cascade . . . but the shortness of our time . . . prevented" (*Life* 1:101). Later, during their final ascent, Cutler observes that "the stones in [the] river were curious, containing talc, starry appearances, and many very light, but we had not the time to examine them critically" (*Life* 1:102). Unencumbered by the goal of summitting, Belknap took his time descending the mountain, noting and estimating the size of a unique precipice and leisurely noting "the sublimity of the everyday" (Lawson, "Elder" 221) and minutiae like "water trickling out from between" a pile of boulders. The most significant result of Belknap's time alone was his refocusing on the details of the mountain landscape, to allow his narrative to transgress the frame of his previous distant perspectives (evident in his tableau-like images of the mountain in profile) and finally to understand the mountain less as a single entity and more as a series of interrelated systems.

> The side of the Mountain, as far as I ascended, is composed of a mass of loose rocks, covered with a deep green moss, in some places as thick as a *bed*. The moss covers the rocks and their interstices, so that in many places you walk on it and it bends under you, and yet supports your weight; but in other places it proves treacherous, and lets you through. . . . This moss on the steep sides of the Mountain serves as a sponge to retain the vapors which are continually brought by winds in the form of clouds against these Mountains, and there deposited. It also preserves the rain-water from running off at once, and keeps the springs supplied with a perpetual dripping. (Papers 5, 3:174 – 75)

The percolating of water through the moss connects the more general proclamations about the area's fertility by a number of expedition members with Belknap's own insistence that the mountains themselves generate weather throughout New England. The fertility and settlement possibilities suggested by the rivers met by the expedition on its approach arise, Belknap asserts here, from the very web of moss that is constantly underfoot in the deepest recesses of the mountain's ravines. Belknap's (however fleeting) connection with Bartram's observations that "reveal and celebrate the fabric of interrelationships . . . in the wilderness" (Branch, "Indexing" 288) is apparent in his movement from a broad tableau to the minutiae of the mountain ecosystem. Like Bartram and his contemporary Jefferson, Belknap actively constructs a bridge from a systemic and timeless Linnaean categorization to a more profound grasp of nature's interconnectedness. In his limning of the relationship between mountainside ecology and water resources, Belknap also echoes Crèvecoeur's critique of the decline in waterpower as a result of the denuded "ancient forests [that] kept the earth moist and damp" (285) This rising chorus of ecological awareness would eventually find its voice in George Perkins Marsh's 1864 *Man and Nature.*

As early scientists, Manasseh Cutler, Daniel Little, and Jeremy Belknap have been said to have written "clumsily" about the White Mountains, but their very "lack of a sense of panorama" (Purchase 141), enabled them to focus their expedition's attentions on the intimacies of place rather than vast, unquantifiable sublime vistas. Eric Purchase has recently argued that Cutler's focus was limited to "the ground immediately under foot" and that he mistakenly "wrote of Mount Washington's shoulders or outcroppings as if they were separate summits" (142). To some degree, the party's naïveté did occlude its ability to fully engage the experience offered by their ascent, but it is in the very transition from broad to specific that one can find value in Cutler's descriptions of "the ground . . . underfoot." Much as his view from the summit framed the vista in familiar, domestic terms, Cutler's representations of his ascent show the blurring of the boundary between local and distant views: "The mountain above the shrubs has the appearance of a close-fed pasture, with many detached rocks rising above the surface. As we advanced we found it to be a mere mass of rocks, covered with a mat of long moss, their crevices and between them filled up with various kinds of vegetables, most of them such as we had never before seen" (*Life* 103).

Whereas nineteenth-century writers became more concerned with destinations and views (which was one of the reasons for the construction of a carriage road, cog railway, and hotel on Mount Washington's summit in the second half of the century), in the focus on the landscape *through* which they traveled, Cutler and Belknap emphasize the distinction between vast open spaces and the places in between. Cutler's own struggle to describe the White Mountains echoes with sentiments drawn straight from Josselyn's enumerative descriptions over a hundred years earlier as Cutler identifies the "number of fish . . . which . . . very readily bit," extensive "tall woods," "finest intervale[s]," and "very well built houses and fine farms" (*Life* 1:98–99). It is in this same narrative, however, that Cutler takes time to look in the spaces between rocks on the summit plateau and catalog the mountain cranberries, Labrador tea, and stunted spruce.

The landscape of the White Mountains, as Thoreau would point out several decades later, after his own visit to the region, provides but little correlation between the regular summit pyramids seen from the distance and a mountain's actual terrain of granite crags and talus. It is the mountains' very topography that works to shape a travel writer's language. For Cutler and Belknap, finally on the slopes of the peak they had for so long seen only from a distance, the text can no longer comfortably present a static, distant representation; the explorers are drawn to look into the mountains' crevices and see what lies therein. The White Mountains, to borrow from Anne Whiston Spirn's landscape poetics, present a *cacophonic* rather than a *euphonic* landscape, thereby challenging writers to explore the mountains' interstices.[10] The nationalist rhetoric of a number of late eighteenth- and early nineteenth-century travel narratives both rearranges the landscape according to established categories of discourse and is similarly transformed by the landscape it seeks to describe. This physical and literary middle ground pointedly illustrates the blurring of discourses addressed by Michel de Certeau as a "sort of void, a narrative symbol of exchanges and encounters" (127), which acts as a *third space* invested with a multiplicity of competing discourses. Landscape's dialogic relationship with language in these texts points to a complex intersection of text and terrain — the work on the page reflecting, shaping, and mediating the national work of landscape change.

"Attending to the grammar of enduring context [of place]," Spirn writes, "entails a response . . . to the physical context of landforms, plants, and plant communities" (181). The dialogic tendencies of landscape writers to act as interlocutors with the landscape, to "allow the landscape to enter *them* in order to be expressed through their writing" (McDowell 381, emphasis mine), suggests further that the landscape, itself a dynamic text, both changes and is changed by the act of writing. Such a negotiation between topography and text, overt in works of later landscape writers, is apparent in zones of contact between landscape and ideology in travel writing published far earlier than Jeremy Belknap's.[11] Whereas W. J. T. Mitchell, using "landscape" as a verb rather than a noun, defines landscape as "an instrument of cultural power" (1), I argue that to perceive landscape merely as a tool is to belie the dialogue that occurs as one is able to see beyond the static scenes of a distant, unreachable mountainscape to the intricacies of a mountain's ecosystem.

By the publication of his third volume of the *History of New Hampshire* in

1793, Belknap is able to reconcile many of the "interstices" of his own experience. This final narrative of the 1784 expedition attempts to combine Belknap's own perceptions with the reports of those, like Cutler and Little, who had summitted the newly named Mount Washington. Although Belknap has the benefit of having read (and incorporated into his now fully encompassing perspective) the words and perceptions of others, the most striking parts of the *History* are most likely drawn from the expedition leader's *departure* from his companions. Belknap's solo descent informs his perception of relationships throughout the forest, where

> trees are seen growing on a naked rock; their roots either penetrate some of its crevices, or run over its surface, and shoot into the ground. When a tree is contiguous to a small rock, its bark will frequently enclose and cover it. Branches of different trees, but of the same species, sometimes intertwine, and even ingraft themselves, so as to grow together in one. (Papers 5, 3:174)

In these moments, where distance from the expedition's expressed goal offers him the clarity of a detailed perspective, Belknap anticipates the synecdoche of a Thoreauvian vertical perception, arguing that "notwithstanding the gloomy appearance of an American forest . . . a contemplative mind may find in it many subjects of entertainment" (6, 3:173). Combined with his gravitation earthward, Belknap's focus on the connections among the individual trees, as he descends through woods that would be described twenty-five years later as "woods, wet, tangled, twisted to a degree almost impenetrable" (*Dartmouth Gazette,* "White Mountains" 2), pieces together the various parts of the forest in a rudimentary view of the mountainside's ecosystem. Whereas other members of the party continued their ascent, preoccupied with reaching the summit, Belknap resigned himself to a solitary retreat to camp but took the time on his walk to notice the minutiae the expansive landscape provided.

Ecological impulses surface in the midst of Belknap's generally broader, exterior descriptions to suggest an inchoate anticipation of environmental texts from the nineteenth century, including those of Thoreau, Muir, and George Perkins Marsh. Marsh, specifically, was among the nineteenth century's most vocal critics of land abuse in the Northeast. He consistently drew attention to connections among forests' "weather, stream flow, and water supplies" to advocate moderation in the unchecked deforestation that competed for resources with a burgeoning tourist industry in the late nineteenth century (McCollough 203). Belknap's focus on similar interrelationships almost a century earlier on the eastern slope of Agiocochook, yet to be named Mount Washington, helps to set a precedent for the tension between the external, superficial perspectives of tourism and other resource-dependent industries on one hand, and on the other close readings of a forest that can seem to "grow together in one."

Upon leaving the White Mountains almost half a century after Belknap's visit, Henry David Thoreau looked back on the peaks of the eastern Franconia range from the artists' colony in Compton,

> surprised by the regular pyramidal form of most of the peaks, including La-fayette, which we had ascended. I think that there must be some ocular illu-sion about this, for no such regularity was observable in ascending Lafayette. ... [W]hen the summit viewed is fifty or a hundred miles distant, there is but very general and very little truth in the impression of its outline conveyed to the mind. (Howarth 277–78)

A distant gaze, though it may offer a picturesque perspective on the mountain landscape, Thoreau argues, does not allow visitors to fully connect with the landscape through which they travel. This sentiment would become popular in guidebooks published in the second half of the nineteenth century, as authors reacted to the huge numbers of train- and carriage-borne tourists who never left the comforts their luxury resorts provided them. Thoreau, who repeatedly consults Belknap's *History* as a cultural and environmental guidebook both in *A Week on the Concord and Merrimack Rivers* (Thoreau) and in his journals (Howarth, *Thoreau*), explicitly challenges the nature of representations made from afar in suggesting that the "very little truth" (Howarth 278) in those works might be tempered by a closer reading of the intricacies and interrelationships of the landscape. Implicit in Thoreau's comment on the deceptive nature of the distant view is a critique of the artist's tendency to seek a perfect perspective that smooths the mountains' rough character and occludes their uniqueness. Tourists and artists visiting the White Mountains in the mid-nineteenth cen-tury were often engaged in the *consumption of views* rather than the *experience of nature*, and Thoreau's comments mark the beginnings of a focus beyond the purview of the average seasonal tourist to an interior landscape. Reflected later by such artists as Albert Bierstadt, Edward Hill, and David Johnson, these concerns would also find their voice in the popular press in the work of writers like Thomas Starr King, who would note in his 1859 guidebook to the White Mountains that tourists "will *gobble* some of the superb views between two trains, with as little consciousness of any flavor or artistic relish, as a turkey has in swallowing corn" (17).

In many ways, Belknap was complicit in an attempt to segregate, box, enclose, and circumscribe the White Mountains, trying to categorize, as well as possible, the region's unique features of climate, elevation, and environment. Indeed, much of the writing that came from the Belknap expedition endeavors to quantify the mountains as so many resources. Daniel Little's preoccupation with the time, Manasseh Cutler's efforts to record temperature and baromet- ric pressure to determine a tolerably accurate altitude for the peak they had climbed, as well as Belknap's own attempts to precisely plot the expedition's course all contribute to an imperial enterprise of categorizing the landscape. The various texts that have been preserved from the expedition serve to reify the agenda of a newly independent American ideology of exploration and ex- pansion northward as well as westward. At the same time, however, Belknap's narratives, like those of his contemporary William Bartram, look beneath the surface to act as a "defense of the region's integrity, not an apologia for con- quest" (Buell, *Environmental* 63). Much like Bartram's work, Belknap's rhetoric acts to interweave the expansionist rhetoric of a new nation, the urgency of scientific discovery, and, to borrow from John Muir, the "grand palimpsest of the world" (93) created by rewriting the mountains from within an imported landscape aesthetic. In reading Belknap, it is useful to take a cue from the geog- rapher Derek Gregory and suggest that the spatial structure of the mountains is "not merely the arena" (120) within which political re-presentation and restruc- turing of the landscape occurs, for the rural environment offers a topographical double-voicedness, wherein the terrain both transforms and is affected by an explorer's agenda.[12]

The complexity of Belknap's narratives, as they draw from eighteenth-century traditions of classification and categorization, as well as presage nineteenth- century tourist and environmental writing, is apparent in his oscillation be- tween distance from and intimacy with the White Mountain ecoscape. The socio-environmental implications of this intermediary position also anticipate the growth of a class distinction between the region's settlers and its future visitors. Participating in a "post-European pastoral perception [that] can, both despite and because of itself, involve a reciprocal process of being defamiliar- ized and instructed by the environmental encounters" (Buell, *Environmental* 77), Belknap reads the expanding logging of the New Hampshire landscape as a social as well as environmental act. He observes in the first volume of *History of New Hampshire* that although "contractors and agents made large fortunes by this traffic . . . the laborers who spent their time in the woods . . . were generally kept in a state of poverty and dependence" (1:150). This growing disconnection between the residents and employees of this working forest and the frequently higher class of recreational visitor would eventually sow the seeds of an economic and ideological dynamic that would become a significant factor in the development of a sustainable land ethic in the next century.

Other late eighteenth-century writers who visited the new nation's rural regions were also drawn to comment on the transformation of the landscape, though often with more aesthetic concerns in mind. During his tour through the northeastern United States and southern Canada in 1795, Isaac Weld noted that "the stumps of the trees . . . on newly cleared land, are most disagreeable objects, wherewith the eye is continually assailed" (*Travels* 1:41). His commentary here draws attention to what would remain a common agricultural practice, similarly condemned by travel and environmental writers throughout the next century. Isaac Weld also embodies the distance between early tourists and residents, observing that to settlers "the sight of a wheat field or a cabbage garden would convey pleasure far greater than that of the most romantic woodland views" (*Travels* 1:41). Weld's appeal to the picturesque, projected onto the American landscape from the aesthetic ideology borrowed to a large degree from Edmund Burke's 1756 essay, *A Philosophical Enquiry into the Origin of Our Ideas of the Sublime and Beautiful*, would become the ideology de rigueur of White Mountains visitors in the nineteenth century. As a means of reading the landscape, the picturesque and sublime are necessarily distancing ideologies that assert that "without an elite consumer . . . there [is] no real landscape" (Brown 57) and that reaffirm the difference between tourist, as a viewer of the landscape, and resident, as a participant in it.

Although principally an explorer, Jeremy Belknap appeals to the emerging landscape aesthetics of his contemporaries as early as 1784, when he asserts that "the most *romantic imagination here finds itself surprised and stagnated*" (*Papers* 5, 3:183), and, in a somewhat more tempered tone in the *History* in 1791:

a poetic fancy may find full gratification amidst these wild and rugged scenes, if its ardor be not checked by the fatigue of the approach. Almost every thing in nature, which can be supposed capable of inspiring ideas of the sublime and beautiful, is here realized. Aged mountains, stupendous elevations, rolling clouds, impending rocks, verdant woods, chrystal streams, and gentle rill, and the roaring torrent, all conspire to amaze, to soothe and to enrapture. (3:39)

As he continues to reconcile his experiences over the nine years between his initial and his final, most polished descriptions of the expedition, Belknap tempers his appeal to the contemporary aesthetic, suggesting practically that the Notch of the White Mountains he describes in this passage is romantic only if one has the leisure to view it as "sublime and beautiful." One might suggest that Belknap's narrative of his expedition invokes Richard Rorty's notion of culture as conversation, though in this instance the conversation is across an ecotone between exterior and interior created by Belknap's situating himself on the periphery. Rather than imposing an imperialist framework onto a landscape, he fashions a view of the White Mountains such that the landscape and framework become merged to create a new environmental discourse.

At this time, both residents and speculators began to understand that tourism could grow into a viable industry unto itself, and settlers themselves often refashioned themselves as entrepreneurs in the tourist trade. Tourists modeling their itineraries and expectations after the recently fashionable European tours to the Lake District in England or the French, Swiss, and Italian Alps, were looking for a place ripe with wild, sublime scenery. The White Mountains' accessibility to Boston, New York, and Philadelphia made them a natural destination.

Edward Augustus Kendall, visiting the White Mountains still early in their development in 1807, found a region very similar to the one visited by Jeremy Belknap, with perhaps a few more settlements and overnight houses, but certainly still a developing region compared with what it would become later in the century. Following conventions of his literary contemporaries, Kendall frames the mountains in the rhetoric of the sublime, offering up numerous "torrents," "deep and rugged ravines," and "steep, narrow defiles" to capture the attention of his readers (175). He paints his scenes with lavish language, for, like Belknap's work, Kendall's *Travels* would likely not be read by many would-be visitors to the region — tourism would not become a significant industry in the region for another twenty years. Even in the early decades of the nineteenth century, the White Mountains were only on the verge of being discovered as a destination for wealthy tourists. In fact, Kendall traveled through the mountains on his way to Vermont, suggesting that the region did not yet merit its own tour. Kendall was content only to look at the peaks from afar, and since he visited the mountains during a snowy November, he would have likely been unable to climb any peaks had he so desired.

While he participates in the same distancing language of his predecessors and contemporaries, Kendall also looks ahead to the area's development. At one of his last stops on the trip through the mountains, Kendall looks back to the slopes of Mount Washington and remarks that "not only pastures, fields, and villages should enliven the expanse of wood, but the forest, while it remains, must necessarily conceal, under its own uniform and sombrous green . . . many bodies of water, which, being laid open and reflecting the light and colours of the skies, would brighten and exhilarate the scene" (187).

In essence anticipating the future clearcutting of those same mountainsides, Kendall's pastoral impulse takes a step beyond Belknap's here to "enliven" the landscape with settlers and farmers (as though they were part of the mountainside itself) and to suggest that the visitor can see all that nature has to offer without penetrating the interior if the exterior is simply removed. In representing the landscape for an urban audience of armchair travelers, Kendall laments that he cannot proclaim the discovery of an earth that "glows with the colors of civilization; the banks of the streams are enamelled with richest grasses; woodlands and cultivated fields are harmoniously blended. . . . And man is still in harmony with nature, which he has subdued, cultivated, and adorned" (Bancroft 269). Kendall visited the region before it had been developed for tourism, and, like Timothy Dwight, who traveled the same route four years earlier, he saw in it the possibilities for an expansion of an agrarian ideal into the wilderness; "it is population, too, and agriculture, that must give to such prospects the beauty and diversity expected from them" (Kendall 178).

Without considering the needs or desires of the very settlers with whom he lodged during his visit, Kendall wanted to clear away the forest cover so there would no distinction between exterior and interior and both could be apprehended from afar. Kendall's agenda of refashioning the mountainsides is not limited to furthering agricultural development on the northern frontier, however; by in effect eliding settler and forest into a single view, Kendall's travel narrative illustrates the beginnings of a separation between resident and visitor that would continue throughout the region's development as both an eventual working forest and a tourist destination.

If Belknap occupied multiple roles of rediscoverer, explorer, and proto-tourist, Kendall is among the region's first self-conscious and self-publicizing tourists. Publishing the account of his many trips throughout the Northeast as a travel narrative, and writing for an audience of upper-class tourists newly armed with European landscape sensibility gleaned from English Romanticism, Kendall looked at the White Mountains through a lens that acted to occlude the difference between viewing landscape as a distant tableau and reaching an intimate understanding of the forest by penetrating its interior. A number of critics have illustrated that the word *landscape* derives from the Dutch word *landschap* and the early English word *landskip*, which referred specifically to Dutch artistic representations of the countryside. Myers asserts that "*Country-side* denoted a place, *landscape* a representation of a place" (70). Although this conception began to wane in the nineteenth century — and to be replaced by a more dynamic meaning, wherein "landscape is not a mere visible surface, static composition, or passive backdrop to human theater" (Spirn 17) — it is precisely this earlier meaning that Kendall evokes when he remakes the western slopes of Mount Washington into a pastoral painting of the European countryside.[13]

The various narratives of Jeremy Belknap's 1784 expedition to the White Mountains illustrate a mediation between the static tableaus of Josselyn's un-approachable wilderness "cloathed with infinite thick woods" and later nineteenth-century concerns with the interiors that early visitors, like Edward Augustus Kendall, could not see beneath the forest canopy. The nature of Belknap's relation to the landscape, then, complicates a reading of his expedition as merely a reductive tool of imperialism. Although the party's involvement in what Mary Louise Pratt terms "anti-conquest," wherein the author's "imperial eyes passively look out and possess" the landscape they traverse (7), is apparent, there is evidence in the various narratives of the expedition of a movement beyond this occupying gaze toward a dialogic relationship with the landscape of the White Mountains. In the first quarter of the nineteenth century, the relationship between writer and landscape continues to be one of dialogue in which, as Anne Whiston Spirn suggests, "ambiguity — layers of landscape meanings — and the metaphors and paradoxes it engenders are a source of rich material for reading and telling" (27). The difficulties presented by the narratives of Belknap's expedition, which attempt to write a dynamic landscape into what was to a large degree a predetermined framework, point to a site of negotiation and dialogue between cultural ideologies and a living ecosystem. This site, an ecotone between an established forest and a variety of pressures — from tourists, residents, entrepreneurs, speculators — would become central in the nineteenth century to defining the relationship between text and topography.

CHAPTER TWO

Economic Topographies

Unsettling the History of Early Tourism
in New Hampshire's White Mountains

 IN THE EARLY YEARS of the nineteenth century, perhaps as a result of Belknap's prototourism, tourists from throughout the Northeast began to venture into the White Mountains, which were now slowly being settled by trappers, farmers, and other entrepreneurs. The turnpike that had been established through the White Mountain Notch, thanks to the persistence and ingenious horsemanship of Timothy Nash and Benjamin Sawyer,[1] inevitably led to the need for overnight houses along this new and direct route from Portland and Portsmouth to northern New Hampshire and Vermont. Along with the traders, merchants, and teamsters such as those Hawthorne cataloged during his 1832 visit were a few tourists eager to be among the first to climb Mount Washington and its yet unnamed sister summits. The earliest guided ascents of Mount Washington were led almost exclusively by members of the Crawford family, whose forebear, Eleazer Rosebrook, had maintained an overnight house since 1803 for teamsters and traders driving along the Tenth New Hampshire Turnpike in the central Notch of the White Mountains (today called Crawford Notch) (fig. 2).

When Ethan Allen Crawford and Lucy Crawford joined their grandfather, Eleazer Rosebrook, in Nash and Sawyer's Location at the foot of Mount Washington in 1817, the Crawfords' location near New England's highest peak had already begun to make their home a popular starting point for aspiring mountain climbers.[2] The rhetoric of a wilderness that flanked the approach to Mount Washington's summit no doubt deterred many casual mountaineers; a *Dartmouth Gazette* article of 29 September 1819 ("White Mountains" 2) is typical, echoing the narratives of Jeremy Belknap's and Darby Field's expeditions in asserting that "obstructions in a steep ascent [in the White Mountains] would, it should seem, deter any one from the labor . . . who possessed less than an iron constitution" (2). Published two months after Abel Crawford and his son Ethan

completed the first footpath to the summit of Mount Washington, the article
makes the claim (most likely as an advertisement solicited by the Crawfords)
that "these difficulties are now wholly removed." As subsistence farmers, traders, and entrepreneurs the Crawfords' enterprise of landscape change located
them in a northern "wilderness" that, as Angela Miller points out, was in the
early nineteenth century a "relative" and "fluid condition within a historical
process" (117). The Crawfords found themselves in the midst of this historical
process, which interwove the landscape with economies of settlement, speculation, and tourism in the construction of what had by the 1830s already become
a "culturally valorized scenic place" (A. Wilson, 50).[3]

ON 17 SEPTEMBER 1818, Abel Crawford accompanied John Brazer of Cambridge, Massachusetts, and George Dawson of Philadelphia on an ascent of
Mount Washington. They began their climb at the home of Abel Crawford,
six miles north of the Notch of the White Mountains, and ascended the ravine
of the Ammonoosuc River on the mountain's southwest side. Abel Crawford,
one of the first settlers in the Notch, served as guide for Brazer and Dawson,
who were only the second visitors to the mountains to hire one of the Crawfords as a guide.[4] Upon reaching the summit after an uneventful climb in what
were apparently fair conditions, the men "placed an inscription in Latin, which
was engraved on a brass plate, and nailed it on a rock."[5] The inscription, in
questionable Latin, was translated by an acquaintance of Abel's son Ethan (for
which the younger Crawford can "vouch not for the Latin or translation being
correct"), and is said to have read:

> "*Altius ibunt, qui ad summa nitunteer.*" — They will go higher who strive to enter
> heaven. "*Nil reputans, si quid superesset agendum.*" — Think nothing be done while
> anything remains to be done. "*Sic itur ad astra.*" — We go thus to the stars. "*Sti-
> nere facto per inhostales sylvas Rustribus pramptis feliciter superrtes. (Eheu quantus
> adest vius sudor!) Johannes Brazer, Cantabrigsensis, Georgius Dawson, Philadel-
> phiensis, hic posuerant ivid Septembris MDCCCXVIII.*" — After passing inhospita-
> ble woods, and surmounting abrupt ledges (how it made us perspire), John Brazer,
> of Cambridge, and George Dawson, of Philadelphia, placed this inscription here
> on the fourth day of the Ides of September, 1818. (39–40)

Most likely out of practicality, Brazer and Dawson had inscribed the plate before commencing the climb, and most likely prior to even arriving in northern
New Hampshire. Never having climbed the mountain before, they nonetheless
anticipated the appropriate reaction to the mountain's summit and affixed it

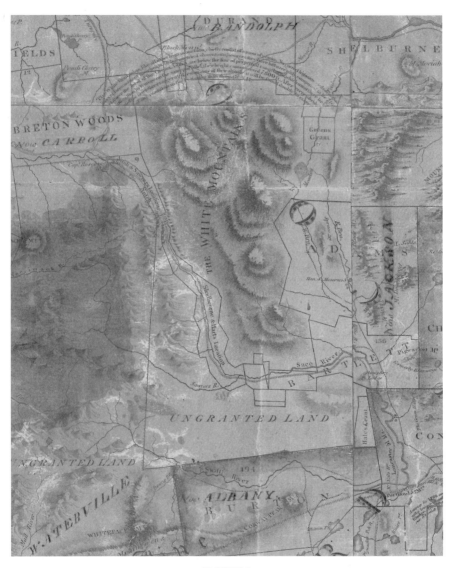

FIGURE 2

Philip Carrigain, *Map of New Hampshire*, 1816, detail. Courtesy
of the New Hampshire Historical Society.

there so others might subsequently share their sentiment (or, apparently lack-ing sentiment themselves, given the generic nature of the lines that begin their inscription, might avail themselves of a pre-scribed one). Not unlike many sev-enteenth- and eighteenth-century explorers of the White Mountains, Brazer and Dawson furnished the experience of reaching the summit with far more rhetorical significance than they gave to the actual ascent. Manasseh Cutler's remarks from the same summit thirty-four years earlier, that the mountains around him resemble the "stacks and cocks of hay" of his native coastal Ips-wich, are endowed with a similarly imported sentiment by which the spectacle of the summit is, in effect, pre-scribed from the climber's own experience. John Josselyn's 1672 *New England Rarities Discovered* similarly invests textual de-scription of the White Mountains with the political implications of locating a newly discovered landscape within an existing discourse. Where Cutler and Josselyn adapted the mountain view to their own rhetorical and perceptual framework, however Brazer and Dawson adapted language from a culture, lo-cation, and class far different from that of the White Mountain region.

As early tourists, furthermore, Brazer and Dawson illustrate a shift from the overt commodification of landscape in exploration narratives like those of Manasseh Cutler and John Josselyn to a focus on the scenery itself. Similarly, their appeal to the transcendental power of a sublime landscape situates their ascent at the beginning of a growing preoccupation with the White Mountains as a fertile scenographic destination.[6] More than merely economic, the nine-teenth-century tourist's sublime gaze (though often generic, pre-scribed, and disinterested) came to reconstruct the viewscape into a "religious, moral, and frequently nationalistic concept of nature" (Novak, *Nature and Culture* 38) that buttressed contemporary westward (and northward) expansion. More than an overt (or from a Kantian perspective, internalized) reaction to specific scenes or situations such as mountaintops, precipices, and expansive vistas, by the mid-nineteenth century the sublime had become enfolded in a larger ideological apparatus of landscape appropriation.

Prior to 1818, aspiring mountain climbers had access to only a few descrip-tions of the White Mountains to guide them and shape their perceptions. Jer-emy Belknap's narrative of his 1784 expedition to Mount Washington, and Ed-ward Augustus Kendall's 1809 *Travels*, as noted earlier, were two of the principal available works of travel literature about the region. In addition, a new detailed map of New Hampshire, meticulously researched and engraved over a thirteen-year period by Philip Carrigain, was made widely available in 1816.[7] The lack of textual grounding notwithstanding, the transformation of the region's literary focus from scientific exploration to scenic exploitation was, nonetheless, abrupt and overwhelming.[8] As a number of mountain towns saw their year-round populations double during the first decade of the nineteenth century, the White Mountains' early settlers witnessed as well a rapid increase in the number of summer visitors in the twenty years that followed.[9] With this inrush of seasonal tourists came a burgeoning appetite for descriptive and prescriptive writing about the mountains. This turned the writing itself into an industry, in which the views became the currency of writers and artists. As early as the 1820s, popular writers like James K. Paulding and Nathaniel Willis parodied the often absurd juxtaposition of natural wonders by an elite tourist class along the northeast's "fashionable tour." Willis's story of two students visiting Niagara Falls and mistaking the towering white façade of a grand hotel for the falls themselves poignantly critiques the frequent replacement of the sublime with the sumptuous.[10] Nathaniel Hawthorne, describing his stay at Ethan Allen and Lucy Crawford's inn in a sketch published in *New England Magazine* in 1835, reveals disdain for the romantic scenic writing that was by then a well-worn cliché. He comments on the generic nature of a "Sonnet to the snow on Mount Washington," penned by one of the party staying at Crawford's: the "lines were elegant and full of fancy, but too remote from familiar sentiment, and cold as their subject, resembling those specimens of crystallized vapor, which I observed the next day on the mountaintop" (*American Travel Sketches* 32). In its description of a generic mountain vista, as in Brazer and Dawson's prewritten inscription in 1818, this later verse places the dynamic, vibrant terrain of Mount Washington into a static (and already overused) frame.

Among the White Mountains' earliest tourists, Brazer and Dawson, whose 1818 climb had been preceded by only a handful of recorded ascents, brought with them the language of popular tourist destinations such as the Hudson River Valley, Saratoga Springs, and Niagara Falls. Like the White Mountains, these other places were not only being physically refashioned by an increase in the number of seasonal visitors, but also ideologically shaped by the very discourses that these visitors used to describe the landscape. Viewing nature thus from a rhetorical remove allowed tourists to separate themselves from the very nature they sought to visit and to participate in what Dean MacCannell identifies as the tendency to see the present as "more unified against its past [and] more in control of nature" (*Tourist* 83). The social narrative of the "tour" grew to become not only a mechanism for landscape change but a tool for social change as well. Indeed, Thomas Cole argued in 1835 that appreciation of American scenery, and participation in the rhetoric of the sublime, could elevate the very social values (and social *status*) of its viewers and help lead them to "healthful streams of true refinement" ("Essay" 100).[11] The tourist sentiments appropriated from Edmund Burke and from the poetry of Wordsworth, Byron, and Shelley — already a staple of the fashionable southern New England tour in 1820 — would become part of the core lexicon of the White Mountain tour in the decades that followed.

More immediately, Brazer and Dawson's climb served to delineate the boundaries in what would become an increasingly complex relationship between seasonal visitors and the region's year-round inhabitants. The brass plate itself wrote the summit experience for an exclusive tourist population; the Latin, familiar to educated upper-class tourists, was unreadable to most White Mountain residents. The theft of the plaque (among other items) from the summit in 1825 underscored what would soon become a very real disparity between local residents and visiting tourists. By removing the plaque as a symbol of tourist encroachment on the local landscape, the perpetrators, residents of the nearby village of Jackson, were implicated in a very literal confrontation between symbolic uses of the landscape and its more practical appropriation. Crawford comments that "mischievous persons" who committed the theft drank "the spirit which we had left there in the bottles . . . robbed the hills of the brass plate, my lead sheet, and everything left there" (*History* 73). The "mischievous persons" were identified and the affair recorded, though Crawford felt "condemned for not prosecuting them" fully for the theft (73). Perhaps Crawford declined to pursue the matter because, despite their crime, the mountain guide nonetheless saw the thieves as more practically minded than the tourists who left the articles, recounting that "the lead, I was told, was run into balls; the bottles, of course, were useful; but what use they could make of the brass, with the Latin inscription thereon, I am not able to say" (73).

Brazer and Dawson's ascent and its aftermath are recorded in the first book-length history of the White Mountain region, Lucy Crawford's *History of the White Mountains*. First published in 1846, Crawford's *History* is a first-person settlement narrative describing the inhabitants, early tourists, topography, and development of northern New Hampshire. As Crawford traces more than thirty years of life in the White Mountains, her emphasis departs from the calculated language of the region's earlier explorers and moves from a focus on the "text as a verbal structure and onto facts themselves" (Franklin 131). The region's relatively rapid settlement enabled Crawford to illustrate the conflicts inherent in the transformation of the region from frontier to tourist destination in a period of three decades. If the quantity of writing about the mountains can be seen as some measure of the explosive growth of the region's tourism, then as the first book-length history and guide to the region, Lucy Crawford's *History* served as a spring for the virtual freshet of guidebooks, histories, and tourists that followed.

Published at the very beginning of a sudden upsurge in White Mountain tourism, Crawford's text presents numerous first- and second-hand accounts of events that are further embellished in later histories and guidebooks. The many texts published after Crawford's that attempt to meaningfully engage the interplay of tourism and the mountain landscape often draw their illustrations directly from Crawford's work.[12] Crawford's accounts of local tragedies, such as the slide that killed the Willey family in 1826 and Nancy Barton's death in 1778, as well as her anecdotes of early life in the mountains, all reappear in modified form throughout the body of White Mountain literature published in the second half of the nineteenth century. As a narrative describing the transformation of the White Mountains from northern frontier to tourist destination, the *History* confronts the very beginnings of the complicated relationships between year-round residents and summer visitors that were beginning to emerge. It is the economy of this relationship that provided the Crawford family's subsistence and the framework for Crawford's *History*. Crawford intimates the overt connection between her family history and the economic and social environment of a developing tourist trade in the introduction to the 1846 edition:

> It may be enquired, by some persons, what has become of Crawford, the Mountaineer, or Ethan of the Hills. It will be the endeavor of the Authoress of this Tale to relate some of his misfortunes and adventures. . . . These facts [Ethan] was unwilling, at first, to have published, as he did not wish to expose those who seemed to be against him: they have been stated in as moderate terms as possible, as we do not wish to injure the feelings even of enemies if we have any such. (ix)

The *History*'s emphasis here on absence — and, later in the text, on resettlement — depicts an environment wherein the economic realities of settlement and entrepreneurship confront the romantic agrarian images presented by the century's earliest visitors, Timothy Dwight and Edward Kendall, and later in the carefully organized paintings by Hudson River School and White Mountain School artists.[13]

Lucy Crawford, who asks her readers in 1846 whether "this same country [can] produce a man now with such wonderful power of muscle and strength of mind" (3) as Eleazer Rosebrook, clearly reflects on the differences between her family and the newly arriving tourists. Her critical view of the mountains' new seasonal residents simultaneously laments the loss of northern New Hampshire's frontier environment to tourist development, and, as a consequence, the loss of the influence of a force that Fredrick Jackson Turner's sweeping thesis would argue at century's end as essential to shaping American identity. Perhaps also reacting to the outmigration of New England farmers to the fertile plains of the Midwest, Crawford's comments at midcentury implicate her family both as settlers, in the trade of subsistence commodities, and as subjects of commerce. The *History*, then, is both a reflection on a life already seen as distant in 1846 (and described at an even further remove by Henry Wheelock Ripley, the 1886 edition's editor, as "the echo of a voice from the misty past" [Crawford 1886 6]) and a critique of the region's abrupt transformation as the White Mountains provided central topoi in the lexicon of the fashionable tour. The *History*'s interwoven narratives of inhabitation, landscape, and tourism reveal the Crawfords as participants not in what Hector St. Jean de Crèvecoeur called the "happy effects which constantly flow . . . from sobriety and industry, when united with good land and freedom" (105), but rather in a negotiation between settlement and a developing speculative, entrepreneurial economy.

The first edition of the history, ostensibly an as-told-to narrative of the Crawford family's life in the White Mountains, presents a first-person narrator whose voice alternates between Lucy Crawford's and that of her husband, Ethan Allen Crawford. The resulting text, infused as it is with anecdotes and personal narratives, can be read as a communo-bio-oratory, which Hertha Wong defines as an as-told-to narrative whose multiple authorship invests the text with the collective history of the entire community. The relationship responsible for this communal production is codified on the book's title page, where the author is identified as "Lucy, Wife of Ethan Allen Crawford, Esq." Although writing a necessarily removed "history," Lucy Crawford's text nonetheless positions the author squarely within her subject matter. She begins the *History* with a description of the Crawfords' progenitors, the Rosebrooks, which she couches in what will become a recurring narrative mode in the text, by describing how they made a "beginning, setting an example for others to follow, suffering many hardships, and enduring many privations" (2). By commencing with a description of her grandfather's family, Crawford both identifies herself as an authority on White Mountain history and creates an inseparable association between the history of the mountains and that of the region's settlers.

The emphasis on the Crawfords' close connection with the mountains in the first chapter of Lucy Crawford's *History* is also apparent throughout the text's chronological narrative, which describes the Crawfords' lives in the Notch from the establishment of the Rosebrooks' first overnight house, through the opening of the Crawford House south of the Notch and Ethan and Lucy's construction of the Notch House in 1828, to their forced departure in 1837. Crawford characterizes her family as almost singly responsible for settling and "improving" the White Mountain Notch during the first quarter of the nineteenth century. "Discovered" in 1771 by Timothy Nash and Benjamin Sawyer, the Notch was first settled by Captain Eleazer Rosebrook (grandfather of Lucy and Ethan Allen Crawford). Rosebrook opened the first overnight house six miles north of the Notch when, in 1803, the Tenth New Hampshire Turnpike was commissioned to facilitate commercial traffic between the seacoast and outlying areas in northern New Hampshire and Vermont.

The first visitors to the Crawfords' houses, as White Mountain historians Guy and Laura Waterman note, "gave little thought to the mountain heights" (*Forest* 40); the road through the Notch, passable by wagons in 1803, was a central route for commerce between the coastal cities of Portland and Portsmouth and the upper Connecticut Valley. As proprietors of roadside overnight houses, the Crawfords were more concerned at first with maintaining a passage *through* the mountains rather than into their interior. Two of the White Mountains' first tourists, Timothy Dwight and Edward Augustus Kendall, though also not inclined to ascend the region's higher summits, did see in the Crawfords the possibility for improving the infrastructure and even the aesthetics of the mountains to facilitate future visits. As I note in chapter 1, Kendall's suggestion in 1807 that "pastures, fields, and villages should enliven the expanse of wood" on Mount Washington's western slopes prefigures later nineteenth-century artists who sought similar picturesque scenes throughout northern New Hampshire. In addition to eliding the work of farming with the creation of the picturesque, Kendall was convinced that Abel Crawford's notion of building a path to the summit of Mount Washington was "work which would save the visitor both fatigue and loss of time" (187). In 1803 Dwight too saw potential in the region's settlers, finding in Abel's father, Eleazer Rosebrook, a "spirit of enterprise" that refashioned the White Mountain wilderness into a romantic agrarian ideal, realizing what James Vance Jr. has termed a utopian democratic landscape. A decade later, the editors of the *Dartmouth Gazette* commended Abel and Ethan Allen Crawford's completion of the first footpath up Mount Washington, claiming that "under the present circumstances" of improvement, more visitors "will be induced to tread" atop the mountain peaks (29 September 1819).

Like his contemporary Kendall, however, Timothy Dwight was also interested in — at least rhetorically — asserting his aesthetic preconceptions on the

White Mountain Notch. South of Rosebrook's inn, Dwight passed several cascades, one of which he describes in his letters as "the most beautiful cascade perhaps in the world":

> The cliffs, together with a level at their foot, furnished a considerable opening surrounded by the forest. The sunbeams penetrating through the trees painted here a great variety of fine images of light, and edged an equally numerous and diversified collection of shadows, both dancing on the waters and alternately silvering and obscuring their course. . . . Everything assumed the character of enchantment; and, had I been educated in the Grecian mythology, I should have scarcely been surprised to find an assemblage of dryads, naiads, and oreads sporting on the little plain below our feet. (*Travels* 100)

By incorporating the description of the cascade into the framework of classical landscape painting — creating a "representation of a given landscape [that] *stands in the place of that landscape*" (Casey 23; italics in original) — Dwight's comments on the region's terrain complicate his adulation of the "rough soil" that "Tempts hardy labour" in a new Republic, which he encourages thus: "thyself revere! . . . declare / What Europe proffers, but a patchwork sway; / The garment Gothic, worn to fritter'd shreds" ("Greenfield Hill" 146). Among the earliest travel writing published about the region, Dwight's epistolary *Travels* illustrates a self-conscious separation from European rhetorical and descriptive traditions. It is telling that Dwight admits (with questionable accuracy, given his former tenure as president of Yale) that he had not been schooled in Greek mythology, and that he paints a picture of terrain "too great" and "too vast" to do anything but rise "with proud supremacy [above] . . . the world below" (98 – 99) where all the works of "Titus particularly . . . are diminished into toys and gegaws" (102). Certainly not the "Switzerland of America" that Thomas Cole and others would describe later in the century, the mountains and their settlers represent for Dwight the potentiality of a new American frontier landscape in which humanity, unlike in the "old world," is "an abundant spring, running and dividing itself everywhere agreeable to the nature and declivity of the ground" (Crèvecoeur 260). This implication of terrain in the construction of the American soul at the beginning of the nineteenth century already situated the textual identity of the Crawfords within an existing nationalist project; their success as entrepreneurs would in some way be a validation of the new Republic's agrarian mythology. Their eventual failure at the hands of real-estate speculators in the 1830s, however, rather than contradicting this myth, as I later discuss, enfolds them in the discourse of "historical relics" themselves, to inhabit the terrain of midcentury place-based writing — textually if not actually.

The work of building the first footpath to the summit of Mount Washington left indelible traces of early entrepreneurship that persist to this day. Much like the self-conscious descriptions of landscape and culture apparent in Lucy Crawford's *History*, the trail itself can be seen as a refashioning of the landscape to suit the demands of visiting tourists. The construction of this path, originally conceived by Eleazer Rosebrook, who reported his idea of building a path to Edward Kendall in 1807, had become an economic enterprise, much like boiling potash, making cheese, and offering lodging to passing teamsters. Ethan Crawford notes how, in 1819, "my father and I made a footpath from the Notch out through the woods, and it was advertised in the newspapers, and we soon began to have a few visitors" (*History* 36). Ethan's advertising and consciousness of the labor of building the path as an economic investment identifies the path as an attraction by which a greater number of visitors would be able to reach the summit and not be held back by the dense forest and its "unfriendly brush" (35).

The footpath, which is still in use today, underscores a growing divide between the region's seasonal visitors and the very topography of the mountains they came to visit. Trail building, first by hotel proprietors and later by hiking clubs, gave a larger number of aspiring mountain climbers access to the higher summits, though at the cost of traveling through the lower forests as though their "unfriendly brush" were but an obstacle to reaching the summit view. Ushered in by the aesthetic sentiment and leisure that enabled well-heeled visitors to take meandering walks through the woods, White Mountain tourists looked to local guides like the Crawfords to lead them along less-traveled paths, where they might follow William Hazlitt's 1822 entreaty in "On Going a Journey" to "shake off the trammels of the world and of public opinion — to lose our importunate, tormenting, everlasting personal identity in the elements of nature, and become the creature of the moment, clear of all ties" (76). Like the proliferation of White Mountain literature in the second half of the century, the very physical act of transforming the landscape so that it, too, might be read, reveals significant changes in land ethics and aesthetics over the course of the mid-nineteenth century. In their encyclopedic history of hiking in the Northeast, Guy and Laura Waterman trace the development of hiking trails to the summit of Mount Washington from 1825, when there were but the two footpaths built by the Crawfords, to 1855, when the peak could be ascended by four separate bridle paths, to 1885, when the summit boasted five footpaths, a carriage road, and a cog railway (*Forest* 85).

Trails often traverse a margin between human and wild, negotiating the individual's perception of the landscape and creating, over time, what Norman Maclean calls a bibliography of the woods. As John Elder discovers as he "hikes" Robert Frost's poem "Directive" in the woods above Bristol, Vermont, logging roads abandoned a century earlier continue to be navigable, as the trails follow the "natural terracing of the slope . . . around the outcrops and erratics that punctuate the syntax of the forest" (*Reading* 9). Much like the way Crawford's *History* traces the contours of social and environmental changes in the White Mountain Notch, the Crawfords' paths mediate between the dense forest, fallen trees, rock ledges, and swollen streams and people's singular desire to pass through these lower regions and reach a mountain's summit. The trail itself serves us as an effective metaphor for the Crawfords' enterprise of negotiating between the landscape that was their home and the summer visitors who came to enjoy it for their "health and amusement" (*History* 55). While seeking a similar middle ground between the Notch's visitors and residents, Crawford offers her narrative to the public as an investment in the hope of a future return.

The publication history of Crawford's book, much like the landscape and family history it recounts, illustrates the transformation of a cultural and literary landscape. First published nine years after the Crawfords' loss of their property in the White Mountain Notch, the *History* appeared in the year of Ethan Crawford's death, 1846. It was not reprinted until 1883, in an edition that corrected many of the typesetting errors of the earlier text and included a new chapter not written by Crawford entitled "The White Mountains: Where to Go and What to See" (195). An 1886 edition printed by a different publishing house added further secondary material, including "carefully selected views" and passages from a few contemporary popular guidebooks (193). Ostensibly intended to create a larger market for the book as a guide to the region, rather than a history, the additional material also overtly interweaves Lucy Crawford's voice with those of later writers. These later editions situate Lucy Crawford's original text at an epic distance from the scores of "modern" late-century guidebooks; in his preface to the 1886 edition, Henry Wheelock Ripley describes Crawford's voice as "from the misty past . . . full of rugged strength and earnest meaning, like the character of the pioneers of the mountains, like the mountains themselves" (Crawford 1886 6). Although merging the Crawfords with the "mountains themselves" elevates the family to the status of local icon, it also strips them of their identity and makes of them simply another stop on the tourist's agenda. As I explore in chapter 3, the guidebook industry flourished after 1850, with no fewer than fifty-three substantial White Mountain guidebooks going to press in the second half of the century. The majority of these books describe the same sites and historical events, often tracing similar topographical boundaries along heavily traveled tourist routes. The resulting intertextual quagmire, wherein sublime views were continually reinscribed on the landscape, was substantially indebted to Lucy and Ethan Allen Crawford's firsthand accounts.[14]

Despite the relatively sparse publication history of the *History*, Lucy Crawford herself revised her 1846 edition after Ethan's death. The first edition did not sell particularly well, and, as Crawford saw her book in part as a venture that might enable her to return to the White Mountains, she began work on a revision that might be more marketable.[15] This never-published manuscript, apparently completed in 1860, the year Crawford reapplied for a copyright, updates and expands the history of the area and includes a broader historical perspective, greater descriptive narrative, and more of an appeal to the region's tourists. Thirteen chapters of the manuscript were kept by subsequent generations of Lucy's descendents until Frederick C. Crawford, who obtained the manuscript in 1951, sponsored a Dartmouth College edition published in 1966. Stearns Morse edited two editions entitled *Lucy Crawford's History of the White Mountains* (Dartmouth 1966; Appalachian Mountain Club 1978), which combine the text of the 1846 *History* with excerpts from Lucy Crawford's 1860 revision (including a fourteenth chapter found later) in a single interwoven narrative.

Lucy Crawford's revision, currently housed in the Dartmouth archives as a loosely bound handwritten manuscript, takes an expanded view of the mountains as a region. It moves away from a focus solely on the Crawford family to sketch a broader picture of the transformation of the White Mountain Notch over the first half of the nineteenth century. Crawford's prefatory note to her 1860 manuscript, contrary to the later editions of Crawford's work published in the 1880s, insists again on the book's function as *history* rather than as one of many guidebooks, its authority implicitly and explicitly bolstered by Crawford's carefully positioned recollections of firsthand experiences in the mountains' early settlement.

The connection by marriage of the author of this work to one of the earliest settlers and her long residence at the mountains gives her advantage for narrating

facts concerning the hardships of the first emigrants to this romantic spot. . . .
Literary fame is no part of our intention. We leave that to those, whose imagination serves them as a guide rather than facts, while we speak of circumstances
coming under our own observation, and from early history.[16] (1860 ms. i – ii)

Crawford's efforts at rewriting the *History* were no doubt in part a reaction to
the numerous guidebooks printed in the 1840s and 1850s, including among others William Oakes's *Scenery of the White Mountains* (1848), John Spaulding's
Historical Relics (1855), Benjamin Willey's *Incidents in White Mountain History* (1856), and the most frequently reprinted nineteenth-century guidebook,
Thomas Starr King's *White Hills; Their Legends, Landscape, and Poetry* (1859).
Crawford witnessed the flood of popular White Mountain guidebooks, many
of which presented a watered-down history of the mountains' settlement, frequently without distinguishing between the Crawfords themselves and the
mountains among which they lived. In addition to trying to precipitate interest in the history of the region's residents, as well as its attractions, Crawford
was no doubt interested in claiming a portion of the newly expanded literary
market for her own. In an effort to create a unique niche for herself, where these
guidebooks catalog a changing landscape seen from the perspective of tourists
and travel writers, Crawford was able to separate herself from her contemporaries and identify herself as a White Mountain resident and therefore as a
unique authority on the events recounted in later texts.

As she fashioned her *History* as the authoritative guide to the White Mountains, Crawford was tempted to speak directly to issues of authorial control. In
a draft revision of her introduction (not bundled with the final manuscript),
Crawford informs would-be readers that

> In some of Mr. [John H.] Spaulding's Historical Sketches [*Historical Relics*] taken
> from my work is true yet in many places he had exagerated he says three public
> houses has been burnt on or near Giants grave since 1805 in this I think he is a
> little mistaken in as my grandparents lived there and I have been acquainted with
> the place ever since a child I never knew of more than two houses being burnt
> there. This he seems to say is fulfilling an old prophesy made by an Indian long
> years ago. [17] (1860 ms. unpaged)

Engaging John Spaulding's popular visitor's guide, Crawford reveals much
about the constructed nature of literary and historical associations in the
White Mountain landscape. Spaulding relegates the Crawfords themselves to
the status of *Historical Relics* and places their story alongside Indian legends

and natural wonders as "solitary pioneer[s] of this mountain wilderness" (15). Later writers also incorporated the Crawfords into their works, eager to populate the mountains, if not with the realities of frontier settlement life, then with "heroic figures — picturesque peasants, noble savages, and hardy yeomen rolled into one" (Brown 67). Nineteenth-century writers and artists frequently sought to populate their landscape representations with literary and cultural associations to rival their romantic European contemporaries. Thomas Starr King, for instance, includes excerpts from Wordsworth, Scott, Tennyson, Goethe, Shelley, and Byron alongside Bryant, Emerson, Longfellow, Whittier, and Lowell to "continue and complete the descriptions . . . or embody the predominant sentiment of the landscape" (viii). King's combined roster of American and European poets illustrates a prevailing tension between the desire to present the public a uniquely American landscape and the felt need to compare the New World with the Old. Thomas Cole, who compared the New World's mountain ranges with peaks in Wales, Scotland, Italy, and Switzerland in his 1835 "Essay on American Scenery," nonetheless saw in the American landscape's distinctly *un-European* wildness the very foundation of American character, suggesting that "American associations are not so much of the past as of the present and future" (108). Lucy Crawford's book reveals a similar dual purpose, though on a more intimate scale. On one level, her *History* retails her experiences as part of a romantic frontier myth — a "frontier nostalgia" that was fast becoming an antidote to what William Cronon sees as the "insidious" and emasculating traits of civilization ("Trouble" 78). But Crawford also looks beneath this embellished exterior at the economic realities of subsistence life as a settler. Despite her reproach of Spaulding for his appropriation of her family's history (and *History*), Crawford is similarly interested in investing her White Mountain stories with cultural associations — and in protecting those associations as her own.

By looking toward the past as well as Cole's "present and future," Crawford's 1860 manuscript tenuously negotiates between competing discourses of settler and tourist. Crawford's claim on the authenticity of her narrative, which contradicts those whose "imagination serves them as a guide" (1860 ms. i), is at times tempered by her desire to compete for the same readership. Although Lucy Crawford claims, as Stearns Morse also notes in his introduction to the 1966 edition of *Lucy Crawford's History of the White Mountains*, to eschew a "literary fame" (xxi), the concluding chapter in the manuscript contains much of the romantic sentiment of texts such as King's *White Hills*, which she might well have read, given her familiarity with other period guidebooks like Spaulding's *Historical Relics*. In its description of a landscape "both sublime and sanctified"

(Novak, *Nature and Culture* 38), the manuscript often draws on a traditionally sublime rhetoric as Crawford laments that "the pen cannot describe, nor the brush of the skillful artists paint so beautiful a picture as nature has spread before us" (1860 ms. 217). This oft-used denial of the possibility of description might be read as an echo of her separation from the "literary," although her evocation of this well-worn literary device and the more thoroughly descriptive passages elsewhere in the manuscript suggest the influence of the newly published tourist-oriented guidebooks. Taking as her model guidebooks like King's *White Hills*, Crawford includes some of her own poetry in her revision of the *History*'s final chapter. As I will discuss further in the following chapter, Crawford's inclusion of verse in her revised *History* echoes King's integration of his own poetry in *White Hills* in an effort to "help persons appreciate landscape more adequately; and to associate with the principal scenes poetic passages" (vii), which further illustrate the breadth of the mountains' iconological significance.[18] Addressing Crawford's forced exile from the White Mountains, the poem "My Mountain Home" seeks not only to make the *History* a more literary work, but also to locate the mountains, as many midcentury guidebooks sought to do, within a more global context. The lines eulogize Crawford's lost home and proclaim

> Italia's soft and balmy air, her azure tinted sky,
> May from her exiled children claim the tribute of a sigh,
> But never can their hearts with deeper feelings glow,
> For their own, bright, sunny land, than I on thee bestow. (1860 ms. 259)

The contextual associations Crawford seeks with these lines echo her contemporaries in their implication of the White Mountains in an existing tourist discourse, where they are often compared to destinations more deeply interwoven with the ligatures of culture and literature — England's Lake District, Italy's romantic ruins, France's Mont Blanc. Sarah Josepha Hale described the American landscape in 1835 as consisting of little else "but huge piles of earth and rocks, covered with blighted firs and fern," and wrote that the "light of song [must be] poured over our wide land, and its lonely and waste spaces 'peopled with the affections'" (*Traits* 90, 91) in effect, writes Dona Brown, calling for "*developing* American scenery" (46). The absence of literary associations with much of the American landscape gave rise to a social anxiety about its significance in comparison with a European countryside echoing with lines from Byron, Shelley, Wordsworth, and others in every glen and dale. Nineteenth-century American guidebook and history writers, including Crawford, sought to reassert their mountain landscape as the "Switzerland of America" by evoking not only imported poetic sentiment — in effect fixing on American scenes (and in American ideology) the reflections of English Romantic poets — but by writing onto the landscape their own often sentimental verse.

As the layered discourses of settlement and tourism in Crawford's text refashion her language for a broader, more literary audience, the content of her narrative effectively traces the widening rift between tourist and resident. The period between the 1820s and 1860s saw a change in the nature and class of mountain visitors from the traders and explorers of early years to well-to-do tourists and artists. Both Lucy Crawford's *History* and its subsequent revision record this distinction, often commenting on the rupture that contributed to the family's eventual departure. She notes, for instance, the inopportune choice of early climbers to wear "fine and costly garments into the woods," which after their climb "looked as if they had been through a beggar's press" (*History* 33). Elsewhere, the manuscript describes the difficulties of daily life in the White Mountains after the turn of the century as "a noble example to that class of ladies, at the present day, whose daily labour is performed in brushing the sidewalks with their silks" (1860 ms. 8).

Later nineteenth-century writers and editors effectively relocated the Crawfords on the periphery of the mountains, clearly defining them as mountain residents and *not* members of their upper-class readership, as I have discussed, by merging Crawford's voice with the mountains themselves and depicting the Crawford family as a "historical relic" as Ripley describes them in the 1886 edition. In the face of this marginalization, the manuscript's explicit appeal to readers is a subversive rewriting of history as social critique that foregrounds the economic realities of a superficially romantic landscape. Where guidebooks and travel narratives explicitly positioned residents and local economies on the margins of the mountain landscape and reshaped the wilderness for a genteel elite, entrepreneurs and landowners refashioned the physical landscape to suit the expectations of that same elite class of visitor. The frequent juxtaposition of opulence with the "experience" of the natural landscape in midcentury hotels and along railways and bridle paths perpetuated the notion of mountains that, as Robert McGrath notes, "were an idea before they were a reality" and were built of "images and words rather than experience" ("Real and Ideal" 59). Lucy Crawford's 1860 manuscript — in its final chapters in particular — compels its readers to see the speculative economies at work beneath the packaged, picturesque tableau of the mountain landscape.

The economic realities of mid-nineteenth century land speculation redefined

White Mountain settlers as marginal to the unimpeded northward progress of the tourist industry. In his book *Places on the Margin*, Rob Shields identifies a variety of peripheral spaces in relation to centers, including the seaside resort and urban center, and the vacation destination as escape from everyday domesticity and commerce. His perception of space involves the notion of binary interdependence; he writes that "'margins' become signifiers of everything 'centres' deny or repress; margins as 'the Other,' become the condition of possibility of all social and cultural entities" (276). This carnivalesque environment is evident in discourse about the "liminal" region of the White Mountains. The tourist industry necessarily interweaves the urban and the wild, primarily in its very construction of the "wild" as a commodity. It is, then, the *illusion* of marginality that the nineteenth-century hotel guests participate in while they inhabit isolated, encapsulated spaces of urban luxury in the mountains, experiencing marginality only on the steps of the hotel's verandah. John O'Grady cautions us not to seek an intermediate position in an imagined duality between a wilderness and the society responsible for the framing, shaping, and ideological construction of that wilderness. Careful attention to Crawford's revisions elicits similar antipathy toward the "intellectual wedge and mallet" (O'Grady 49); in the 1860 revision of the *History of the White Mountains*, Crawford integrates discourses of settler and tourist in an attempt to maintain her family's identity in the face of a growing tourist industry.

By admonishing popular writers for plagiarizing her *History*, Crawford knowingly resists being a subject of tourist discourse. By the conclusion of her chronological narrative, Crawford has redefined her text as a partly economic, speculative exercise, and she reexamines her own position as a subject of the tourist economy. Chapter 14 in the manuscript (the 1846 book contains only ten chapters) is titled "The manner in which Mr. Crawford lost his mountain home. Mr. Crawford's death. The way the children managed to obtain a living." It details the financial hardships as a result of which, she writes, "we were deterred from a return to our mountain residence" (Morse 212).[19] Perhaps incited by her daughters, Crawford seeks to make the facts of the family's forced exile "plain to public minds" and to "speak names openly" so that their situation might be perceived more favorably by the public (Morse 212).

Ethan Crawford's plans to expand and improve his inn, as Eric Purchase also notes, required capital investment that the Crawfords' subsistence income could not manage. The resulting debt with which the Crawfords were burdened (a debt that had been mounting since the fire that destroyed their home in 1818) left them vulnerable to persuasive land speculators, who were continually trying to manipulate the Crawfords' land holdings in their favor. Eventually arrested in Lancaster for failing to pay his debts, and compelled to sell his home for $300, Ethan Crawford moved with his family to Guildhall, Vermont, in 1837. Reflecting on these days and on the manipulations of later speculators, which finally prevented the family's return to the White Mountains, Lucy Crawford writes, "we were so closely held in these merciless manacles of injustice we were like the reptile under the crushing foot of the sullen serf with not even the power to squirm" (Morse 217). In her striking remarks, locating her family beneath even the "foot of the sullen serf" in the social economy of the White Mountains in the 1830s and 1840s, Crawford offers her readers a view of the economic relationships that exist just outside the frame of so many carefully wrought landscape paintings, engravings, and descriptions whose preoccupation with sublime and picturesque scenes belies the realities that confront the region's inhabitants. The proliferation of an upper-class tourist apparatus across the region was presented as almost inevitable, as the mountains became economically, physically, and rhetorically more accessible. As much as the northern frontier that Timothy Dwight celebrated in the first decade of the nineteenth century as a "source of American democracy and national character" (Cronon, "Trouble" 76), this "romantic ideology of wilderness leaves precisely nowhere for human beings actually to make their living from the land" (Cronon, "Trouble" 80).

Among the more distinguished groups to climb Mount Washington with Ethan Crawford was a party of men from Lancaster, New Hampshire, who made their ascent in 1820 with the intention of naming the summits surrounding Mount Washington.[20] From the high mountain's summit, they "gave names to several peaks, and then drank healths to them in honor to the great men whose names they bore, and gave toasts to them" (*History* 40). During a jovial and well-supplied "orgy of mountain-naming," the "Lancastrians" gave names to Mounts Adams, Jefferson, and Madison north of Mount Washington, and to Mounts Monroe, Franklin, and Pleasant (now Eisenhower) south of the peak.[21] After christening all the unnamed peaks they could identify, the party of "distinguished characters" called upon Ethan Crawford, whom they had hired as a "guide and baggage-carrier" and "loaded equal to a pack-horse," to join them in their toast-making (38). Crawford comments, "as this was a new thing to me, and not being prepared, I could only express my feelings by saying I hoped all of us might have good success and return to our respective families in safety, and find them in health" (40). While the democratic space of rural and wild northern New England may well have contributed to the national character promoted by Crèvecoeur and Jefferson and longed for by Hawthorne, apparent in these early visits is the assertion of more *civilized* social structures on a rural landscape. When Benjamin Willey, writing for an audience of upper-middle-class tourists of the 1870s, offers idealistically that "no oppression . . . can ever exist around the White Mountains" (295), residents like the Crawfords had largely been pushed to the margins of the tourist economy — as the "wilderness came to reflect the very civilization its devotees sought to escape" (Cronon, "Trouble" 78). The social and economic gap between the Lancastrians and their guide is inscribed on the landscape itself as they — if somewhat haphazardly as a result of an abundance of "O-be-joyful" — gave names to mountains that overtly brought the physical nature of the mountains to serve the discourse of the new nation.[22]

While the Crawfords labored to accommodate a growing number of summer visitors by transforming the physical landscape of the White Mountain Notch through cutting paths, maintaining roads, and expanding their lodging capacity, Lucy Crawford similarly manipulated the mountains' social landscape in her *History*. Crawford uses her very narrative of the Notch's early settlement as currency in the expanding tourist economy. As much as the Crawfords themselves were exploited by land speculators, Lucy Crawford sought to exploit her family's position as the Notch's first settlers and mountain guides for financial reasons so that they might eventually return to their "mountain home." The narrative currency of her family's history in the Notch, and of Ethan's exploits in particular, is measured throughout Crawford's *History*. Ethan came to represent, both in the *History* and (thanks largely to Lucy's efforts) in later guidebooks, the epitome of the hearty backwoodsman — an image that prompted popular guidebook author Thomas Starr King to proclaim in 1859, "Noble Ethan Crawford! . . . What a flavor of wild mountain life, what vivid suggestions of the closest tug of man with nature . . . do we find in his adventures and exploits" (223). It was this image, too, that brought visitors to the Crawfords' inn to seek Ethan as a guide for their climbs. Lucy's descriptions of Ethan's extraordinary feats work both to commemorate her husband, who died in the same year the *History* was published, and to contribute to her book's salability in the increasingly competitive guidebook market.

As early as 1855, popular guidebook author John Spaulding began to blur the boundaries between the Crawford family and the mountains that were their home when he noted that "the name of E. A. Crawford is deeply chiselled upon the rocks of this granite Mount built by nature (Mount Washington)" (17). More recently, Dona Brown gives credit to Crawford for being a primary instigator of tourism's growth in the White Mountains. She writes, "Crawford was the inventor, the organizer and the driving force of the White Mountain tour" (44). Eric Purchase asserts similarly, "almost single-handedly, Crawford transformed the White Mountains from a barrier to commerce into a great attraction for wealthy travelers" (25). Although the Crawfords were able to at least marginally take advantage of a growing tourist industry, it is an overstatement to attribute the region's development to their work. It was the very influx of these affluent travelers, after all, that eventually led to Crawford's forced departure from the mountains; upper-class tourists were interested in greater luxury in their lodgings than could be provided by Ethan Crawford, whose inn, wrote Mary Jane Thomas about her stay at the Crawfords' in 1831, offered only "fare and accommodations . . . of the most primitive character" (Thomas 49).

In the 1820s and 1830s, the Crawfords found themselves inhabiting the region both as settlers reliant on the fruits of the landscape to sustain them, and as tour guides and innkeepers to their affluent visitors. Aspects of the Crawfords' multiple roles can be seen in the dynamic development of their White Mountain Notch farmstead and inn. This mulifaceted existence can be traced in the architecture of nineteenth-century farm buildings, in which the multiple roles played by farmers in the region was "reflected in the rambling, multipurpose, connected farm buildings" (Wallace 20). Despite constantly adding rooms and outbuildings throughout the mid-1820s, Crawford reports that they used one room, which was "half the bigness of the house . . . as a kitchen, a victualing room, a sitting room, and when crowded, a sleeping room" with "a cookstove in a woodshed adjoining the house" (68). By 1832, however, Crawford writes, "we now suffered for want of house-room . . . . and frequently [Lucy] would give up her own bed and lie down herself upon the floor" for the benefit of their guests (150). Lucy Crawford notes several times her husband's concern about not being able to provide sufficiently for their guests. When a carriage road is proposed from Ethan Crawford's up the west side of Mount Washington, he decides to give up the project, and a much-needed $200, noting

> I was already under so much embarrassment I did not feel able to build an addition to my house, and I well knew that if I made this road, and did not have suitable accommodations for those who would be likely to come, it would only be imposing on the public to have a road to the Mountain and not have house room enough to make those comfortable who came to stay with us. (*History* 44)

Although the Crawford family might have been among the first to capitalize on the new commercial value of the landscape, and to cater to what Brown calls "a new sort of customer" (43), like many modern small rural entrepreneurs, their enterprise fell victim to commercial pressures from outside northern New Hampshire. Years later, an advertisement in the 9 July 1878 edition of *Among the Clouds* declares about the greatly expanded Crawford House at the head of the Notch (rebuilt in 1859) that "No other Hotel in America is so near to a score of natural wonders, and, while standing in a region given up by common consent to solitude, perfect rail communication is now made with all the routes of the country, and every comfort and luxury obtainable is applied to the guests."

The relatively primitive inns of which Lucy and Ethan, and Ethan's brother Tom Crawford, were the proprietors simply could not compete with this developing class of grand hotel. The burgeoning hotel business drew speculators and investors from urban areas to the south, including Boston, New York, Philadelphia, and Baltimore. As I will further explore in later chapters, these new hotel proprietors catered likewise to visitors from those same cities, thereby creating in the White Mountains a displaced urban center, where the predominantly urban, upper-class tourists were able to stay the whole summer and yet be in continual contact with "the cares and anxieties of Wall-street and State-street" (Willey 301).

In the eyes of both early visitors like Timothy Dwight and later generations of tourists, the Crawford family was "native" to the mountain region. Later writers wrote the Crawfords into their descriptions, and today, as evidenced by the proliferation of the family's name among the area's features — Crawford Notch, Mount Crawford, the Crawford Path, Mount Tom (Crawford, Ethan's brother), Mount Tom Brook, Crawford Brook, Ethan Pond (and trail) — attest, the name continues to live on. Notably absent from this list, much like the absence of her authorial hand from the 1846 *History*, is Lucy. The slippage between explorer and tourist witnessed by Ethan and Lucy Crawford in their account foregrounds the distinction between native and tourist that frames so much contemporary discussion. "The tourist," asserts environmental critic Neil Evernden, for instance, "can grasp only the superficialities of a landscape, whereas a resident reacts to what has occurred" (99). The pretourist White Mountains were inhabited (rather than visited) by individuals engaged directly with the landscape in commerce and industry. Crawford's *History* recounts a number of stories about local feats of "improvement," including that of Richard Garland, who, in his effort to support a farm for his family, frequently walked "thirty-one miles, and half the distance with a load" each day to borrow a neighbor's plough "while he the same day did a great day's work" piling timber and ploughing his newly cleared plot (173). Eleazer Rosebrook, as Timothy

Dwight notes, exemplifies the frontier settler, "station[ing] himself in absolute wilderness" (qtd. in Kilbourne 74). His son Abel Crawford and grandson Ethan Allen Crawford were likewise connected to the landscape they inhabited as "part of a place," and their nicknames — they were often called the "Mountain Patriarch" and "Giant of the Hills" respectively — drive home the point. Their identities thus became inherently interconnected with the mountains themselves, embodying the history of the landscape in their own histories. This description of the Crawfords persists through the publication of a variety of guidebooks to the White Mountains in the 1850s, 1860s, and beyond, in which Ethan and Abel Crawford become immortalized as fixtures of the landscape. As late as 1916, Frederick Kilbourne identifies them as part of the landscape itself as he exclaims of the Crawford cemetery near the gravel mound known as the Giant's Grave at the foot of Mount Washington: "what more fitting resting-place for the remains of the pioneer[s] could have been found!"(75). The iconic status of the Crawfords is also echoed in subsequent representations of White Mountain locals. The mountain guide and backwoods settler become frequent figures in tourist discourse, both as romantic images of "man's oneness with nature" and as voices of authority providing inside knowledge about the White Mountain landscape.

Lucy Crawford's many drafts and revisions of her 1860 manuscript of the *History of the White Mountains* reveal attempts to come to terms with her place in multiple discourses and her desire both to be true to the landscape of her "mountain home" and to the tourists who, by 1860, were visiting the Crawfords' Notch by the hundreds. By integrating historical and personal anecdotes with more overtly informational chapters presenting "Routes to the Mountains. Towns about the Mountains. Their accommodations for travelers. Best views from surrounding towns," Crawford's manuscript blurs the generic boundaries between settlement narrative and guidebook. Though she evidently had in mind publishing the book as an "acknowledge[ment] to the public for their benevolent patronage" (1860 ms. 240) even in 1846, by 1860 the burgeoning guidebook market may have convinced Crawford to shorten some of the more extensive anecdotes herself in favor of factual, informational chapters more appropriate for a regional tourist readership.

Mid-nineteenth-century visitors to the White Mountains, in their quest for a truly sublime, if already well-worn, experience, relied on histories like Crawford's to offer, much as Brazer and Dawson's inscription had done decades earlier, an appropriate rendition of the scenic view. Guidebook writers often accommodated this impulse, offering, like Thomas Starr King, whose popular *White*

Hills was first published only thirteen years after Crawford's *History*, "to help persons appreciate landscape more adequately" (*History* vii). As in the clearly defined chapters in Crawford's 1860 revision, King divides his description of northern New Hampshire regionally according to what he identifies as the four prominent river valleys in the mountains (Pemigewasset, Saco, Androscoggin, and Connecticut). King himself notes that he would have preferred "to arrange the volume by subjects instead of by districts," but he felt that this would make the book less "valuable" (and indeed less salable) as a "guide to particular landscapes" (vii). Providing literary access to the landscape for tourists who often passed through the mountains in two or three days was a paramount concern of writers in the second half of the century, and, in keeping with this editorial trend, the clearer organization and detailed chapter headings in Crawford's 1860 revision would also have offered an easy way for readers to access specific information.

Crawford's position astride two often-conflicting genres — one that foregrounds the identity of the region's settlers and their relationship with the landscape and another that marginalizes the two in favor of hotels, railways, and attractions — is apparent throughout her 1860 revision. For example, although she admonishes the rapid tour, writing in 1860 that "an hour, nor a day is not sufficient to study this vast book of nature" (1860 ms. 218), Lucy Crawford also facilitated access to her own narrative by including detailed chapter headings in her revised history. The 1846 edition titled only the first two chapters, as they connect to the Rosebrook and Crawford family. The manuscript version introduces headings for all the chapters that detail the events described therein, such as "Chapter VIII — The storm of 1826. The great slide from the mountains. The destruction of the Willey family. Mr. Crawford's loss." The inclusion of headings both draws on period conventions and enables readers to extract specific information from the book rather than having to read lengthy unidentified sections. Moreover, entirely new chapters included in the manuscript attempt to further quantify the mountain experience for visiting tourists; a newly added thirteenth chapter catalogs climatic data in "thermometrical tables" (two of which are, ironically, copied from J. H. Spaulding's book), routes to the mountains (and their lengths), as well as a selection of accommodations.

It is most significant that the newly added chapter headings illustrate Crawford's desire to appeal to a larger audience, one with a seemingly insatiable appetite for sensational narratives about family hardships (chapter 3) and disasters (chapter 4), including the Willey slide (chapter 8) and other deaths in the mountains (chapter 12). At the same time, Crawford's view toward a broader audience, as revealed at least cursorily in the chapter headings, changes the history's focus from the Rosebrook and Crawford families to a history of their inherent connection with the mountain landscape. John Mudge, editor of the 1999 reprint of Lucy Crawford's 1846 *History*, writes that her later revision added "material in order to make the book more a history of the White Mountains as a whole rather than a history of the Crawford family" (x). Inasmuch as Crawford's desire to broaden her readership is undeniable, a close reading of the 1860 history provides clear evidence that in both editions Lucy Crawford saw little distinction between her family's history and that of the mountains.

Lucy Crawford's manuscripts and revisions illustrate that her work in revising her *History* (and, as a consequence, her history) compelled her to balance the earlier domestic focus on family and social history with an appeal to her new readers by integrating the language and conventions of contemporary guidebook writers. As subsequent revisions layer, integrate, and excise certain sections of text, the appeal to an audience of tourists removes much of the domesticity apparent in the earlier version of the *History* — scenes that would have appealed more to potential settlers than to genteel seasonal visitors — and places the region's history within the context of a more familiar tourist discourse. Still, as I noted earlier, Crawford's authority as witness to much of early White Mountain history remains the same and continues to provide the framework within which she re-places certain events into language that caters to the competitive guidebook market of the mid-nineteenth century. Events that become codified in the discourse of tourism in the second half of the century were often (as was the case with John Spaulding's *Historical Relics*) revisions of Lucy Crawford's earlier accounts. Among the more romantic, tragic events that fit well into tourists' desire for sublime experiences were the death of the Willey family in an 1826 rockslide and the tragic death of Nancy Barton by exposure during a journey to Portsmouth on foot in the White Mountain Notch in the winter of 1778. Particularly in Lucy Crawford's telling of Nancy's story, there is an evident transformation from the first version of the book (which was the first publication to contain a complete account of the events) to the second. The 1846 text introduces the story as follows:

> I have heard it said by the people of Portsmouth that when children were at play
> and happened to fall out with each other, the worst punishment they could inflict
> upon their mates was to wish them up at the White Hills, as that was considered

the worst place in the world by them. Perhaps their minds had been affected by the story of Nancy, who perished in the woods in attempting to follow her lover. (*History* 106)

The 1860 manuscript inserts additional text to read:

> It will be recollected by those who have visited the spot, that the stream so called, as "Nancy's Brook," is about one-half of a mile below the Mt. Crawford House, taking its rise far up the mountain, tumbling its waters over large precipices as it descends down through the heavy forests below. But few small streams so readily attract the attention of the traveller as this; time has suffered this stream to cut deep channels varying from ten to thirty feet, giving the appearance of flumes. It is by nature a wild spot, and taken in connection with the death of Nancy, the eye naturally rests upon the scene. (1860 ms. 124)

Where Crawford's original introduction frames Nancy's story in a more social and domestic setting by connecting the story with children's play, her revised version removes the tragedy from the domestic sphere into a place that is "by nature a wild spot." Much as in John Spaulding's *Historical Relics* and Thomas Starr King's *White Hills*, Lucy Crawford's later passage makes clear the connection between landscape and event by suggesting that the stream's precipitous falls and deep channels themselves echo the tragedy of Nancy Barton's death. The sublimity of the landscape couples the events with the topography to reinforce the effect on the visitor whose "eye naturally rests upon the scene." By deemphasizing the earlier text, Crawford also makes apparent that she has read the works of her contemporaries and is similarly writing to an audience interested in a pre-scribed, and in many ways generic, sublime experience. Although the manuscript excludes much of the anecdotal detail that invests the published *History* with its intimate flavor, Crawford was unable, finally, to separate mountain and family. Boston publisher Nathaniel Noyes wrote to Crawford that her 1860 manuscript

> contains much that would be interesting to the visitors to the mountains nowadays, and much that would be of no interest at all to them, as there is a different class of persons go there now from what there did 10 years ago. There is too much that relates personally to your family, to interest and please visitors who now go there I think, but as a whole it is quite entertaining. With a number of good illustrations it would sell to some extent, although I am free to confess that if you would give me the copyright today I would not publish it. (Crawford papers, Ms. 626, Box 1)

As her 1860 revision makes clear, the histories of the Crawfords, Rosebrooks, and other early settlers and the history of the mountains among which they lived are inseparable. It is precisely in the details of settlement life, however, that Crawford's original *History* helps to populate a landscape that later guidebook writers and artists often portrayed solely for its sublime content, relegating its residents to the margins if they represented them at all. Noyes's letter illustrates one of the problems central to Crawford's revision process as she tried to both present an undistorted view of her family's history in the Notch and to reposition her text in the prevailing discourse of contemporary guidebooks — to perpetuate the arcadian myth of settlement sought by visiting tourists and enwrap her narrative in what Ripley in the 1886 *History* called its "olden, homely, quaint speech . . . full of rugged strength and earnest meaning" (6).

Notwithstanding her best attempts to expunge details of family life from the manuscript, Lucy Crawford found that publication eluded her. As her correspondence with prospective publishers and her illustrator, Marshall M. Tidd, reveals, her reasons for not publishing the manuscript were principally financial. Although Crawford did commission Tidd to sketch nine scenes highlighting incidents from the *History*, she was able to pay his $49 fee only over a two-year period, and she never made arrangements to have the sketches engraved (fig. 3). In what seems a final attempt to step outside her position as resident (though then exiled), Crawford hoped to incite interest in her project from Harriet Beecher Stowe, whose own *Uncle Tom's Cabin* had then been in print for several years.[23] Crawford wrote to Stowe in the late 1850s, "as you are a writer I should like to have you look over my work & write a sequel & perhaps you may in looking over the old albums find something in them that will be interesting to the public" (Crawford papers, Ms. 626, Box 1).

Crawford's appeals to outside assistance with the project seem ironic, however, as it was Crawford's assertion of authorial control that is one of the most significant revisions apparent in the 1860 manuscript. The later text appropriates Ethan's first-person voice (and possible collaboration with Lucy Crawford's daughters) and presents it as a first-person narrative in Lucy's own voice. Taking control of the text empowers her to revisit and revise specific incidents, at times revising the narrative to highlight her own accomplishments, but more often to foreground the roles of the first women visitors to the mountains in the early nineteenth century. The middle ground between tourism and a persisting subsistence economy inhabited by White Mountain residents in the 1810s and 1820s gave Crawford the experience to write about the mountains from both settlement and tourist perspectives. Annette Kolodny describes a domes-

FIGURE 3

Carrying a Lady down Jacob's Ladder. Woodblock drawing by Marshall M. Tidd. In a letter to Lucy Crawford dated 13 February 1860, Tidd responds to Crawford's apparent concern that the landscape is not sufficiently wild: "You mention the scene at Jacob's Ladder as not being rough enough. Those are mere outline sketches and of course cannot give the rocks in detail as they will be when finished on the wood, and I will see that it is corrected in the drawing." Courtesy of the Dartmouth College Library.

tic fantasy on successive western frontiers that, though it placed women beside men (though not necessarily with the same motives), did not allow them to participate in it. "The dream of a domestic Eden," writes Kolodny, "had become a nightmare of domestic captivity" (9). In contrast with this prevailing gender division in the frontier experience, Lucy Crawford shared with her husband much of the exuberance (as well as the work) offered by climbing the mountains around their home. Although not apparent in the published version of the *History*, Crawford's connection (and the connection of her female guests) to the mountains becomes clearer and indeed a more substantial part of the text in her later revision.

Women mountaineers were quickly becoming significant members of the White Mountain summer community. In an 1877 *Appalachia* article, Mrs. W. G. Nowell contemplates clothing "which could be feminine and yet be adapted to exploring even primeval forests," since skirts had "proved themselves so inconvenient and so dangerous." Nowell continues to assert that "relieved of the excessive weight of her ordinary dress, [a woman] could carry upon her back, by the aid of straps, at least fifteen pounds," and that "many ladies take great pride in carrying their own burdens" (183). The 1860 manuscript's expanded accounts of early women climbers on Mount Washington can thus be read as both an assertion of Crawford's *own* identity as woman in the wilderness and an appeal to an expanding audience of women readers. A close reading of a few of Crawford's modified narratives of early female ascents of Mount Washington will serve to illustrate the growing importance Crawford gave to women in her descriptions of these early climbs.

Of the first women to attempt an ascent of Mount Washington in September 1821 (three sisters with the last name of Austin), Crawford writes that they "were ambitious and wanted to have the honor of being the first females to place their feet on this high, and now, celebrated place" (*History* 47). Crawford extends her account of the ascent in the 1860 manuscript by adding the romantic rhetoric typical of midcentury guidebooks, writing, for instance, how "the prospect from the summit is boundless and the variety of scenery so great as to chain the eye upon different objects, hour after hour" (1860 ms. 59 – 60). Her addition of quintessential tourist discourse — the climbers perceived the "country round about to appear like [a] map at their feet" (1860 ms. 59) — suggests that, though she provides a lengthier description of the women's climb here than in the 1846 edition, Crawford is also concerned with the salability of the new book in a market overrun by guidebooks filled with colorful and often overwrought descriptive language. Crawford's role as refashioner of the historical record again serves to complicate her text. At the same time as she writes to compete for a rapidly growing tourist audience, she refocuses her narrative on the role of women in the mountains. As she does elsewhere in the manuscript, Crawford amends her earlier commentary on women climbers, here deleting her earlier assertion that "there was not left a trace or even a chance for a reproach or slander excepting by those who thought themselves outdone by these young ladies" (*History* 48).

Four years later, in August 1825, a gentleman and his sister arrived at the Crawfords' with the intention of climbing Mount Washington. Crawford notes that "although she received no encouragement from those who knew her intentions, still she insisted upon the undertaking" (1860 ms. 91). Lucy Crawford accompanied the party in what was her own first ascent of the peak, and, despite a period of poor weather, the climbers were able to summit the peak on the third day of the ascent. Upon completing their successful climb, the "ladies [Lucy Crawford included] considered themselves richly paid" for their efforts (1860 ms. 93). Crawford again extends her descriptions in this revised section, thus underscoring the women's success in the ascent rather than their difficulties. Indeed, she concludes this section of the manuscript not by asserting, like her husband in the *History* (at least as she gives him voice), that "never after this did we persuade ladies to follow their example; but discouraged them whenever we could, endeavoring to prevent them not to attempt it, as we thought it too much of an undertaking" (75), but by ending simply "they were the second party of females that had ever attempted to make the ascent" (1860 ms. 93).

A final episode serves to illustrate not only Lucy Crawford's overt revisions of female ascents, but also her selective editing of the material she frequently excerpted from the inn's logbook. On 27 August 1825, a party of two men and three women, led by Dr. John Park of Boston, arrived at the Crawfords' to climb Mount Washington. Three of the climbers, among them Dr. John Park's daughter Louisa Jane, successfully reached the summit in what Dr. Park described as "the midst of a dismal hurricane [with] no prospect." Despite the adverse weather, Park is careful to insert an early adoption of European tourist rhetoric, suggesting that "certainly our situation partook much of the sublime, from our known elevation, the desolation around us, and the horrors of the tempest. . . . I never saw any thing more furious or more dreadful than this" (*History* 78). Reflecting on this climb more than a decade after publishing her first *History*, Lucy Crawford chooses to quote more selectively from the inn's logbook than in the first, published version. Although she, too, integrates the language of the sublime into her 1860 revision of the *History*, Crawford excises the following passage (included in the published editions toward the conclusion of John Park's log entry): "Gentlemen, there is nothing in the ascent of Mount Washington that you need dread. Ladies, give up all thoughts of it; but if you are resolved, let the season be mild, — consult Mr. Crawford as to the prospects of the weather; and with every precaution, you will still find, *for you*, a tremendous undertaking" (78).

By entirely leaving out this passage, Crawford truncates Park's own comments to bolster her own agenda of foregrounding the expedition's success, rather than focusing on the difficulties of the ascent. Clearly keeping her new audience of women readers (and tourists) in mind, Crawford deliberately edits her original *History* to refocus sections of the narrative on women's accomplishments in the mountains, in effect acting as an advertisement for future visitors. Crawford was catering to a generally expanding female readership. Short-lived early nineteenth-century women's magazines like the *Lady's Weekly Miscellany* (1805 – 1808) and the *Ladies' Literary Cabinet* (1819 – 1822), which were devoted to fiction, music, and miscellany, had by midcentury evolved into magazines with more substantial articles, often about women's education, as well as fiction by the century's prominent authors. *The Ladies' Magazine*, founded by Sarah Josepha Hale in 1838, and *Godey's Lady's Book*, later edited by Hale, are prominent examples of widely read serials in which Crawford may have seen potential readers for her own work.[24]

As the only female author of a White Mountain history, Crawford, who was keenly interested in her book's financial success, saw the need to cater to an expanded audience. In the second half of the nineteenth century, women were very often seen as mountaineers comparable to men. As early as 1869, the popular writer William "Adirondack" Murray advocated that women assume their place on mountain trails. A decade later, Moses Sweetser wrote of women on White Mountain paths that "it hardly needs to be stated that American ladies can accomplish nearly everything which is possible to their sturdier brethren."[25] Such an empowering environment led Emily Thackray to opine in 1889 in one of the region's daily summer newspapers, the *White Mountain Echo*, "In the conservative masculine mind, particularly of Europe, it has been a mooted point whether a woman could climb, camp out and 'rough it,' with any pleasure to herself or comfort to the 'lords of creation.' But to-day in America, things are greatly changed; mountain-tramping has become a 'fad among ladies and they are encouraged by their brothers, their cousins, and their uncles'" (qtd. in Brown 123).

Lucy Crawford's appeal to her potential women readers is nonetheless

couched in her critique of the growing class distinctions apparent as the northern frontier was transformed by the northern tour. In 1846 Crawford writes of
Grandmother Rosebrook's relocation to Monadnock, New Hampshire (later
renamed Colebrook), "what courage must this woman have possessed, after
being so many years among relatives . . . and changing them for the woods!"
(*History* 10). By 1860 Crawford makes of Rosebrook an example "to that class of
would be ladies at the present day whose daily labor is performed in brushing
the sidewalks with their silks" (1860 ms. 8). Crawford's respect for her husband's
grandparents arises from a combination of Christian upbringing and her belief
in the transformative properties of life on the frontier. It is this life that she
longs for and longs to return to as she seeks her "mountain home" in the Notch
after losing it in 1837. The frontier life she experienced in her youth, and even
the simplicity of early life in the White Mountain Notch, had by then been sup-
planted by the commercial interests of the tourist industry. The "simple life"
of settlement existed only as a romantic ideal packaged for visiting tourists.
From her perspective in the 1850s, Lucy Crawford connects her grandfather's
"hardships and privations" on the northern frontier with America's success
in the Revolutionary War. She observes that "the life of the backwoodsman
produced courage and a spirit which fitted him to stand up before the enemy
and dare to maintain that right which by God's law belonged to him, Liberty"
(1860 ms. 11).

Domestic fiction writers of the mid-nineteenth century often looked to the
frontier for their material. In particular, as Kolodny explains, they wished to
escape an urban social environment in which women's traditional domestic
roles were being replaced by more modern, mechanized definitions of domesticity. Removing their heroines to distant frontier settlements enabled writers
to "displace the gilded mansions and sordid tenements of New York, the dor-
mitory dwellings of the New England mills" with the "relaxed domesticity"
of the frontier cabin (Kolodny 168). The myths of settlement life these novels
perpetuated ignored, by their very nature as domestic fantasy, the economic
realities of land speculation and the inequitable relationships between absen-
tee landlords and the subsistence lives of their tenants. What more realistic
portrayals of frontier life by women offered readers, despite guidebook author
Benjamin Willey's "cheering reflection" in 1855 that "no oppression . . . can ever
exist around the White Mountains" (295), was the reality that "class and caste,
opinion and prejudice" had followed society to the frontier; "migration to the
frontier did not release Americans from the burden of history to shape society
wholly anew" (Kolodny 139). As much as Crawford sees in the mountains the

opportunity for women to participate in adventure to the same extent as the men in their parties, she joins her contemporaries Henry Ward Beecher and William Murray in maintaining that settlement life offers a more pious, equitable, and character-building existence than would a more urban environment.

THE PRETOURIST White Mountain landscape as described in Lucy Crawford's *History* is topographically marginal, arranged according to towns that lay on the periphery of the higher, less accessible regions. Jeremy Belknap's 1784 circumambulation of Mount Washington delineated both in his narrative and on his sketch map of the expedition, for instance, a clear boundary between the "tour" and the mountain interior. Less than half a century later, the Crawfords staked their livelihood on tourists' desire to penetrate that very interior, thereby emphasizing the beginnings of a topographical and economic shift between margin and center. With the transformation of the region's commerce from resource-based and agricultural industries to tourism and recreation, the wildness that had existed on the periphery of the mountain region was made central — even, as I have noted, in guidebooks and on maps. Synchronous with this transformation of the wilderness at the margin into an accessible, consumable center, is a similar shifting of settlements like the Crawfords' to a peripheral existence.

In light of Lucy Crawford's inability to republish her *History of the White Mountains*, as it would have been of "no interest at all" to prospective readers, it is tempting to read popular nineteenth-century guidebooks like Thomas Starr King's *White Hills* and John Spaulding's *Historical Relics* as antipodes to Crawford's *History* and as exemplars of the mechanism of an exploitative tourist industry. Such a reading, however, homogenizes a more complex cultural and natural landscape. Artists and writers in midcentury, while retailing the settler as yet another "relic" in a commodified landscape, present more complicated views of the natural and economic landscapes of the White Mountains. As the numbers of seasonal visitors increased simultaneously with an increase in development and the beginnings of a prolific logging industry, writers and artists attempted to reconcile their roles as tourism promoters with the ensuing impact on the very landscape they were promoting. Throughout the layers of this rhetorical ecosystem there resound echoes of an inchoate ecological awareness that interweaves the multiple discourses of tourism, settlement, industry, and environment.

CHAPTER THREE

The Sublime and the Sumptuous

The Currency of Scenery and
White Mountain Tourism

ON 16 JULY 1858, on his way back to Concord at the end of a three-week trip to the White Mountains, Henry David Thoreau stopped in the popular artist's village of Campton at the southern edge of the range. Looking back at the Franconia Mountains he had climbed the previous day, Thoreau remarked that when seen from that distance,

the Franconia Mountains show three or four sharp and regular blue pyramids, reminding you of pictures of the Pyramids of Egypt, though when near you suspected of no such resemblances. . . . Twenty-five miles off, in this case, you might think that the summit was a smooth inclined plane, though you can reach it only over a succession of promontories and shelves. (quoted in Howarth 278)

Thinking back on his own climb of Mount Lafayette, the range's highest peak the day before, Thoreau remarked that in contrast to his distant perception of the peak as a "regular blue pyramid," the "surface was so irregular that you would have thought you saw the summit a dozen times before you did" during an ascent of the mountain's final treeless mile (quoted in Howarth 277). In fact, Thoreau lamented that he had to convey to a fellow climber the bad news that the summit, though apparently near, was quite far off. Thoreau, who famously declared about his summit experience in "Ktaadn" that "The tops of mountains are among the unfinished parts of the globe. . . . Only daring and insolent men, perchance, go there" (641), admits about Lafayette that "the summit of a mountain . . . is not, after all, the easiest thing to find, even in clear weather" (277). Lafayette, at 5,260 feet only 10 feet lower in elevation that Katahdin, was in the mid-nineteenth century a far different outing. While, by his own estimation, Thoreau was part of only the fifth recorded ascent of the Maine peak in 1846, Lafayette boasted a pair of well-worn hiking trails and bridle paths and a summit refuge. In the decidedly not "unhandselled" world of New Hampshire's popular peaks, Thoreau nonetheless finds it "surprising how much more bewildering is a mountain-top than a level area of the same extent" (282). Despite the taming of the peak by the proprietors of the nearby Profile House, the mountain resists an easy ascent and, as Thoreau makes clear, resists straightforward description as well.

Thoreau's 1858 remarks in Campton—from which he admits "there is but very general and very little truth in the impression" of the mountains—are ironic, since the village had become a popular artists' colony precisely because it "apparently affords the best views" of the Franconia Mountains Thoreau had just visited (Howarth 278). In the years after Thoreau's sojourn, Campton claimed artists such as Frank Shapleigh, Edward Hill, George Albert Frost, and Samuel Gerry among its visitors (fig. 4). The broad vistas presented in these artists' paintings of Franconia Notch do indeed depict the Franconia Mountains as the regular pyramids that smooth over the details of the mountainside. Hiding beneath what a half-century earlier Edward Kendall disparagingly labeled the "uniform and sombrous green" of the forest lie the complex details of an undulating landscape that cannot be captured in either paintings or maps made from a distance. Throughout the late nineteenth century, representations of the White Mountains in distant, expansive views proliferated in guidebooks and in magazine and newspaper articles, as well as in paintings made by visiting artists. As representations of vast western landscapes came before the gaze of the armchair tourist after 1870, the mountain summit also began to develop as a generic symbol. Apparent in some commercially distributed representations of the White Mountains, the "emergent, operatic western vision" (McGrath, *Gods in Granite* 168) of landscape often precipitated an artificial elevation of White Mountain peaks despite their accessibility as a potentially knowable landscape. The oft-invoked appellation the "Switzerland of America" suggested to tourists that, indeed, part of their visit was concerned not with New Hampshire at all, but with the potential of seeing beyond the White Hills to more exotic locales. Examples of this generic perception of the White Mountains were widespread into the late nineteenth century and persist to this day as local businesses often appeal to visitors' preconceptions of "mountains" with no engagement of the White Mountains' real topography. This pervasive late-century phenomenon can be seen quite strikingly in an illustration of the Mount Washington Carriage Road for William Cullen Bryant's 1872 *Picturesque America* (fig. 5). Perhaps resulting from an acquiescence to the reality that the White Mountains are clearly *not* the Switzerland of America, stylized representations of the region occasionally crop up in commercial im-

FIGURE 4
Samuel Gerry, American (United States) 1813–1891. *Valley of the Pemigewasset*, 1858.
Bequest of Henry C. Lewis. Courtesy of the University of Michigan Museum of Art.

ages throughout the nineteenth and twentieth centuries. In his poem "New Hampshire," Robert Frost would also agree, although with more accurate topographical knowledge, that New Hampshire's "mountains fall a little short" (170). He laments

> the sad accident of having seen
> Our actual mountains given in a map
> Of early times as twice the height they are —
> Ten thousand feet instead of only five —
> Which shows how sad an accident may be.
> Five thousand feet is no longer high enough. (169)

As I discuss below, the shift to an aesthetics of a *specific* landscape can be traced to the integration of artistic and scientific descriptions with the publication of Charles Hitchcock's *Geology of New Hampshire* in 1874. The tension between the distant view and an intimate experience of place, though most evident in paintings and prints, is also apparent in textual narratives of the tourist experience, which often packaged the mountains as commodities upholstered with the rhetoric of the sublime.

Explorers and proto-tourists at the turn of the nineteenth century had labored to place the White Mountains within the language of an expanding

FIGURE 5

S. V. Hunt, *The Mount Washington Road*. Illustration for *Picturesque America*, 1872, edited by William Cullen Bryant. Courtesy of the New Hampshire Historical Society.

nation. The tourists who arrived on their very heels drew on a similarly pre-existing discourse — in this case on an increasingly accessible narrative of sub-lime experience — to reshape the mountain viewscape as a commodity. As the rhetoric of the fashionable tour was imported into northern New Hampshire, the explorer's "solar eye," seeking to quantify and re-present the landscape as real estate, was steadily transformed into a sentimental, though still ideo-logical, gaze. The tourist's impulse to view a landscape through the lens of a guidebook perpetuated a distance between observer and place, thus inevitably valorizing the summit as the aesthetic apex of the visitor's experience, in what Dean MacCannell identifies as a trinity of tourist, site, and interpretive marker (*Tourist* 41). By the 1850s, frequently visited summits in the White Mountains numbered fewer than half a dozen. Visitors would most often reach these sum-mits on horseback, by carriage, or later, by cog railway. The majority of visi-tors found the *experience* of the climb itself something to be avoided. Edward Kendall suggested the emergence of the summit as a destination (rather than the climb as an experience) during his 1807 visit. At that time, he welcomed Eleazer Rosebrook's notion of building a footpath up Mount Washington's western slopes as "a work which would save the visitor both fatigue and loss of time" (187). Rosebrook's vision would quickly be more than realized; the summit of the White Mountains' highest peak would boast two footpaths by 1821, a bridle path by the mid-1840s, a carriage road by 1861, and a cog railway by 1869.[1] The easy accessibility of mountain summits was often signaled by the construction of mountaintop hotels and shelters; Mount Washington itself had two by 1853, and by 1860 ten structures of varying degrees of luxury were dis-tributed among the mountains' highest accessible summits. The summit pros-pect quickly became an integral (and expected) part of the late-1800s tourist experience. Echoing a common sentiment, in 1881 the avid White Mountains tramper Marian Pychowska saw fit to complain, regarding the summit of 3,300 ft. Mount Kineo, that the view left much to be desired, as "the clearing of the top has not been done as thoroughly as I hope it will be one day" (Rowan and Rowan 63).[2]

Many visitors to the region were drawn to the higher mountain summits, from which the "bewitching world" below was transformed into a "text that lies before one's eyes" (de Certeau 92). But many tourists were equally content to look upon the mountains from afar; they often moved along the valley floor in a direction prescribed by guidebook writers, hotel promoters, and, later, steamship and railway line managers. Popular entry points to the mountains were most often the grand hotels, either the Profile, the Glenn, or the Crawford House.[3] The choreography of tourists' movement through the mountains echoed Jeremy Belknap's own circumambulation of Mount Washington in 1784. While Belknap, over the course of his twelve-day expedition, explored the intricacies of the mountain landscape and interacted with local residents (particularly while hypothesizing about the mountains' year-round whiteness), his genteel nineteenth-century followers were most often isolated by a pervasive tourist apparatus from mountain residents as well as any hardships in their exploration.

The sentiments of tourists in the second half of the century were both codified in and manipulated by the proliferation of guidebooks to the White Mountains published after the late 1840s. As we have seen, Lucy Crawford's 1846 *History of the White Mountains* was soon followed by William Oakes's *Scenery of the White Mountains* (1848) and John Spaulding's *Historical Relics* (1855). Benjamin Willey distinguished his 1856 *Incidents in White Mountain History* by writing extensively about the rockslide that took the lives of his brother's family in 1826. Thomas Starr King's *White Hills: Their Legends, Landscape, and Poetry* (1859), the most popular of this era's guidebooks, is as its subtitle might suggest, a monumental attempt to populate the White Mountains with a diversity of literary associations drawn from European and American poetry. Later publications like Moses Sweetser's 1879 *Views in the White Mountains* provide greater insight into the mechanism of tourism. Samuel Adams Drake's 1882 *Heart of the White Mountains* describes an exuberant post–Civil War landscape, wherein the mountains embody a "delightful sense of freedom!" (5). As I will discuss in this chapter, later guidebook authors like King, Sweetser, and Drake became more reflective and aware of themselves as participants in the tourist-driven culture of the late nineteenth century, as they write more critically about intersections of tourism, promotion, railway development, logging, and environmentalism.

White Mountain guidebooks published between 1850 and 1880 were necessarily engaged in the enterprise of attracting and guiding summer visitors who often arrived in the mountains with an established set of aesthetic and sentimental preconceptions. Despite (or sometimes because of) their economic ties to the perpetuation of tourism as an industry, their rhetorical treatment of the White Mountain landscape reveals a significant interweaving of economy, environment, and ideology in the northern New Hampshire — and indeed American — landscape of the nineteenth century. Nineteenth-century guidebook writers, some of whom were local residents, and others of whom were avid explorers of the mountains' interior, often negotiated between visions of a culturally shaped landscape that does "not have to be painted on canvas — it need only be 'framed' by an appreciative spectator" (Byerly 55) and a desire to narrate the *experience* of visiting the mountains. By merging acts of appropriation, transformation, and commodification of the landscape, guidebook writers situated environmental writing at the crossing of multiple discourses of national ideology, commerce, resource development, and environment that echoed the contact between people and the world they inhabit.

One of the White Mountain publications that most significantly merged travelogue, scientific treatise, and guidebook was Thomas Starr King's *White Hills*. King's book, although it established itself as the principal guidebook for White Mountain tourists, is not a typical guide. Its more than four hundred pages of descriptive narrative, anecdotes, poems, and images present a comprehensive guide to approaching the mountains through a particular landscape aesthetic. *The White Hills* not only offers specific frames for a characteristically picturesque or sublime vista but also suggests the best time of day for observation, as well as the exact sentiment the viewer should have while looking upon the scene. Such a strictly prescribed aesthetic response, though a welcome aid to many tourists (as evidenced by the book's multiple editions), imposes a framework that marginalizes imperfections and selectively re-presents the "contents" of a scene in terms appropriate for a sublime or picturesque view. Packaging the mountainscape in this way emphasizes the apparatus of tourism and the distance of the tourists from the place they are visiting as well as the tourists' desire to *do* the mountains in the same way everyone else *does* them. Moments of interpretive didacticism in King's *White Hills* seek to standardize the visual experience for all tourists. Such an agenda adumbrates the popularization of picture postcards that would follow less than two decades later and resembles a nineteenth-century version of our contemporary scenic vista or "Kodak picture spot." King's own commercial impulse, to write a timely and well-received guidebook, inevitably made him a participant in the economics of the viewscape. In his study of the development of twentieth century tourism, Alexander Wilson notes that as "scenic value" became a "monetary concept," "sightseeing was no longer an individual activity. . . . It was the organized mass consumption of familiar landscapes" (42). Dona Brown similarly regards the late nineteenth-century White Mountains as a place involved in "mass-consuming scenery" (60). As participants in the considerable commercial enterprise that White Mountain tourism had become by 1860, authors like King helped to cultivate a public fascination with *the* view and with the ability to capture that view of the landscape rather than to experience movement through a landscape.

In a typically didactic selection, King describes how readers should ideally view the region's highest peaks, the Presidential Range. He begins by declaring that the mountains look best from one particular spot on the road:

> If the bright foreground of the meadows golden in the afternoon light, and the velvety softness of the vague blue shadows, and the hues that flame on the peaks of its lower ridge, and the vigor of its sweep upwards to a sharp crest, are not enough to perfect the artistic finish of the picture, a *frame* is gracefully carved out of two nearer hills, to seclude it from any neighboring roughness . . . and to narrow into the most shapely proportions the plateau from which it soars. . . . [Moving] a quarter of a mile, either way . . . spoils the charm of the picture by breaking the frame. (8–9)

Fixing the tourist in only *one* particular place effectively locks the individual and landscape together, though at the same time denying the landscape its "natural" extent or the tourist the freedom to *tour*. The artifice of landscape evident in this passage illustrates the growing practice of mediating the mountain landscape for tourist consumption. By suggesting that the view requires further "artistic finish," King emphasizes his ability to imaginatively re-present a scene for his audience in an effort, as he argues in *The White Hills'* preface, to "help persons appreciate landscape more adequately" (vii). King's assertion that the landscape *requires* human intervention in order to achieve aesthetic perfection also points to a key distinction between King and his contemporaries. By pointing to the importance of actively positioning oneself before a viewscape, King also argues for slow, repeated observation of the mountains to obtain their fullest understanding: "many a person may pronounce upon the tone of a picture, that it is not natural," he argues, "who has no conception of the scale and freaks of color which a fortnight reveals among the mountains" (72). Thus, while it largely epitomizes the packaging for mass consumption of the viewscape prevalent at midcentury, King also attempts to present vistas that address both the (upper-class) reader's knowledge and appreciation of art and the "rough" world at the margins, here partially occluded by a well-positioned "frame."

As suggested in chapter 2, *The White Hills* divides its description of northern New Hampshire topographically according to what King identifies as the four prominent White Mountain river valleys, the Pemigewasset, Saco, Androscoggin, and Connecticut. In the preface to the guidebook, King notes that

> It would have been more to the author's mind to arrange the volume by subjects instead of by districts, and to treat the scenery under the heads of rivers, passes,

ridges, peaks, &c. But it was found that such a distribution and treatment, although it might have given the book more artistic unity, would have made it less valuable on the whole, than to construct it as a guide to particular landscapes, and a stimulant to the enjoyment of them. (vii)

It is King's emphasis on what is absent from his guidebook, more than his outline of its contents, that helps to distinguish his *White Hills* from the works of his contemporaries. The preface reads like an apology for an author whose language, although firmly situated within the discourse of tourism, belies an interest in the details of the landscape. King acknowledges Benjamin Willey's *Incidents in White Mountain History* and the work of the botanist Edward Tuckerman, whose list of mountain plants was, the author laments, excised due to the book's excessive length. Such a cross-generic intertextuality, though not unique among late nineteenth-century guidebooks, when read alongside his more overt critique of the mechanism of tourism, illustrates King's desire to connect his aesthetic discourse with local perspectives (of Willey, a White Mountain resident) and with more elaborate details of the region's flora.

Of course, the *absence* of these sections from King's *White Hills* clearly locates the author squarely in the gap between an appeal to the environment and the economic realities of a tourist industry at its zenith. Throughout the guide, King attempts to bridge this gap between the rhetoric of the popular guidebook, which endeavors to "direct attention to the noble landscapes that lie along the routes by which the White Mountains are now approached by tourists" (vii), and a nascent awareness of tourism's environmental impact on the mountains, as he seeks out places where the "steeds of fire and steam do not vex the air . . . with any echoes as yet" (17). As implied in its preface and made explicit throughout, *The White Hills'* focus is on developing the reader's *perception* of the landscape rather than on representing the reality of the mountains—a perception built principally of "images and words rather than experience" (McGrath, "Real and Ideal" 59). In his preface, King outlines his guide's organization as a catalog of mountain scenery, and a guidebook is in many ways just this: a catalog of artifacts, a document of possession. Although it fell to early explorers like John Josselyn and Darby Field to enumerate the fertile lands and potential riches the mountains offered, mid-nineteenth-century guidebook writers like King turned their rhetorical gaze on the region's scenic wealth.

Dona Brown notes that in the 1850s, "naming and unnaming the features of the landscape was only the beginning" of the business of generating associations (65). King certainly participated in the fad of (re)naming that began in

earnest in 1820 with the naming of the peaks surrounding Mount Washington
and continued until even the smallest rock outcroppings often carried the name
of nineteenth-century explorers or artists.[4] He also adopted historical events
and individuals to enrich his readers' vision of the White Mountains and to
validate the mountains' own cultural value as the "Switzerland of America." By
layering language borrowed from European aesthetics with American events
and places, King refashioned events in White Mountain history to fit into an
increasingly complex aesthetic and ideological landscape.

It is constructive to look closely at King's treatment of one particular event
of White Mountain history in order to highlight his frequent layering of borrowed and local materials. The story of Nancy Barton, whose tragic 1778 death
is recounted in numerous regional histories, like the Willey family tragedy,
provided mid- and late-century writers with historical associations to rival
their European counterparts. King's account of Nancy Barton's death in *The
White Hills* clearly adumbrates Lucy Crawford's 1860 description of the event,
which I discussed in chapter 2. In his version, King asserts that

> In Scotland, a highland pass, so wild and romantic as that from Upper Bartlett to
> the Crawford House, would be overhung with traditions along the whole winding
> wall of its wilderness; and legends that had been enshrined in song and ballad
> would be as plentiful as the streams that leap singing towards the Saco, down
> their rocky stairs. But no hill, no sheer battlement, no torrent that ploughs and
> drains the barriers of this narrow and tortuous glen, suggests any Indian legend.
> One cascade, however, . . . is more honored by the sad story associated with it,
> than by the picturesqueness of the crags through which it hurries for the last
> mile or two of its descending course. It is called "Nancy's Brook"; and the stage
> drivers show to the passengers the stone which is the particular monument of the
> tragedy, bearing the name "Nancy's Rock." (184)

This passage layers a number of conventions of nineteenth-century American
landscape rhetoric. Initially, King laments that the largely empty landscape is
devoid of associations that would be found throughout Europe. He frequently
attempts to bring these into his text by quoting passages from Byron, Wordsworth, and Goethe, along with a number of American writers, although often
quite awkwardly, since the associations are about and from elsewhere.

The section of *The White Hills* that includes the story of Nancy Barton is
framed by poems by Charles MacKay and Elizabeth Barrett Browning. Browning's "Lessons from the Gorse," which concludes the section, is another ex-
cellent example of King's seeding of the White Mountains with inappropriate

associations. The gorse (*Ulex europaeus*) is a flowering shrub native to Europe and currently considered an invasive, noxious plant in the United States.[5] The gorse's proclivity for more temperate climates make it unlikely, had gorse already been widely disseminated in the 1850s, which is doubtful, that its spiny yellow flowers would have made their way to the slopes of the White Mountains. The chapter at the end of which King included Browning's poem is, somewhat ironically, an overview of the "Vegetation of the White Mountains" written by the botanist Edward Tuckerman. Tuckerman begins his chapter: "The predominant Life in the mountains is always Vegetable Life. This . . . is sure to be beheld and felt, — and studied, too, by those who seek the inner truth of the outward" (230). King's own agenda as a guidebook writer can be identified in pointing his readers toward the "inner truth of the outward," though his drive toward associationism and his indebtedness to the rhetoric of the sublime in fact often *separates* his readers from the facts of the landscape.

Writers such as King often enriched specific mountain localities by overlaying them with literary and historical associations removed from the local historical context of the place. In a satiric look at nineteenth-century guidebooks in their 1930 *Book of the White Mountains*, John Anderson and Stearns Morse admit that they do not treat their predecessors nor "their lubrications altogether reverently" (264) as they warn readers that ascents in the mountains are "as frequently imperiled by precipitous language as by the more obvious dangers of topography. Fastidious sightseers may be more easily frightened off by a sudden metaphor than by the most unexpected slide" (16).

Such symbolic transformations of local landscapes of course further removed the actual landscape from the discourse of tourism and the mountain region's cultural history from the eyes of visitors. An additional example from King's *White Hills* may help to illustrate the complexity of this symbolic process. Four miles north of Abel Crawford's inn in the White Mountain Notch, a small stream called Cow Brook flowed into the Saco River. Likely named after some incident of bovine imprudence (or impudence), the brook was known to the Notch's residents, the Crawfords and the Willeys, only at its confluence with the Saco. They regarded it principally as another impediment to maintaining a summer road through the Notch. In 1858 Henry Wheelock Ripley, a North Conway writer and artist, and Mr. Porter of New York, were informed of a waterfall on Cow Brook a mile from the road.[6] King, finding the name of Cow Brook "unpoetical" (207), suggests the new appellation of Avalanche Brook in memory of the 1826 Willey disaster to more appropriately place the stream in the context of a visitor's tour. Perhaps named by the Willeys themselves when they lived and farmed in the area between 1825 and 1826, the transnaming of the brook from utilitarian to symbolic serves to underscore the sublime rhetoric of the place, much as the Willey family came to represent the sublime experience sought by visitors to the Notch. The pair explored the brook and indeed found a waterfall and cascade not far from the road. These they named Sparkling Cascade and Sylvan-Glade Cataract. The falls on Avalanche Brook, though already christened by Ripley and Porter, were renamed Ripley Falls in King's toponymic reorganization of the stream (Porter's name, though originally associated with the ravine through which the brook flows, has since been largely forgotten). Tourists working their way northward through the Notch (as was the usual direction) either by carriage or, later, by train, would cross Avalanche Brook shortly before reaching the Willey House site. The brook would then act as a fitting epigraph to the next chapter of their visit. By investing even the White Mountains' less substantial natural features with symbolic value, King effectively writes the landscape's details into a larger narrative of tourism's development and visitors' expectations. King's narrative describes the development of the White Mountain landscape in microcosm; a local informant draws attention to a previously "unknown" dramatic natural feature, which is then "discovered" by upper-class visitors and subsequently aesthetically and toponymically reframed by a visiting writer.

King's renaming of mountain features is complicated by his own critique of a similar spate of naming earlier in the century. "What a pity that the hills could not have kept the names which the Indian tribes gave to them" (20), he intones when describing what Waterman and Waterman call the 1820 orgy of mountain-naming of the peaks of what is now known as the Presidential Range (Waterman and Waterman, "Reverends" 44). Comparing northern New Hampshire's place names to those among Maine's highest mountains, King asserts that " 'Whipple's Grant,' and 'Hart's Location,' and 'Israel's River,' and 'Knot-Hole' road, are not so redolent of poetry as crystal Ambijejis and Katahdin and Millnoket" (31). Although he longs to recover Native American names and stories to write into his descriptions of the mountains, King's impulse is nevertheless for more romantic than accurate visions of precolonial northern New England. Missing from his lament is any meaningful engagement of the Abenaki's history, save for noting their absence. This lapse implicates King in the prevalent discourse of cultural appropriation of the time, in which the role of Native Americans "was to pose—and disappear" (Krupat 38). Much like the Vermont that John Elder explores in *Reading the Mountains of Home*, New Hampshire, too, "was held to be an in-between place" for Native American tribes, and by the nineteenth century, as larger native groups began to be forced onto reservations, smaller groups like the "Western Abenakis did actually seem to disappear, in the eyes of outsiders at least" (Elder 204–5). Of course, this erasure (and subsequent nostalgia for what it occluded) was part of a codified systematic removal of native peoples from agriculturally and economically desirable American regions. For writers like King, Native American cultures represented what his contemporary John Spaulding labeled "historical relics" of an idealized but disappearing past, in which they served as "sources for a literary construction of a vanishing way of life rather than as members of a vital continuing culture" (Larzer Ziff quoted in Vizenor 8).[7] King's ability to interweave the discourse of a resource-based tourist economy with a sensitive engagement of place reveals both his participation in tourism's refashioning of the landscape for its own aesthetic and economic agendas and his awareness and frequent critique of that very transformation.

The critical view of tourism held by a number of mid- to late-century guidebook writers like Thomas Starr King, Moses Sweetser, and Samuel Drake did much to complicate the homogeneity of tourist discourse in which they were explicitly involved. As I note in chapter 1, this critique grew from seeds sown by early regional writers like Jeremy Belknap, Timothy Dwight, and Edward Kendall. An apparent rhetorical difference between the earlier texts and the flood of guidebooks and histories published after 1850 was the attempt of the latter to establish a balance between creating a physical frame through which readers could access the viewscape and exploring the intimate landscape beyond the borders of that frame. More than a few White Mountain paintings from the middle and late nineteenth century reveal a similar struggle between objectification and engagement. Many of the artists influenced by the Hudson River School took skills practiced in the Catskills and elsewhere to northern New Hampshire. In the 1820s and 1830s, Thomas Cole's "natural" landscapes, from which tourists and residents were often conspicuously absent, trained audiences to "read landscape at the same time that they obscured the constructive role of the self in the process of interpretation" (Myers 77). The second generation of Hudson River School artists and their contemporaries built upon the nationalist and didactic mode developed by Cole, depicting in the White Mountains "not the wilderness itself, but the idea of wilderness" (Purchase 75). This often required effacing undesirable details (such as people or buildings) or reorganizing houses and farms in the foreground to fit a picturesque ideal.

Such is the case in Benjamin Champney's 1865 painting, *Mount Washington from the Intervale* (fig. 6). Champney, considered by many the founder of

FIGURE 6

Benjamin Champney, 1817 – 1907. *Mount Washington from the Intervale*, 1865.
Collection of Samuel and Shelia Robbins. Courtesy of the
New Hampshire Historical Society.

the White Mountain School of painting, was immediately struck by the scene
and admitted in his autobiography that he had rarely seen "so much beauty
and artistic picturesqueness brought together in one valley" (103). Champney's
depiction of what became almost a visual cliché in mid- to late-nineteenth-
century art shows an idyllic picturesque scene whose manicured and practically depopulated middle ground belies much of the landscape and population
history of the area. Champney's good friend John Frederick Kensett painted
the same expansive view of the Mount Washington massif in 1851 during their
visit to North Conway (Champney had painted a small oil sketch of the scene
at the same time). Kensett's painting, *Mount Washington from the Valley of
Conway*, was popularized in an 1851 engraving by James Smillie, and the scene
was reproduced many times in paintings, in prints, on maps, and in books
(including *The White Hills*). In the mid-nineteenth century, Mount Washington attained enormous popularity as a national symbol of a much-venerated
American hero. Donald Keyes ("Harmony") points out that Kensett himself
"chose Mount Washington as his vehicle to create a poignant patriotic and
spiritual symbol" (84).[8] The particular view of the peak depicted by Kensett,
Champney, and others combined this nationalism with an ideology of progress

in a prosperous agrarian landscape. The agrarian idealism that valorized the hewing of fields, farms, and villages from the wilderness of the White Mountains embodied what Timothy Dwight had revered as a "spirit of enterprise and industry, and perseverance" (*Travels* 96). This far-reaching representation of the mountains exemplified artists who depicted a popular "idea of wilderness" (Purchase 75) and perpetuated a tourist industry that would itself threaten the picturesque images of White Mountain School painters.

When Benjamin Champney first visited the White Mountains with Kensett in 1851, the two artists produced similar paintings of Mount Washington from Sunset Hill, just to the east of the village of North Conway. Kensett's *Mount Washington from the Valley of Conway* and Champney's *Mount Washington from the Meadows in North Conway* both depict a more populated foreground than Champney's 1865 work, illustrating a closer connection to Thomas Cole's agrarian ideal. The luminist qualities of Champney's later works, in their depiction of a "nearly airless" mountain atmosphere (Keyes 97), better illustrate the distanced, abstracting perspectives presented in period guidebooks and promotional texts. As tourism in the region reached its peak in the 1870s, attitudes such as those Champney expresses in *Mount Washington from the Intervale* worked to both aesthetically efface local residents from the canvas and guidebooks and to marginalize them in the local economy. Thomas Starr King echoed Champney's sentiment when he wrote about North Conway in 1859 that "if some duke, or merchant-prince with unlimited income, could put the resources of landscape taste upon it, adorn it with cottages, hedge the farms upon the meadows [and] span the road with elms . . . the village might be made as lovely a spot as it would be possible to combine out of the elements of New England scenery" (155–56). Drawing explicitly from European landscape sentiment, King effaces the existing inhabitants, whose barns, as he writes, often tarnish the most "sightly places," and repopulates the view with what he believed should be there. This notion of populating a landscape not with local working-class residents but with an idealized representation of their homes, farms, and fields is common in both travelogues and in guidebooks like King's *White Hills*. As is the case throughout his book, King again reveals his position as both participant in the tourist industry and a chronicler of its environmental effects. With tourism's almost exponential growth in the second half of the nineteenth century, artists like Champney and Albert Bierstadt also reflected on the potential environmental devastation that the continuing increase in tourism might precipitate.

Despite the prevalence of a homogenized view of the diverse mountain environment popularized in Kensett's view of the North Conway intervale, some artists nonetheless became inspired by the underlying landscape. They may well have been prompted by ideas that led the state's geologist, Charles Jackson, to argue for the inherent relationship between his discipline and painting. "The artist who represents a mountain correctly upon a canvas," wrote Hitchcock in 1874, needed to "thoroughly understand the features of our scenery" (589). Painters and, later, photographers built upon concepts popularized by George Perkins Marsh who, in his 1848 address before the Rutland County, Vermont, Agricultural Society, articulated attitudes about the inherent interconnections among forest, river, and soil that had been percolating among a number of his contemporaries. Adumbrating the sentiments of Susan Fenimore Cooper, who, in her 1850 book *Rural Hours* decries "an indifferent sort of husbandry . . . in which neither the soil nor the wood receives any attention" (89), Marsh argued that the current state of silviculture was a "mistake of cosmic proportions" (R. Judd 94).[9] Similarly concerned with tourism's effects on his beloved scenery, in his 1900 memoir Champney reflected on the transformation of the picturesque scenes around his beloved North Conway cottage, writing "in anterailroad days North Conway and its surroundings [were] vastly different from what the tourist finds it today" (Champney 156). The multiple resource-based industries of tourism, logging, and charcoal production, as well as the vestigial practice of making potash, all threatened the very forests that Bierstadt, Champney, and Kensett — along with Asher Durand, Thomas Hill, Aaron Shattuck, and others — were coming to the mountains to observe.

Renowned for his expansive, nationalist Western landscapes, despite their frequent "wholesale departures from topographic fidelity" (Casey 11), Bierstadt was also drawn to the interiors of the Northeast's mountain landscape. His 1863 *Mountain Brook* (fig. 7) offers a clear contrast to the paintings of some of his contemporaries. Bierstadt's work is often read as symbolic of a distant but attainable peace beyond the "decay and adversity" of the Civil War — indeed, the belted kingfisher in the center of the painting is, according to John Audubon, the only kingfisher to have resided in both Confederate and Union states (Simon). Beyond the painting's political symbolism one also finds a very real concern with the intricacies of the forest, which, for Bierstadt and other artists, expressed the essence of the White Mountains more than the spectacular, sublime vistas popularized by the tourist industry. *Mountain Brook* is an example of a more extensive refocusing on the intimacies of place within the White Mountains, negotiating between the antipodes of what Janice Simon calls the mountains' "dual power" of expansive vistas balanced by intimate forest scenes

(93). Works including David Johnson's 1851 *Study, North Conway, New Hampshire*, the stereoscopic views published by Albert Bierstadt's brothers Charles and Edward, and later works like Edward Hill's 1880 *Ravine Brook*, all valorized the details of the landscape and contributed to a burgeoning environmental awareness that complicated the otherwise overtly touristic rhetoric of paintings, photographs, and guidebooks.

Winslow Homer was among the artists whose work, painted while visiting the White Mountains as the environmental impact of tourism was becoming evident, helped to bolster support for a growing environmental awareness. According to Robert McGrath, Homer's visits to the White Mountains in 1868 and 1869 influenced popular artists to reposition the human subject in the center of the canvas. "Homer's radical shift from the face of nature to the facts of tourism," as McGrath notes, may indeed show the landscape as a "mere backdrop for the artist's exploration of human agency" (*Gods in Granite* 154), but it also illustrates the reality of the tourist's exploration of the expansive tableaus painted by artists of the Hudson River and White Mountain Schools. Paintings like Homer's *Bridle Path, White Mountains* (1868) and *Summit of Mount Washington* (1868) show tourists participating in active outdoor recreation *in* the mountains rather than simply gazing *on* them from afar. Similarly, Homer's *Mountain Climber Resting*, completed in 1870, places a climber squarely in the center of the mountain landscape as active participant rather than as passive observer (fig. 8). The valley below the climber's precipitous perch recedes into the distant background as the figure (and pursuit) of the climber, reclining before nature much like Michelangelo's Adam, refocuses the viewer's attention on the action of interacting with the landscape, in effect bridging the gap between distant and intimate observation. By exploring this space between the "dual power[s]" of the mountain landscape, artists like Homer, Hill, and Bierstadt — along with guidebook writers such as King, Samuel Drake, and Moses Sweetser — began to draw attention to these issues of development and its environmental effects. As I discuss in chapter 4, their ideas merged with growing public sentiment expressed by late-nineteenth-century writers and outdoor enthusiasts like Frank Bolles, Bradford Torrey, Lucy Larcom, Isabella Stone, and Marian Pychowska, eventually leading to protective legislation such as the 1911 Weeks Act and the creation of National Forests nationwide.

The crags, ledges, and ravines that compose much of the White Mountain landscape, as Thoreau pointed out after his own visit to the region, offer but little correlation with the regular pyramids the mountains resemble from a distance. The mountains present a discordant and varied landscape that challenges writ-

FIGURE 8
Winslow Homer, American, 1836–1910. *Mountain Climber Resting*, 1868 – 1869.
Cooper-Hewitt, National Design Museum, Smithsonian Institution.
Gift of Charles Savage Homer, Jr., 1912-12-98.

ers to explore the mountains' unfamiliar places; the region's very topography necessarily contributes to travel writers' literal and literary engagement of the landscape. For Manasseh Cutler and Jeremy Belknap, finally on the slopes of the peak they had for so long seen only from a distance in 1784, the text could no longer comfortably present a static, distant representation; the explorers were drawn to look deep into the mountain's crevices and see what lay therein. Visitors to the mountains almost a century later often found themselves situated between these distant and intimate readings of nature. As the rapid growth of tourism and other resource-based industries began to demonstrate more conspicuously the consequences of unbridled road, railway, and hotel construction on the mountain ecosystem, artists and writers were attracted to the largely unexplored (and unexploited) places in the White Mountains' interior. Travel guides by writers like King and his contemporaries, Benjamin Willey, Samuel Drake, and Moses Sweetser, are similarly balanced between rearranging the landscape according to established categories of discourse and being simultaneously transformed by the landscape they seek to describe.

One of the essential tenets of ecocriticism maintains that the distance inherent in a casual observer's (particularly a tourist's) perception of the environment perpetuates a culturally determined disconnect between individual and landscape. The place-conscious Wyoming writer Gretel Ehrlich's suggestion that "landscape cannot exist without an observer" (17) is a useful articulation of both this distance and the constructed nature of the landscape being observed. Frequently, visitors to northern New Hampshire would be drawn to — or, more appropriately, directed to — sites of inhabitation and human experience. Where artists from the Hudson River School visiting the White Mountains would remove or rearrange local residents in their works, guidebook writers of the same period might integrate residents into a catalog of spectacles to be consumed as a part of a "White Mountain experience." The Willey House, Nancy's Brook, the Crawford House, the Mount Washington Cog Railway, and the many resort hotels that crowded the mountains' periphery were but a few of the human artifacts that could be found on the itinerary of a typical White Mountain tour. The turn-of-the-century writer and avid entomologist Annie Trumbull Slosson often found herself a de facto tourist attraction during her butterfly collecting visits to the summit of Mount Washington. On one busy summer afternoon, Slosson overheard a woman reading through her list of sights before departure to make certain she hadn't missed any: "Printin' office, Lizzie Bourne's grave stun, the Tip-over House and — there I ain't seen the old bug woman!" Slosson adds sardonically that "I did not introduce myself and nobody pointed me out. So the disappointed sight-seer was dragged reluctantly to the train, her golden opportunity lost" (qtd. in Boardman 51). Thomas Starr King is conscious of the difference between "an experience in the mountain region, as our party were then enjoying it for a week" and Ethan Allen Crawford's "early acquaintance with its hardships and solitude." Yet he notes how the Crawfords, by the 1850s valued principally as "historical relics," were gawked at as a "specimen of the first settlers . . . of the wilderness" (222). As the White Mountains became more popular among upper-middle-class tourists in the late 1850s, the tourist apparatus made "of itself its principal attraction in which the other attractions are imbedded" (MacCannell, *Tourist* 48).[10] The mountains, their wildlife, and, as is apparent from the examples above, their residents, were codified as so many "relics" and thus made peripheral to the visitors' search for the sublime experience.

By fashioning the White Mountain landscape into a site to be observed from afar and consumed as a viewscape, the region's promoters perpetuated a separation of the *perception* of place from the *reality* of the mountain environment, thus creating a present "more in control of nature [and] less a product of history" (MacCannell, "*Tourist*" 83). The textual and topographical refashioning in which artists, guidebook writers, hotel proprietors, and promoters were en-

gaged veiled the landscape behind a rhetorical distance that, as the ecocritic
Alexander Wilson writes, "permits us the luxurious delusion of being neutral
observers with the ability to manipulate a distant environment" (122). An 1872
advertisement for the Profile House in Franconia Notch is typical of the period's promotional language in that it depicts the hotel as a civilized enclave
from which one can simply look out *onto* the mountains, without venturing
into them:

> A welcome sight, indeed, is the Profile House to the weary traveler, as it greets his
> vision at the twilight hour. All nature seems hushed in repose, and naught but
> the sighing of the wind in the tree tops far above disturbs his meditation. How
> vast and how mighty seem the everlasting mountains, whose summits are lost to
> him in the darkness of night! . . . It is completely shut in by the mountains which
> rise almost from its doors to a great height . . . . Such wildness and grandeur the
> tourist has seldom seen, and he never tires in gazing upon the varied forms of
> beauty which, on every hand, meet his view. The hotel . . . has several times been
> enlarged to meet the growing popularity of the place, until it will now accommo-
> date 500 guests. The parlor is eighty-four by fifty feet, and 460 yards of carpeting
> are required to cover its floor. A band of music is always in attendance for the
> pleasure of guests, and dancing forms one of the attractions of the place during
> the evening hours. Here is a telegraph office, and the mails are received daily, so
> that guests, though away from the larger places, are not altogether outside of the
> comforts and luxuries of home. (*White Mountain Republic*, 29 March 1872)

Hotels such as the Profile House enabled their visitors to look out from an
expansive verandah and, in an act akin to Mary Louise Pratt's "anti-conquest"
(39), let their eyes "box the compass" and passively possess what they see (Harrington 5). But as Thoreau observed in 1858, the representational distance between observer and the observed perpetuated by artists working from places
like Campton is difficult to bridge. The gain, Wilson surmises, may be "objectivity, but the loss is any notion of interrelation between the elements of the
visual field. We see only what is, not how it came to be" (122). Richard Taft and
Charles H. Greenleaf, proprietors of the Profile House, intended not only to
build a grand hotel, but also to mediate the visitors' engagement with the mountains. The leisure culture of the late 1870s for the most part had eschewed the
"rather time-consuming and labor-intensive work of scenic touring" (Brown
72) in favor of more passive recreation. Tourists were content to gaze up at the
mountains from between the Profile House's three-story Doric columns.

Grand resort hotels imposed a class consciousness and an architectural social order that served, the proprietors hoped, to domesticate the wilderness in which they served as sentinels of urban sophistication. The hotels, themselves participating in the "grand life of self-display" (Tolles 19), worked to commodify the landscape by organizing and encircling it within a constellation of similar, well-appointed structures. In his unique 1882 narrative guidebook *The Heart of the White Mountains*, Samuel Drake makes of the mountains a series of discrete interior spaces. Echoing John Ruskin's assertion that mountains "seem to have been built for the human race as at once their schools and cathedrals" (qtd. in King xviii), Drake writes of the village of North Conway, "Nature has formed here a vast antechamber into which you are ushered through a gate-way of mountains upon the numerous inner courts, galleries, and cloisters of her most secluded retreats" (39). Within these sumptuous sites, which mirror the expansive salons of the region's resort hotels, visitors can connect with the landscape by referring back to popular paintings and engravings of fashionable scenes.[11] Drake maintains that "one cannot turn in any direction without recognizing a picture he has seen in the studios, or in the saloons of the clubs" (42). Indeed, even elements of the climate are separated from their natural setting, such as when, after an 1876 winter ascent of North Conway's Mount Kearsarge, he surveys the snow-laden scene and remarks, "talk of decorative art!" (49).

Drake's representation of the mountains as a domestic, built environment in effect domesticates the wilderness and facilitates the reader's transition from hotel foyer to forested mountainside. His emphasis on the forest's interior, however, also emphasizes its symbolic significance, often in contrast to more expansive, sublime viewscapes. Whereas Albert Bierstadt's paintings of the interior of the White Mountain landscape created a symbolically potent space upholstered with the visual rhetoric of a national tragedy twenty years later, Samuel Drake similarly focused his attention on the interior spaces of the landscape as he explored the mountains from "chamber to chamber, and from cloister to cloister" (159). In his aptly titled *Heart of the White Mountains*, Drake reveals that his interest in the "decorative art" of the mountains' interior is part of a developing relationship with the forest environment.

Drake often underscores the text's emphasis on the landscape beneath the forest canopy by incorporating illustrations of forest scenes by W. Hamilton Gibson. The author's description of an ascent of Mount Washington through Tuckerman Ravine (the same route by which Jeremy Belknap's party climbed the peak in 1784) thus focuses on the "confusion and havoc" of the "primitive forest" on the mountain's lower slopes (98). In an apparent attempt to involve the reader in his climb in this section of the book, on one page Drake divides

wood. Time and again we found the way barred by these exasperating windfalls, and their thick *abatis* of branches, forcing us alternately to go down on all-fours and creep underneath, or to mount and dismount, like recruits, on the wooden horse of a cavalry school.

But to any one loving the woods—and this day I loved not wisely, but too well—this walk is something to be taken, but not repeated, for fear of impairing the first and most abiding impressions. One cannot have such a revelation twice.

THE PATH, TUCKERMAN'S RAVINE.

FIGURE 9

William Hamilton Gibson, *The Path, Tuckerman's Ravine*. Illustration for *The Heart of the White Mountains*, by Samuel Adams Drake. Courtesy of the New Hampshire Historical Society.

the text diagonally from lower left with an image of the group's climb through the forest (fig. 9). The image breaks the text's otherwise fluid, consistent typography, coercing readers to themselves stumble over fallen trees and through undergrowth to follow the course of the narrative. Reading, thus, becomes akin to scrambling through the woods: "Time and again we found the way embarred by these exasperating windfalls, and their thick *abatis* of branches, forcing us alternately to go down on all-fours and creep underneath, or to mount and dismount, like recruits, on the wooden horse of a cavalry school" (157). In its obvious invocation of military images, as well as in its very typography, this passage foregrounds both the arduous nature of the climb up Mount Washington and the sense of the climb itself as a conquest. Drake's interweaving of images from the recent Civil War with the language of tourism, furthermore, makes of his White Mountain climb more than a common mountain tramp. The ascent becomes a symbolic struggle through tangled woods beyond which he foresees an emergence onto the airy summits above that embody "a delightful sense of freedom!" (5). Many of the climbs described in *The Heart of the White Mountains*, during which the mountains become an allegory for the potential of America's future, are reminiscent of John Muir's 1867 thousand-mile walk through a landscape in ideological repair.

Although the mountain's summit may symbolize a salvific light beyond these woods, Drake's scramble through Tuckerman Ravine, like the reader's own scramble through the topography of Drake's text, suggests an experience with and within nature—not simply a passing through an environment, but participating in it. Like Belknap's narrative of his curtailed ascent nearly a century earlier, for Drake the forested lower slopes are given nearly the same attention as the rocky windswept summit, even appearing in a separate chapter from the trip to Mount Washington's summit. Shortly after his struggle with the "*abatis* of branches," Drake offers readers insight into the interconnections he sees around him:

> I recall no mountain-path that is so richly diversified with all the wildest forms of mountain beauty. At first our progress through primitive groves of pine, hemlock, and birch was impeded by nothing more remarkable than the giant trees stretching interminably, rank upon rank, tier upon tier. But these woods, these countless gray and black and white trunks, and outspread frameworks of branches, supported a canopy of thick foliage, filled with voices innumerable. (158)

The striking ecological perspective in this passage that highlights the interdependence of trees and wildlife in the forest canopy points to a growing awareness of environmental relationships introduced in the earlier work of Marsh and Thoreau, among others. In its outline of a developing awareness of the forest ecosystem, *The Heart of the White Mountains* also involves human visitors as participants in a larger ecological context. Drake's movement up the slope (much like his reader's) parallels the development of his own land ethic as he moves from conquest to interaction and finally to a sense of preservation, cautioning those who would follow him to "tread softly! . . . Step lightly! You expect to hear the crushed flowers cry out with pain" (158).

Like Drake's Mount Kearsarge and Bierstadt's *Mountain Brook*, many sites in the White Mountains were destined to become larger-than-life symbols of the nineteenth-century American landscape. As Thomas Starr King's would-be visitor makes a short detour from the "regular Conway road" to the shore of what is today Chocorua Lake, the author meaningfully introduces the reader to what he describes as the "two Chocoruas," "nearer alike than the Siamese twins" (140). Whereas the peak on the horizon presents a "rocky, desolate, craggy-peaked substance," its reflection in the lake's surface creates but a "wraith of the proud and lonely shape above" (140). The two summits before the viewer, characterizing the separation between the mountains and their representation, provide an apt illustration of the dual nature of King's *White Hills*. The mountain's very location in the southernmost range of the White Mountains makes it both readily visible to the passing tourist and uniquely situated to divide the mountains from the lowlands. To the south lies a "charming lowland aspect" that Thomas Cole complained was "sublime but not a scene for the Canvass — too much like a map" ("Sketch" 28). The north confronts the visitor with "ridge after ridge" of "nothing but mountains" (King 141). The topographical and figurative play in King's description distances the view from the experience of climbing the mountain, the accessibility of which had not improved significantly in the quarter-century since Thomas Cole's climb in 1828, which he described as being "as perilous as it was difficult" ("Sketch" 28). While valorizing the "craggy-peaked" nature of Chocorua's summit (fig. 10), the mountain's relative inaccessibility (it was climbed only "now and then" even in the 1840s and 1850s [141]) contributes to the distance between viewer and viewscape and empowers the author to seed the mountain's slopes with literary and artistic associations.[12]

King presents Mount Chocorua as an exemplary summit: "It is everything that a New Hampshire mountain should be. It bears the name of an Indian chief. It is invested with traditional and poetic interest. In form it is massive and symmetrical. . . . And it has the fortune to be set in connection with lovely water scenery" (141). Even Henry James, who in 1904 was content to look up

FIGURE 10
Mount Chocorua, 2005. Photograph by the author.

at rather than ascend the peak, noted that it was "duly impressive and duly
. . . overwhelming" (19). King's ordering of Chocorua's attributes occludes the
physical mountain beneath layers of literary and historical association. The description of the mountain in *The White Hills* relies less on firsthand experience
than on artistic and literary descriptions of Chocorua and other peaks. He does
lament, however, that, despite Chocorua's virtues, the absence of a poetic rendition of the mountain's namesake legend, "Chocorua's Curse," detracts from the
visitor's overall experience. Even though "Mr. Whittier has not told it in verse"
(145), to appease his audience's desire for a retelling of the legend King reprints
much of Lydia Maria Child's short story, "Chocorua's Curse" (Child, *Coronal*),
originally published in the 1830 edition of *The Token*.[13]

"Chocorua's Curse" tells the story of the Indian prophet Chocorua, whose
son was killed after he accidentally consumed poison that the Campbells, a
family of colonial settlers, had left out to exterminate a "mischievous fox" (165).
In revenge, Chocorua kills Cornelius Campbell's wife and children while Cornelius is away from home. Upon his return, Cornelius follows Chocorua to the
summit of his namesake mountain and shoots him atop the summit ledges.
With his dying words, Chocorua declares "a curse upon ye, white men. . . .
[T]he Evil Spirit breathe death upon your cattle! Your graves lie in the war path
of the Indian! Panthers howl, and wolves fatten over your bones!" (166). Child's

story, likely inspired by Thomas Cole's painting of the mountain (an engraving of which accompanies "Chocorua's Curse" in *The Token*) and perhaps by Henry Wadsworth Longfellow's 1825 poem "Jeckoyva," presages in many ways later critiques of settlers' and tourists' impact on the White Mountain landscape. In her retelling of the legend, Child elides the Pequaket Chocorua with his namesake mountain, thereby paralleling his eventual demise with the Euro-americans' settling of the mountain wilderness. Although Child invests the characters of Chocorua and Cornelius Campbell with similar traits, perhaps to place them on an equal footing, in the end "Chocorua's Curse" reverts to an account of strife between noble savage and independent settler. A counterpoint to the alternatives to eradication presented in Child's 1824 revolutionary *Hobo-mok*, "Chocorua's Curse" reveals the ire of "Indian animosity" that is "always the same" and implies that the murder of the region's native residents, be it inadvertent or deliberate, is inevitable.

Despite her attention to collisions between culture(s) and nature(s) in the story, however, Child, like King, is disappointed by the dearth of literary associations connected with the peak. "Had it been in Scotland," she writes, "perhaps the genius of Sir Walter would have hallowed it" (162), thereby foreshadowing her own story's recognition alongside Thomas Cole's depictions of Chocorua as part of a landscape grown "quite densely populated with imaginary figures, romantic stories, names, and associations" by 1860 (Brown 70). Indeed, the mythology that "invested" Chocorua is apparent throughout the nineteenth and early twentieth centuries, from Longfellow's "Jeckoyva" to Ethan Allen's *Legend of the Curse of Chocorua* to Joseph Fred Hall's *Legend of Chocorua*. In each retelling of the story, the overt connection between Chocorua the Pequaket and Chocorua the mountain persists. By the middle of the twentieth century, Cedric Whitman's 1945 epic narrative poem "Chocorua" virtually fuses the Indian with the mountain. After the death of his son, Chocorua declares

> Like the great oak I hooked myself to these hills,
> Clamped my roots to the lowest rock;
> They lopped my branches, they left me
> A crooked spine sticking naked in the air.
> . . .
> I will become this mountain and bear down forever
> On their heads my angered shadow. (3.112 – 139)

King's contemporary, Benjamin Willey, includes both an unattributed reprinting of Lydia Maria Child's "beautiful story" and what he believes is the "correct account of Chocorua's curse" in his 1857 *Incidents in White Mountain History* (271). In contrast to Child's story, Willey's "correct account" pits Chocorua against a "miserable white hunter" who would shoot the Indian for the "price of his scalp" despite Chocorua's pleas. Chocorua's curse and subsequent suicidal leap from the summit ledge illustrate, far more than Child's story, what was seen as the inevitability of the "disappearing Indian." As I discussed earlier, the absence of Native Americans from, and the subsequent reintroduction of Native American images and stories into, the White Mountain landscape epitomizes Louise Erdrich's recent paraphrase of Custer's infamous aphorism to read "the only interesting Indian is dead, or dying by falling backwards off a horse" (124).

In addition to refashioning the White Mountains to fit within the ideational framework of the tourist industry, guidebooks sought examples of the sublime in every recess and wove the landscape's natural features into a rhetorical fabric of literary association, spectacle, and commercialism. Even the tragic circumstances of some of the region's early settlers became suffused with the vocabulary of the sublime and beautiful and of an emerging environmentalism. In the summer of 1826, Samuel and Polly Willey, along with their five children and two hired men, lost their lives in an avalanche, which, though responsible for what Samuel's brother Benjamin would see as the "complete" destruction of the area, left their house unscathed. The significance of this slide, and the publicity it generated for the White Mountains, has been discussed extensively, both in nineteenth-century guidebooks and in contemporary critical readings of White Mountain history. Eric Purchase, for instance, argues that the "Willey disaster marks the start of a new American awareness of landscape" by creating a locus for the sublime in America (1). Dona Brown similarly sees the significance of the slide by noting that it was through this event that the "Crawfords got their first big break" in the tourist business (44). Comparing the White Mountains with the contemporary resort destination of Niagara Falls, John Sears notes that the Willey disaster was far "richer in cultural meaning" than any incident at Niagara, and he credits the slide with helping to "establish the fame of the mountains" (74).

The symbolic significance of the Willey tragedy is undeniable. Even in the months that immediately followed, the event was couched in a "verbal gothicism" that dwelled on the horror expressed by the landscape so soon after the tragedy (McGrath, *Gods* 10). The paintings and engravings inspired by Thomas Cole and Henry Cheever Pratt, who visited the Notch in October 1828, helped both to establish the place of the tragedy in the American psyche and to further

FIGURE 11

Anthony Imbert, 1794/95–1834. *Distant View of the Slides That Destroyed the Whilley [sic] Family, the White Mountains,* ca. 1828 – 1829 after the work of Thomas Cole, 1801 – 1848. Albany Institute of History & Art. Gift of Edith Cole Hill (Mrs. Howard) Silberstein, great-granddaughter of the artist.

redefine the White Mountains in appropriately sublime terms. Cole's visit, during which he produced the now lost *Distant View of the Slides That Destroyed the Willey Family* (see Anthony Imbert's version [fig. 11]) helped to convince him of the aesthetic significance of the White Mountains as a place where one could find the "sublime melting into the beautiful [and] the savage tempered by the magnificent" (Cole, "Essay" 103). Nathaniel Hawthorne's popular short story, "The Ambitious Guest," first published in 1835, continued to promote the tourism of tragedy. John Anderson and Stearns Morse, in their 1930 *Book of the White Mountains,* observe, "for years afterwards the Willey House was a Mecca for the curious, the sentimental, the romantic" (171). John H. Spaulding informs readers in 1855 that a "commodious two-story hotel has been erected near this spot, and thousands each season come to stand upon the rock that saved the famous old Willey House" (*Historical Relics* 58). After 1850 guidebooks devoted considerable type to descriptions of the tragedy and the landscape it helped to shape, as well as to lengthy speculation about the Willey family's final moments. As early as the 1840s, visitors (and their readers) regarded the Willey Slide as a fixture requiring no introduction.[14]

Benjamin Willey, Samuel's brother, wrote extensively about the White Mountains and published a guidebook to the region entitled *Incidents in White Mountain History* in 1856. Understandably, Benjamin is particularly concerned with the landslide that killed his brother's family. His description of the event, comprising about forty-five pages, a full 20 percent of his guide, offers three possible scenarios of how the family might have perished and focuses to a large degree on the emotions the Willeys must have been feeling at the time of the tragedy. Benjamin emphasizes that "it is impossible for anyone now living, or anyone who lived at the time of this destruction, to [empathize] with the agonies of spirit" felt by the Willey family. He adds that, although we "may strain our conception of mental horror and impressions of soul that might come upon us under the most startling forms of impending death, . . . after all, we should fail entirely of coming to the dreadful reality" of the event (138). Nonetheless, his preoccupation with their emotional state also serves to underscore the contemporary tourists' desire to reenact the experience (as much as possible) and feel those same emotions. To a substantial degree, Benjamin Willey's narrative helps to guide readers (and visitors) through an emotional landscape more than a physical one. Much in the way that King's *White Hills* coaches the reader in how to view the landscape, Benjamin Willey instructs us on how to feel about it.

Despite Benjamin Willey's close connection to those who died in the rockslide, at the conclusion of his own description of the tragedy he resorts to the rhetoric of tourism. Suggesting that, finally, "we cannot do better, perhaps, than . . . the words of Byron" (139), he shifts his attention from the White Mountain Notch of 1826 to a land wherein "the quick Rhone . . . has cleft his way" (140). Willey thus does much to relocate a very personal tragedy into a landscape of what Dona Brown calls "mass-produced" associations (48). Building associations by inscribing an imported poetic sentiment on an American landscape, he becomes, finally, like Hawthorne's young man, sporting an "opera glass set in gold" (*Sketches* 29), moved to read from Byron on the way through the Notch.

Although Benjamin Willey felt compelled to reach across the Atlantic to effectively describe the events of the death of his brother and his family, the Willey tragedy did become the subject of several much reprinted American poems. For instance, at the conclusion of his description of the Willey tragedy, King quotes Thomas W. Parsons's 1855 poem "The Willey House." The poem's own extensive publication history is itself a comment on the significance of the

Willey tragedy for the literature of tourism. First printed in *Putnam's Monthly Magazine* shortly after it was written, the poem was reprinted in its entirety in King's guidebook, then served as the touchstone for Parsons's 1875 *Willey House and Sonnets*, and finally appeared in Parsons's *Collected Poems* in 1893. In 160 lines, "The Willey House" depicts both the bucolic setting of the Willey house and the drama of the 1826 tragedy.

> A happy home it was of yore:
>   At morn the flocks went nibbling by,
> And Farmer Willey, at his door,
>   Oft made their reckoning with his eye.
>
> Where yon rank alder trees have sprung,
>   And birches cluster thick and tall,
> Once the stout apple overhung,
>   With his red gifts, the orchard wall.

Despite the detailed speculation about the events of 28 August, like much literature of tourism, "The Willey House" re-places the house and family into a traditionally pastoral topography, drawing, as Eric Purchase points out, many of its images from Horace's *Odes*. There is no mention in Parsons's poem of the three-story 40' × 70' hotel abutting the old Willey House built by Horace Fabyan in 1845. In the poem's apparent disregard for the changes in the land since 1826, Purchase reads Parsons as "exert[ing] no awareness of how tourism had affected the Willeys" (115). The poem's empty landscape, however, illustrates a consciousness of the very visible tourism of Parsons's day. Parsons leaves out the tourists, as we can see in the passage below, but this is not a sign that he is ignorant of them; he is simply re-placing the Willey house in what he sees as a more appropriate picturesque frame. Though variously emblematic of the imported sentiment of the Notch's midcentury visitors, "The Willey House" also participates in the very economy of tourism that is notably absent from its description of the tranquil precalamitous landscape. Near the beginning of the poem, Parsons draws his readers' attention to the White Mountain Notch as though it were a picturesque hollow, beckoning them to

> See that cottage in the glen,
>   Yon desolate forsaken shed —
> Whose mouldering threshold, now and then,
>   Only a few stray travellers tread.

> No smoke is curling from its roof,
> At eve no cattle gather round,
> No neighbor now, with dint of hoof,
> Prints his glad visit on the ground.

Parsons's verse sheds significant light on midcentury perspectives on the Willey slide not in spite of its apparent ignorance of the "influence of the city and market economy" (Purchase 115), but precisely because of the poem's conspicuous effacement of tourists from the scene. In a discourse of landscape that valorized "artifacts rather than facts" (McGrath, "Real and Ideal" 59), Parsons's textual artifact, much like King's larger topographic catalog, fixes the landscape within an aesthetic discourse that echoes earlier paintings by Henry Cheever Pratt and Thomas Cole.[15] Leaving out evidence of the apparatus of a bustling tourist enterprise, Parsons locates his poem within a discourse that seeks to define the tourist experience in terms of an appropriate viewscape.

In an overt example of his propensity for building associations, King asserts that the "tremendous walls" of the Notch are transformed, "touched by terror, reflected from the Willey calamity" (202). This mountain pass, described thirty-five years before the slide by Jeremy Belknap as containing "almost every thing in nature, which can be supposed capable of inspiring ideas of the sublime and beautiful" (*History* 3:39), epitomizes the intention of guidebook authors and tourism promoters to tie physical places to histories and events in order to refashion the mountains as a region rich with local significance. It is perhaps this idea that suggests to King, as he leaves Parsons's poem to continue his description of the Notch, that "there is little need now of any detailed or elaborate description of the wildness and majesty of the Notch" (202). Adhering to his topographical choreography of the White Mountain tour, King moves northward through the Notch, allowing the narrative of the event to speak for the landscape, thereby successfully investing text with toponymic symbolism.

By the conclusion of King's section on the Willey area of the Notch, the event itself had already receded, as it had for visitors by the 1850s, from its significance as a tragedy that took the lives of nine people to a largely symbolic occurrence to be cataloged as a "historical relic" beside the Crawfords in John H. Spaulding's 1855 book. Samuel Eastman echoed Spaulding's sentiment in his popular 1858 *White Mountain Guide Book* when he described the Willey House as a "showcase" that was not worth the "trifling expenditure" of the twelve and a half cent entry fee charged by the proprietors (Eastman 79). Dona Brown argues that by the middle of the nineteenth century, the "White Mountain region and the cult of scenery were transformed by their own success" (70).

As I discussed earlier in this chapter, the resort hotels that continued to increase in number through the late nineteenth century certainly enabled tourists to view the mountains from within sumptuous surroundings, thus separating them from the wilderness beyond the edge of the hotel veranda and perhaps attenuating their need for a sublime experience. The decline of the sublime in the White Mountains, however, as epitomized by a refashioning of the Willey tragedy as mundane, also points to a larger national revision of wilderness perception. The expansion of agricultural lands westward and northward in the mid-nineteenth century precipitated an ideological and industrial "war with the wilderness" (Thoreau qtd. in Nash 102). Roderick Nash traces the rising clarion call for preservation through the second quarter of the nineteenth century from John James Audubon to James Fenimore Cooper to Francis Parkman and Thoreau. All these writers cite the increasing clearing of and building in wild lands as pointing to the "prospect of a totally civilized America" (Nash 102).[16] It is just such a civilized wilderness that the White Mountains had become by the 1850s, created as much by the artist's brush and writer's pen as by the continuing construction of lavishly appointed hotels.

King himself surmises that in the case of the Willey Slide, "the waste of the mountains is not destructive, but creative" and that "in the long run the ravage of the avalanche is beneficent" (204). King's ministerial hand is evident here as he concludes, "apparent disorder is overruled by the law of loveliness" (205). Here we can once again see the author's situatedness between competing forces of "market and economy" on one hand and a nascent environmentalism on the other. His vacillation between critique of and complicity in a tourist landscape aesthetics and ethics is apparent in his reading of the event's tragedy through Parsons's poem simultaneous with an attention to the slide's reshaping of the landscape to create an even more spectacular vista for the visiting tourist. To inform his aesthetic (and indeed moral) transformation of the Willey tragedy into a "creative" event, King draws on John Ruskin's *Modern Painters*. Ruskin traces the transformative hand of painters who, "among the debris of Swiss mountains," were, despite the landscape's "breaks and disturbances," able to depict a "natural unity [that] is so sweet and perfect" (204). It is while traversing the contested rhetorical terrains of promotion and preservation that *The White*

Hills presages the contentious dialogue among tourists, entrepreneurs, lumbermen, politicians, and scientists that would eventually lead to the passage of the Weeks Act in 1911 and the creation of the White Mountain National Forest.

If the sublime spectacle of the 1826 Willey Slide marked the beginnings of tourism's refashioning of the White Mountain environmental, social, and economic landscapes, it is useful to look at a parallel event at the height of White Mountain tourism to consider how the perspective of the industry changed over the sixty intervening years. On 10 July 1885, the residents of the town of Jefferson, approximately twenty miles from Crawford Notch and just north of the Presidential Range, witnessed what has become known as the Cherry Mountain or Stanley Slide. Since the slide occurred at the height of tourist season near numerous boardinghouses and resort hotels, comparisons to the 1826 rockslide that killed the Willey family and two hired men were inevitable. Immediately after the slide, local year-round and seasonal newspapers ran stories ranging from the sensational to the scientific.[17] On 18 July the *White Mountain Echo and Tourist's Register* ran the following headline on its front page:

The Stanley Slide.
Wonderful Transformation on the Slope of Cherry Mountain.
A Deep Gorge Cut.
New Cascades Formed, and Forty Acres Covered with Debris.
Several Miraculous Escapes.
Counterpart of the Renowned Willey Slide,
Travelling Two Miles in Three Minutes.
A New Feature for Sight-Seers.

Accompanied by an image of the White Mountain Notch, the site of the Willey tragedy (likely to convey a not-so-subtle impression of a connection between the two events), the *Echo* article narrates the events of the Cherry Mountain Slide, describing the extensive destruction of Oscar Stanley's property and livestock and the severe (and ultimately fatal) injury of Stanley's employee, Donald Walker. As suggested by the multiple layers of the article's headline, the rhetorical and iconological landscape through which the slide ran its course was a complicated one. Sensational tourist literature would be cobbled together with economic realities of North Country farming (and late-nineteenth-century farm abandonment) and a new scientism in mountain exploration for several years to follow. The *White Mountain Echo* article cited above, for instance, concludes its description of the events of 10 July with an appeal to the paper's core readership; if the slide itself is not sufficiently interesting to the visitor, a scramble up the slide's path is "amply rewarded by the charming view of [Mount] Jefferson."[18]

Charles Hitchcock, author of the 1874 New Hampshire geologic report, asserted in a followup *Echo* article of 22 August that the slide was "destined to be as memorable in the annals of White Mountain history as the famous Willey slide of 1826." Although the events may have been geologically similar, Hitchcock's predictions about the Stanley Slide's longevity in the public consciousness proved far from the mark. Akin to the 1826 Willey Slide in that it was precipitated by an abrupt yet unremitting "cloudburst," the slide on Cherry Mountain traveled between one and a half and two miles from the mountain's summit through Oscar Stanley's farm, "completely demolishing a partially built house, a large barn, fatally injuring [Donald Walker], killing several cattle and smaller domestic animals." The slide was a significant topic at the Appalachian Mountain Club's Boston meeting in October 1885, giving rise to a report printed in the club's journal *Appalachia* (Knox) and in the *White Mountain Echo* of 24 July 1886. The timing of the slide at the height of the summer tourist season, the proximity of the event to a number of hotels, and the site's visibility from a nearby railway led to its exploitation by the media and public. Hitchcock himself slips into the discourse of tourism when he concludes his *Echo* article by noting how "the locality may be reached most conveniently by way of the Whitefield and Jackson R.R."

Where the Willey tragedy had time to concretize as an "event" and find a place in the discourse of tourism, however, the Stanley Slide had no such opportunity and was immediately the center of attention. In a letter to Isabella Stone written on 19 July, nine days after the Stanley slide, Marian Pychowska, a frequent summer boarder in nearby Randolph, wrote

> The Owl's Head [Cherry Mountain] slide seems to have made a great noise all over the country. New York and Chicago papers both had full accounts. Quite a party went from here to visit it last Tuesday and my aunt and uncle saw it of course from the train in passing. My mother and I have inspected it only from a distance. This morning as we drove to Gorham to church we met almost innumerable vehicles. All Gorham seemed on its way to the slide. (Rowan and Rowan 223)

Despite this immediate popularity, or perhaps as a result of it, the Stanley Slide was not destined to achieve the same stature as the Willey Slide before it. Of course, the human tragedy of the Willey disaster far outweighed that of the slide on Cherry Mountain, and the Willey's intact home both left a monument for future visitors and added to the symbolic significance of the earlier event.

Tourists visiting the site (and sight) of the later tragedy did not have the benefit of historical distance afforded to midcentury visitors to the Willey House. No one remained to give a firsthand account of the Willey Slide, and hypotheses about the 1826 August night pervaded histories throughout the middle of the nineteenth century. This speculation, caused by a lack of firsthand information about the Willeys' last night, became a catalyst for the cascade of historical narratives, short stories, and poems. No such reaction followed the destruction of Oscar Stanley's farm. In the shift from event to cultural artifact, the Cherry Mountain Slide was perhaps too much in the foreground to remain in the public consciousness for long.

The obvious differences between the two slides notwithstanding, the "Stanley Slide," and the response to and representation of it, is worth exploring because of its timing and the immediate, overwhelming impact of tourism on the tragedy. That its popularity was short-lived and would in no way have the same legacy as the Willey Slide became evident fairly quickly. Frederick Kilbourne's 1916 book *Chronicles of the White Mountains* describes the event only sparingly in a single paragraph. Although he notes that Donald Walker lost his life, the death becomes only an item in a catalog of other items lost to the slide: "it wrecked the house, killed several cattle, and mortally injured Donald Walker, one of the farmhands." Kilbourne continues his narrative, writing that "for years the vast scar of this slide, known as the 'Stanley Slide,' was plainly visible from Jefferson, but of late years it has become overgrown again and so is now much less conspicuous" (304). By the middle of the twentieth century, while public interest in the Willey Slide persisted, mention of the Stanley Slide in White Mountains literature continued to wane dramatically. The 1930 Anderson and Morse *Book of the White Mountains* contains no mention of the event, whereas one of the last general White Mountain histories to be published, Ernest Poole's 1946 *Great White Hills of New Hampshire*, grants the slide only a single sentence: "Most of them [slides] were small affairs, but the Cherry Mountain Slide in 1885 sent a million tons of earth, rocks and trees thundering down." No mention is made of specific damage or death that resulted (103).

Shortly after the Willey Slide in 1826, the site began to attract a diversity of people to the White Mountains, including tourists, as I have mentioned, simply wanting to witness where the disaster occurred. It also appealed to writers such as Hawthorne and guidebook authors eager to place the event in proper context, as well as scientific writers like Charles Jackson, Charles Hitchcock, and Joshua Huntington (Hitchcock's assistant), each contributing to different versions of New Hampshire's geological report, and the early environmentalist and conservation writer, George Perkins Marsh. Scientific writing about the mountains in the nineteenth century often overlapped considerably with tourist discourse. Thomas Starr King's popular guidebook, for instance, shared much with scientific reports. Hitchcock's 1874 *Geology of New Hampshire*, among other contemporary publications, drew on King's guide for its more colorful descriptive sections. As I mentioned earlier, in an effort to add historical and scientific validity to *The White Hills*, King included two chapters by the White Mountain botanist Edward Tuckerman, "Exploration of the White Mountains" and "The Vegetation of the White Mountains." Correspondingly, in one section of his geological report, Hitchcock refers to a locale that was "one of the favorite points of view with Starr King, who regretted that so few persons among the great travelling public ever attain to it," adding, more in the language of a guidebook rather than of a geologic treatise, "it is of easy access, by a carriage-drive of a dozen miles from Gorham or a walk of a mile or two from the Milan station on the Grand Trunk Railway. There is a country inn at Milan, where travellers are always welcome" (608).

A more complex example of intertextuality among disciplines can be read in the writing of the Vermont-born environmental activist George Perkins Marsh. Marsh, who had found throughout the landscape of northern New England the "effects resulting from an injudicious system of managing woodlands," argued in his 1848 address before the Rutland County Agricultural Society that the "loss of the primeval forest left a void in the spiritual as well as the economic scheme of rural life" (Merchant, *Ecological Revolutions* 1). Marsh refined his ecological ideas in his seminal 1864 work *Man and Nature*. In it, he asserts the "mutual relations and adaptations" of both the "organic and inorganic world[s]" are so subject to the "terrible destructiveness of man" that the "harmonies of nature are turned to discords" (36–37). Marsh's connection of land abuse, overlogging, erosion, and watershed pollution (by silt — a byproduct of all these things) to loss of viable waterways induced him to view even the Willey disaster as an illustration of similar human effects on the wilderness. The slide, he writes, "may have been occasioned by [logging], or by the construction of the road through the Notch, the excavations for which, perhaps, cut through the buttresses that supported the sloping strata above" (228). Marsh conjectures that the Willey Slide was wholly a result of human transformation of the landscape, including logging, road building, and rock blasting. A longstanding and vocal conservationist who wrote and lectured on the issues of sustainable agriculture and silviculture before the middle of the century, Marsh was, however, incorrect about the events in 1826. As Eric

Purchase notes, the road through the Notch required significant work only several miles north of the Willeys' home, and logging was not done in the area on a large scale until half a century *after* the slide (151). Despite his work with deforestation and erosion, and the pollution of watersheds in the Northeast as a result of environmentally destructive logging practices, Marsh's vigor led him to a certain narrowmindedness that attempted to blame all destructive natural events on humankind.

What we *can* read in Marsh's argument, however, is that the event, though not precipitated by human interventions in the area's environment (which were fairly limited at the time, as logging would not play a major economic role in the area until some forty or fifty years after the landslide), was overwhelmed by a focus on its cultural significance. As a result, the slide was removed from its natural environment and placed into a carefully constructed framework that appropriated the natural event and repositioned it as a cultural one, re-plete with sublime awe and associative value. In this migration from event to myth, environmental concerns raised in Marsh's treatise are lost along with practical questions such as "why the Willeys were in Crawford Notch in the first place" (Purchase 152). These are replaced by speculation about the "horror of that night to the doomed family" (King 194) and by a reverence of the spot as a sublime archetype. The "spiritual" and "economic" interests involved in places like the Willey site became progressively more interconnected as the economics of tourism and a burgeoning resource-extraction industry increas-ingly came into conflict with the spirituality of a sublime experience sought by tourists. As I have noted, by the 1860s issues of human impact, preservation, and recognition of forests as ecological systems were beginning to find their voice in unlikely venues such as guidebooks, where the rhetoric of tourism was complicated by the obvious effects of that very tourism on the landscape the authors were describing.

Although the purpose of King's guidebook was to sell both itself and the White Mountain region to tourists (tasks in which it succeeded marvelously), it also gave voice to midcentury conservationist sentiment as it appealed to read-ers' understanding of the White Mountains as a particular place and not merely something to be consumed. King was conscious of the physical and social ef-fects that both tourist and timber economies have on a landscape to which he nonetheless continued to draw visitors. Although *The White Hills* is critical of the tourist, who "gobbles" the scenery as if it were "his dinner," King's explicit critique of local resource-based economies becomes evident in his lament over a wildness lost to an expanding economy. An excerpt from John Greenleaf

Whittier's 1848 poem "The Bridal of Pennacook" that King includes near the beginning of *White Hills* does not comdemn the tourist trade, but rather local agriculture and industry:

> What a pity it is that our great hills
> Piled to the clouds — our rivers overhung
> By forests which have known no other change
> For ages, than the budding and the fall
> Of leaves — our valleys lovelier than those
> Which the old poets sang of — should but figure
> On the apocryphal chart of speculation
> As pastures, wood-lots, mill-sites, with the privileges,
> Rights and appurtenances, which make up
> A Yankee Paradise — unsung, unknown
> To beautiful tradition; even their names,
> Whose melody yet lingers like the last
> Vibration of the red man's requiem,
> Exchanged for syllables significant
> Of cotton mill and rail-car! (32)

Whittier's elegy for a wild landscape being lost to "pastures, wood-lots, [and] mill sites" points very specifically to the commerce of a working landscape and to the language used to name and order it. Drawing on imagery similar to that of the vanishing Indian of Chocorua's Curse, Whittier merges native and nature to mark the mournful loss of both. When the guidebook was first published in 1859, large-scale logging in the White Mountains was only in its earliest stages. The transformation of the forest economy, also traced in the poem above, from clearing for farmland to clearcutting for timber, had been critiqued only a decade earlier by George Perkins Marsh and was only beginning to be noticeable to summer tourists. His inclusion of this passage locates King in the middle of a contested terrain — in one moment critiquing the effect of spectacle-hungry tourists and local resource-based economies on the landscape, and in another, as a guidebook author, drawing more visitors to the region by his very nature. Implicit in his critique of tourists' perfervid "gobbl[ing]" of viewscapes and summit experiences and his directive to refocus on the forest's less frequently visited interior is a nascent environmental consciousness, which, by the late 1850s, had begun to find advocates among King's contemporaries.

As I noted in chapter 2, Lucy Crawford, who, along with her husband Ethan, had spent many years exploring the area around the notch that would bear their name, also urges midcentury tourists to take time to properly digest their mountain experience. In her 1860 revision of *History of the White Mountains*, she asserts "an hour, nor a day is not sufficient to study this vast book of nature." Benjamin Willey appeals similarly to time-pressed tourists in his 1856 *Incidents in White Mountain History*: "it is utterly impossible to know what the White Mountains are by whirling through Conway, and Glenn, and Notch, and Franconia, in a week" (290). Charles Hitchcock echoes King's own language when he informs would-be visitors to Mount Washington's summit that "except by a thorough inspection of what seem small areas, he cannot appreciate the immense number and variety of objects visible. He can spend a full month in observing, and discover some new feature every day" (620). Moses Sweetser similarly laments the loss of a locale whose "charm was broken forever" by the intrusion of railway lines (Sweetser, *Views* unpaged). Later writers declare how the "tourist hordes" who arrive each summer in a "torrent of cars" speed through the mountains without taking the time to see what King calls the letters of nature's "infinite alphabet" (394).[19] Such criticism of the tourist trade by its very promoters points to a considerable increase in the number of visitors in the 1860s and 1870s, which precipitated the expansion of resort hotels, railway spurs, bridle paths, and mountaintop buildings. The rapid economic growth throughout the Northeast in the 1860s occasioned many to escape the "quest for success . . . through the new summer vacation ritual" (Tolles 77) and seek refuge in the well-appointed hotels of northern New Hampshire. This perennial outmigration from Northeastern urban centers prompted a competition among hotel proprietors and promoters to create the most enticing destination for a growing class of wealthy guests.[20]

Among Thomas Starr King's numerous contemporaries and competitors was Moses Sweetser, author of the most extensively published nineteenth-century book of White Mountain photographs and descriptions, his 1879 *Views in the White Mountains*. With ten distinct editions all published in a single year, and a complicated interplay between the book's photographs and textual descriptions, Sweetser's enterprise limns the increasingly intertwined layers of tourism, commerce, and preservation. *Views in the White Mountains* was printed by a company in Portland, Maine, owned by the Chisolm brothers. The Chisolms were both publishers and newsagents for the railroad that provided access to White Mountain hotels. At the same time, one of the brothers, Hugh Chisolm, was owner of a large paper mill that sometimes clear-cut stretches of mountainside that the tourists riding into the mountains on trains were coming to see.

Although the Chisolm brothers went to significant lengths to commission

Sweetser, a well-known and respected White Mountain historian and travel writer, to pen their descriptions, his portrayals are very often disconnected from the visual images in the book. For example, in characterizing his own love for the mountains, Sweetser asserts that the book will describe the "highest and remotest peaks, and their deepest and most terrible ravines." Of the twelve photographs in the book, however, only two are of an untrammeled mountain landscape. Sweetser cannot seem to reconcile the building of the railroads and hotels with their visual and environmental impact on the mountains. In one example, a photograph of the Mount Washington Cog Railway approaching the summit is meant to be a depiction of a memorial to the death of Lizzie Bourne, which is situated on the margin of the photograph, to the right of the tracks (fig. 12). The background of the book's publishers makes the focus of the images on the commercial aspects of the mountains understandable. Sweetser's descriptions, however, contain often-explicit critiques of the increase in development that the book's images celebrate. In the same guide whose pictures illustrate a reverence for the railway, Sweetser writes, "when railroad-builders, those Goths and Vandals of our age, reached North Conway, and stretched their rigid trestles and gravel-banks across her exquisite meadows, the charm was broken forever." But at the same time as he decries the loss of natural beauty, he locates the residents of the region as working for the tourist enterprise, as if the whole of the White Mountains was constructed solely for the pleasures of the wealthy tourists who summered there each year. He explains that throughout the region, "there are scores of paths cut through the forests and upon the mountains by the hotel-keepers and villagers, for the sole object of making easy the ways to scenes of grandeur and beauty."

Moses Sweetser's critique of White Mountain railroads in the pages of a book sold in trains traveling over those very tracks, King's engagement of the forest's interior in addition to popular summit viewscapes, and Benjamin Champney's celebration of the White Mountains' "dual power" (Simon 93), along with similar works by many of their contemporaries, struggled to record and redefine a landscape that was being transformed at the very moment when they described it. The devastation wrought by extensive clear-cutting in northern New Hampshire is well documented by historians, environmentalists, and even timber industry representatives. At the end of the century, tourists demanding all the trappings of an urban environment among the White Mountains necessarily found themselves at odds with others who sought more pristine natural surroundings. Tourism's expectations, combined with the incipient environmentalism I trace in this chapter, and, in the century's final decades with the

FIGURE 12
Lizzie Bourne's Monument, on Mount Washington. Published in
Moses Sweetser, *Views in the White Mountains*, 1879.

logging industry's massive and sudden transformation of the landscape, produced a complex dialogue between these competing perceptions of land use.
The tourist industry's desire for an unoccluded, properly framed window onto
a sublime wilderness, was, at the end of the nineteenth century (much as it remains today) at the center of a political discourse concerning the appropriate
management of the "land of many uses."

As early as 1848, George Perkins Marsh addressed the growing imbalance
between land use and abuse among New England farmers. Even before the explosion of White Mountain tourism in midcentury, articles in publications like
the *Farmer's Monthly* began to reflect on the inevitability of development and
on forests that would eventually succumb to the logging industry. By the turn
of the century, writers in the popular press added their voices to a campaign to
stop overdeveloping the forests. In the May 1909 issue of *Colliers*, Earnest Russell described the J. E. Henry Company as "butchering the beautiful forest of
that [Zealand] valley and doing the most reckless lumbering I have seen in the
mountains" (qtd. in Belcher 212). Thomas Will wrote of the Zealand Valley in
1907, "the writer has surnamed this 'Death Valley'" (qtd. in Belcher 98). Joseph
B. Walker similarly described forest abuse in the same area in 1891, noting,

"As one now looks upon the two towering sentinels of fire-blasted rock which mark the opening of this valley, there blazes into his mind, in letters of living fire, the terrible inscription which Dante in his *Divine Comedy* placed over the entrance arch to hell, — All hope abandon ye who enter here" ("Our New Hampshire Forests" 13). Though proponents of conservation for very different reasons, these writers illustrate a change in sentiment toward the landscape, away from overuse and in the direction of a conservationism that would lead to the 1911 Weeks Act and eventually the creation of the White Mountain National Forest.

As debate about New England's northern forests in the late twentieth century shapes future perceptions of recreation and industry in New Hampshire's national forest, the discourses of center and of margin continue to reconstruct the landscape, both textually and physically, for particular social and economic agendas. Much as the manipulative hand of nineteenth-century artists and writers grew transparent to summer tourists, and they grew to see representations as truths, we need to remain critical of the tricky relation between representation and reality (or, as Eric Purchase would have it, between reality and realty) as we continue to negotiate a complex interweaving of perceptions, industries, and ideologies.

CHAPTER FOUR

Alone with Scribe and Staff

Rewriting the White Mountains,

1870 – 1900

THE SOUTHERN BOUNDARY of the White Mountains is roughly delineated by a range of mountains stretching from Mount Chocorua near the Maine state line toward the Pemigewasset River to the west. Immediately to the west of the peak celebrated for its association with "Chocorua's Curse" rises its neighbor, Mount Paugus, named by the poet Lucy Larcom for the Sokosis leader, and known locally as Old Shag or Toadback.[1] Spring runoff from both peaks swells Paugus Brook on its course toward the Bearcamp River to the south. The notch through which Paugus Brook runs presents a challenging obstacle to hikers; during a traverse of the range in 1925, Brooks Atkinson suggested that those who attempt to climb the two thousand feet from Paugus Brook to its namesake summit are "by no means numerous or altogether wise" (Atkinson and Olson 68). Today a hiking trail winds from a trailhead at the end of Paugus Mill Road through third-growth forest, past a pile of sawdust and industrial detritus that marks the site of an old lumber mill along Paugus Brook, and northward to the former village of Albany along the Swift River.

The toponymic and topographic sediment that layers this eastern end of the Sandwich Range complicates what might at first appear to be the simple act of hiking through the notch. The artifacts that litter the site of the old Paugus Mill — tin stovepipes, stone foundations, and fuel cans painted with a barely distinguishable Mobil Pegasus surrounding an immense mound of sawdust — suggest that the site had been home to a logging operation as recently as the mid-1950s. An array of wooden scaffolding buttressing sections of Paugus Brook nearby, however, hints at earlier use. According to the oral histories collected by Marjory Gene Harkness in the mid-1950s for the *Tamworth Narrative*, a mill operated on or near that site between 1907 and the mid 1920s, chiefly exporting oak pilings to serve as foundation for reclaimed land in East Boston.

In the late 1880s Frank Bolles, who had purchased a summer home in the nearby village of Tamworth Iron Works, engaged his Tamworth neighbor Nathaniel Berry in a quest to find what he thought to be a "lost trail" northward along Paugus Brook to the Swift River, believing this to be a significantly shorter route from Tamworth to Conway. Berry, a "farmer, lumberman, hunter, trapper, surveyor, carpenter, and public-spirited citizen," whose family had lived on the same Tamworth farm for at least two generations, himself recalled a road through the notch when he was a boy around 1850 (Bolles, *At the North* 45–46). Roughly a mile north of Berry's farm on Paugus Brook (almost precisely where today's mill site remains visible), Bolles and Berry entered a "clearing of an acre or more" that was home to "the ruins of a saw-mill" where in the years before the Civil War there had stood "two or three slab houses" and a "stable where the lumberman's oxen had been kept in the winter nights." Bolles's narrative of the expedition in his 1893 (first edition) book *At the North of Bearcamp Water* makes it clear that he and his companion passed through an industrial landscape that had long since been abandoned to the hardwoods of the New England forest; Bolles noted how the "strong, quarrelsome blackberry had mastered the sawdust" (48).

Although the date of the site's earliest use is unclear, what is apparent is that the same site on the banks of Paugus Brook had been used for a sawmill on at least two if not three separate occasions between 1840 and 1960. Leaving their own marks on the forest floor, the hikers who pass through the sparse mixed hardwood forest of beech, birch, and maple past the site today are provided with precious little historical context save for National Forest Service signs threatening eager souvenir hunters with a hefty fine, signs whose only interpretive function is to designate this as a "historic site." The future of industrial artifacts in National Forest wilderness areas has recently been a contentious topic among White Mountain historians and the National Forest Service. While there are vocal proponents for rewilding wilderness areas by removing logging artifacts, Littleton, New Hampshire, writer Mike Dickerman argues that the White Mountains occupy a "permanent place in local logging annals" and thus despite legislative designations, many places defined as 'wilderness' "will never be . . . pristine wilderness area[s]" (*Why I'll Never* 135). We cannot, of course, undo more than a century of logging history simply by hauling industrial detritus out of the woods. Its place in White Mountain wilderness areas is interwoven with the forest that has reclaimed its landscape. In old logging camps far from any road, trees have grown to maturity around stovepipes and through steel bedframes to syncretize industrial and wild in an inseparable union. Evidence of logging history in places like Paugus Notch contributes to the rich, multifaceted natural, cultural, and economic history of the region, an example of what William Cronon calls "the full continuum of a natural landscape that is also cultural" (quoted in Mitchell and Diamant 232).[2]

The vestiges of industry littering the forest floor at the base of Old Shag and at the edge of the Sandwich Range Wilderness are now partially obscured by the framework of the region's new industry of tourism and forest recreation. Trails impel a linear progression across a landscape, whereas its history might more appropriately be understood by tracing an archaeology of the complicated, intersecting layers beneath the forest duff. Much like the decades of accumulated sawdust at the mill site, the Paugus Brook valley is layered with the frequently competing ideologies of recreation, resource extraction, preservation, and regulation. Bolles's narrative interweaves these discourses with the language of romantic regionalism to create a nexus of environmental experience, what John Muir, in *A Thousand Mile Walk to the Gulf*, described as "one grand palimpsest of the world" (93). Describing the ecosystem of the American Southeast, Muir admitted that his ability to read the landscape was incomplete: "Our limited powers are . . . perplexed and overtaxed in reading the inexhaustible pages of nature, for they are written over and over uncountable times, written in characters of every size and color, sentences composed of sentences, every part of a character a sentence" (93). Sifting through the strata of cultural and environmental artifacts both at the Paugus Mill site and throughout the fin-de-siècle White Mountains reveals an intersection of many discourses, a platial intertextuality that resists straightforward definition. What John Hanson Mitchell has called the "greatest trespass of all" (10), to pause on the hiking trail, perhaps to step off and explore the margins of the thoroughfare, is to consciously trace the interwoven threads of place and time.

In 1892 Charles E. Fay, an enthusiastic member of the Appalachian Mountain Club and an inveterate explorer of mountain ranges throughout North America, had completed his project of building a footpath and shelter on the summit of Mount Passaconaway, just to the west of Mount Paugus.[3] In an article printed shortly thereafter in the Appalachian Mountain Club's journal, *Appalachia*, Fay contemplated the consequences of his trail building, asking "was it justifiable to love the mountain not less, but climbers more?" and "was it not a breach of confidence to plan for the wholesale invasion of [the mountain's] privacy, and to aid in making it a readily accessible peak?" As if in response to his own queries, he decided to descend the peak not on his newly built trail, but along a neighboring trackless ridge, in order, he writes, to "prolong the luxury of the forest to the last possible moment" (318). Fay's concerns about the extent of trail building and the expansion of tourism in the late-nineteenth-century White Mountains illustrate a tension between a steadily diminishing wildness and continuing expansion of tourism into a landscape where, as Frank Bolles forebodingly observes, the "scream of the distant locomotive whistle seems ominous of impending crowds" ("Three Days" 1).

The year after Charles Fay's climb on Mount Passaconaway, as Frank Bolles's book *At the North of Bearcamp Water* was being published, Frederick Jackson Turner famously declared the closing of the American frontier. Although Turner's remarks focused primarily on the end of decades of perfervid western expansion and saw such a closure as a portent of change in American social and political values, visitors to northern New Hampshire like Fay and Bolles found a landscape on the verge of a similar transformation. By the 1890s the "daunting terrible" wilderness John Josselyn had described in the late seventeenth century had been chiefly subdued by the progress and industry of America's expansionist ideology; "the frontier was moribund," writes Roderick Nash; "wilderness [was] no longer dominant" (145). The "new product that is American" that Turner claimed was created by the physical and ideological confrontation of the human and wild at the frontier was clearly losing its place of origin (Frederick Jackson Turner 4). A decade after his oft-cited recognition of the frontier's close in 1893, Turner declared further, "the great supply of free lands which year after year has served to reinforce the democratic influences in the United States is exhausted" (261). While visiting Eleazer Rosebrook's overnight house at the foot of Mount Washington in 1803, Timothy Dwight was impressed by the "enterprise . . . industry, and perseverance" required to hew a living from the region's dense forests and poor soil (*Travels* 96). In the period of the grand resort hotel's greatest prosperity, from roughly 1870 to the turn of the century, the frontier experience in northern New Hampshire was also diminishing, as railroads and hotel proprietors continued to aggressively develop and promote the White Mountains as a premier resort destination for upper-class urban tourists. The prosperous economic climate encouraged the almost-unchecked development of hotels, many of which could accommodate more than two hundred, and sometimes more than five hundred, guests each night. These grand resort hotels — which were often equipped with "new recreational alternatives" such as bowling alleys, rifle ranges, casinos, and tennis courts (Tolles 143) — effectively imported urban economic and social sensibilities into a wilderness setting. Some late-century tourists, having just realized the means to vacation in the mountains, looked with some disdain at the environs of "the guide book tourist" (Whitman 132) and set themselves up in inns and boardinghouses at the margins of the larger, luxurious resort hotels, in order to better seek adventure among the hills.

The prevailing economic and social forces that continued to expand the region's tourist capacity in the late nineteenth century helped to foment an environmentally minded reaction to the unchecked growth of railways and hotels as well as to the simultaneous development of a prosperous logging industry. The same motivations that drove most tourists away from cities to the White Mountains — as a "remedy to the ill effects of city life" (Strauss 277) — also encouraged writers like Frank Bolles and his contemporaries in the White Mountains, including Bradford Torrey and Annie Trumbull Slosson, to begin to explore the overlapping narratives of tourism, nature, and inhabitation that were indelibly written upon the landscape. After the formation of the Appalachian Mountain Club in 1876, avid trampers and club members including Charles Fay, Isabella Stone, Marian Pychowska, and Edith Cook all took to the mountains and recorded the details of previously unexplored terrain. Within these often very detailed articles also percolates a growing critique of what they saw as an increasing conflict between tourist and logging industries and the natural resources upon which they were based.

All enthusiastic explorers in their own right, these fin-de-siècle White Mountain writers responded to social, political, and economic motivations that created a situation fertile for the germination of seeds sown by earlier environmental writers such as Marsh and Thoreau. Writing in a period when the often overstated sublime rhetoric common in the writing of King and his contemporaries (which was adopted by Lucy Crawford in her 1860 revision), was "considered in bad taste" (Brown 72), Bolles and his contemporaries were drawn to the interiors of the mountain landscape, intent more on actively exploring untrammeled wilderness than on looking at the mountains from a hotel verandah. More than simply a period of aesthetic change, however, the last quarter of the nineteenth century saw the White Mountains as a contested resource vied for by hotel and railroad entrepreneurs as well as by a largely unregulated logging industry. Regional and national economic forces combined to enable the rapid development of luxurious grand resort hotels throughout the mountains and to persuade local residents to move from their subsistence farmsteads to the promise of more fertile lands in the Ohio River Valley.

The new generation of more environmentally aware visitors remained on the periphery of the White Mountains' increasingly affluent resort hotel culture, and it was as a result of that culture's very expansion that they often sought refuge in less frequently explored areas of the mountains. Incited both by the increasing urbanization of parts of the mountains' wilderness and by the environmental destruction caused by massive logging operations, these trampers explored the blank spaces on maps of the region and filled them in with what one of them described as "actual measurement of sole leather" (Pychowska 265). A number of the more vocal participants in this wave of exploration were women who, perhaps spurred by the club's acceptance of women members at its second meeting in 1876, helped to shape environmental discourse at the end of the century. The often pathless forests embraced by the Appalachians created a place where women were able to dwell, at least temporarily, outside a socially appropriate domestic sphere. Perhaps seeking a frontier environment at the periphery of the region's burgeoning hotel culture, late-century women explorers discovered (or recovered) a place that reinforced the "intense individualism, expansion of work roles, and independence" that Anne LaBastille sees in women's work during the same period on the western American frontier (21). The late-century White Mountain landscape, layered with often competing discourses of tourism, logging, and a nascent environmentalism, created an ideal environment for both women and men who were looking to recapture the "excitement of the frontier or the war which had passed them by" (Strauss 272), though occasionally at the cost of disregarding the region's local residents. This wilding impulse empowered explorers like Bolles and Fay to look behind the static, sublime tableaus of their predecessors and begin to see the mountains as an interconnected ecosystem of human and nonhuman elements — one that, in the face of unchecked industrial expansion, called for preservation.

Charles Fay suspected, perhaps, that his zealous trail building in the 1890s might lead to the overuse that some summits are subjected to today, when the popularity of hiking has, according to some estimates, made southern New Hampshire's Mount Monadnock the second most climbed mountain in the world after Japan's Mount Fuji. In many ways, however, hiking, like trail building itself, can represent a middle ground between the human and the nonhuman rather than simply an intrusion into the wilderness. Writing about literature of the landscape traversed by the Appalachian Trail, Ian Marshall points to the trail itself as "negotiating between human and wild" (193), at once constrained by the undulations of mountain topography and clearly constructed, while also leading to specific natural or cultural/historic sites valued by trail architects and subsequent visitors. In one respect, trails like those developed by Charles Fay or Frank Bolles are meant to fashion an experience: in Bolles's case, to foster a return to a romantic, pretourist past, and in Fay's, to underscore the importance of *climbing* a mountain rather than simply arriving at the summit ("whoever would not prefer to go . . . to the summit by his own effort is not worthy to set foot" on it [Fay 316]). While trails might be seen as a metaphor for human interaction with the wilderness by mediating between the human desire to penetrate the wilderness and the topography of the terrain underfoot, trails also impose a linear order on a varied landscape. Trails are often shaped with regard to what consensus dictates ought to be seen — which summits, waterfalls, ponds, and rock ledges are determined to have value. As with most aesthetic and experiential fashions, scenic value changes over time, and many backcountry destinations fall into disuse, leaving behind the remnants of another forest industry. Logging roads — like the one Bolles refashioned into a hiking trail and then, with the help of others, into a bridle path — are similar, though they often exist far longer in the landscape's ecological memory: Rails, railway ties, bridge timbers, indeed remnants of whole logging camps exist throughout the White Mountains. Where an abandoned hiking trail might turn into a raging watercourse each spring and contribute to local erosion, former logging railroads transect vast areas of wilderness in straight lines miles long, and tote roads, still visible from many White Mountain summits, traverse mountainsides like gradations on a topographic map etched on the land itself.

Whether we use trails to access remote waterfalls and lakes or to reach striking topographic features, we are participating in an existing discourse that is, itself, a negotiation between economic and environmental concerns. From the establishment of the first trail to the summit of Mount Washington in 1819, footpaths in the White Mountains have historically been connected to recreation and an economy of tourism. In the mid-nineteenth century, the few established hiking and bridle paths existed principally as commercial endeavors of a locality's hotel proprietors. The Crawford Paths (1819, 1821), the Davis Path (1845), and Glenn House Path (1852) were built by hotel owners to meet a growing demand for access to the summit of Mount Washington. In the later half of the century, though, competition among hotels grew so intense that individual paths were no longer appropriate, and hotels would often use one another's paths, thereby profiting from significant labor on the part of a trail's architects. Guy and Laura Waterman point out that, as a result of this commercial focus, even as late as 1900, White Mountain trails were generally clustered around hotels and inns with few connecting links between them (*Forest* 227).

By the 1870s hiking and bridle paths to the region's most popular destinations like Mount Washington, Mount Lafayette, Mount Willard, and Mount Moosilauke had become well established. The last quarter of the nineteenth

century saw a proliferation of trails, many resulting from science-oriented expeditions. The expeditions by Charles Hitchcock and others to create the 1874
state-sponsored *Geology of New Hampshire* traversed untrammeled wilderness
to reach places seldom visited. Others, Charles Fay and his fellow Appalachians
among them, would often follow these rough paths and further develop them
as hiking trails. Paths most often led to or through interesting features or vistas, but sometimes the paths were more utilitarian in nature. As I mentioned
earlier, the Bolles Trail, still bearing the name of its rediscoverer, shows quite
plainly the transition of a trail's use from practical to recreational. Bolles was
motivated by a story about a road connecting the mountain village of Tamworth and the Swift River valley to the north. Equipped with the remnants of
this story, Bolles persuaded Nathaniel Berry to accompany him on an expedition to try to retrace the narrative of the "lost trail."

Over the course of his journey, Bolles reveals a change in his own perspective on the forest as the two men make their way through the woods to the hut
on the other side of the Sandwich Range and then back to Tamworth. Bolles
begins his account by saying that the forest is dark and dismal, comparing it
to precolonial visions of the landscape, akin to "the grotesque forest pictures
which are produced so frequently in German woodcuts" (*At the North* 50). As
the party of men ride on horseback northward from the center of the farming community, Bolles remarks on the contrast between the pastoral valley
and the forest at its northern edge: "as we drove away from fields, roads, and
the surroundings of habitations, animal life grew less and less abundant, and
plant life less varied" (47). An avid ornithologist, Bolles reads the changing
landscape through its bird as well as its plant life as he and Berry move from
the open fields to an almost reverentially silent interior: "as we entered the forest," he writes, "bird music ceased, few flowers decked the ground . . . and not a
squirrel disturbed the quiet of the endless aisles" (48). It is only when the group
reemerges from the forest that the flowers at the edge of the woods beckon,
"brilliant as jewels." "Anything more in contrast with the gloom of a northern
forest," Bolles adds, "would be hard to discover" (60). The distinct line with
which Bolles differentiates the picturesque nature of fields and farms from the
darker wilderness at its edge points to the writer's desire to further domesticate
the village's surroundings. It is Berry's story of a lost winter road through the
forest that enables Bolles to envision such a taming of the forest's wildness.

As Bolles and Berry approach the top of the pass, forward progress becomes
increasingly difficult, and any vestige of the old logging road is lost. At that
point, it is only the story of the "man and woman in a sleigh who had once

crossed this frowning barrier" that sustains the pair's "hopes of finding a pass which could be opened to wheels" (52 – 53). The chaotic landscape of lumbered and storm-felled trees presents potential for romantic history as Bolles and his companions pass by the remnants of lumber mills and derelict houses and follow the "curious ribbon of saplings" (55) that marks the course of the old road.

> It was easy to imagine the snow piled high upon the hills, smothering the brooks and burying the rough spots, and to fancy that over the trampled snow the woolly and steaming oxen came to drink of the water, while a sturdy French Canadian broke the ice with his axe and drank at the spot where from under the snow the spouts led the water into his end of the dugout. The cattle are dead, the axe has rusted, the Canadian has been killed in a brawl . . . but the brook still murmurs over its pebbles. (56 – 57)

The transition from working forest to romantic tableau apparent in this passage is indicative of Bolles's move toward rewriting the landscape in light of its history, be it factual or embellished. In her exploration of the layered cultural and natural terrains in the desert Southwest, Leslie Marmon Silko traces the interpenetration of land and story among the people of Laguna Pueblo. She writes that every feature of the land is connected to a story, and thus each natural artifact becomes inextricably connected to the story of the Pueblo culture. One cannot walk through the landscape around Laguna, she writes, without reading the narratives in the rocks, mesas, and arroyos. In his own narrative, Bolles sees the land *as* the story, and he attempts to remake the land to fit the stories he had heard about the Paugus Brook valley. Like Silko's depiction of a land layered with stories of place, Bolles finds in the dilapidated lumberman's cabin the stories of a recoverable past. He wants to reconnect the recovering White Mountain forest with remembered stories of French Canadian lumbermen and sleigh rides from Tamworth to Albany. Bolles foresees a future in which he might relive that original journey from Tamworth to Albany on horse-drawn pung, so he is re-creating the mountains to construct a place from his imagination. Bolles does eventually realize his mythic landscape as he concludes his narrative with a description of an almost ceremonial procession of "nearly a score of axes, hatchets, and savage machettas [which] resounded upon the trees and shrubs which encroached upon the road. Behind the axemen came several horses, each bearing a rider as courageous as she was fair" (61).

Frank Bolles's fascination with the romantic story of preindustrial White Mountains comes at a historical period when, in the face of increasing industrialization throughout the Northeast's metropolitan centers, urban readers who might not have had sufficient means to take the extended holidays away from home promoted by Henry Ward Beecher and William "Adirondack" Murray often sought respite in the literature of country life. This late-nineteenth-century fascination with rural sketches was typified by the romantic regionalism of works such as Sarah Orne Jewett's 1877 *Deephaven* and 1896 *Country of the Pointed Firs*, Alice Brown's 1895 *Meadow Grass: Tales of New England Life*, and, starting in 1877, by the sketches, poems, and stories published in the *Granite Monthly*. The economic situation that helped to cultivate the popularity of these publications influenced a number of White Mountain writers, including Bolles, to explore the complex terrain of the mountains as both an actual and an invented place.[4] Annie Trumbull Slosson, William C. Prime, and Bradford Torrey frequented the paths and railways around Franconia Notch in the White Mountains' northeast corner, and John Greenleaf Whittier, Lucy Larcom, and Bolles himself were regular visitors to the Chocorua region in the southeast. Whittier and Larcom were seasonal tenants at the Bearcamp River House in West Ossipee from 1868 until the hotel was consumed by fire in 1880. The early-twentieth-century editor Eugene Musgrove adds that, despite the destruction of the Bearcamp River House in 1880, Whittier and Larcom's connection to the area is written indelibly upon the local landscape: "Whittier Peak (named by Sweetser) towers near by, the West Ossipee railroad station is now Mount Whittier, and the hamlet Whittier is not far away; Mount Larcom is further west" (336–37).

In their day, Bolles and Torrey were frequently compared favorably to both Thoreau and the more contemporary John Burroughs. Reviews of Bolles's first published book of peripatetic essays, *The Land of the Lingering Snow*, note that the book recalls the school of Burroughs, Torrey and Abbott," written by "a naturalist who [was] at the same time something of a poet and philosopher" (*Hartford Courant*, 28 November 1891).[5] Although Bolles's literary career was relatively short (he died in 1894 at the age of 38), through his numerous letters to the *Boston Post* under the pseudonym O.W.L., which were later compiled in his two books of essays (one posthumously), he was able, like Burroughs, to "transport to (sub)urban parlors intimate scenes from the northeastern edgelands" (Buell, *Writing* 145).

Much as he exported rural images into urban reading rooms, Bolles similarly imported romantic ideas about the working New England landscape to his seasonal northern home. Bolles was instrumental in changing the name of his adopted village from Tamworth Iron Works, after the area's early-nineteenth-century industrial history, to Chocorua. In December 1886, only a few months after the Bolles family was able to move into its summer home on the north shore of Chocorua Lake, Frank Bolles lamented that "so placid a hamlet should be chained to so harsh a name" ("Three Days" 5). Three years later, Bolles circulated four separate petitions among village residents to have the name changed. Residents generally favored East Tamworth as a potential appellation, since "Chocorua was hitched to enough things already — a mountain, a lake, a river, a hotel, and a library" (Casarotto, unpaged). Thus, although he was successful at first, the name alternated between Tamworth Iron Works and Chocorua five times before it was changed for the last time in 1897.[6] By prompting the name's change, Bolles further demonstrated his desire to remake the village and its environs into the romantic tableau depicted by artists such as Thomas Cole, Frederick Church, and Benjamin Champney during their earlier visits to the White Mountains. By renaming the town after the area's most prominent natural feature, Bolles explicitly implicated the town in the discourse and economy of tourism rather than of its industrial history.

The mountain at the foot of which Bolles spent the last eight summers of his life became something of an altar to what Bolles saw as essential in a pastoral retreat. One is reminded, by Bolles's toponymic and iconological refashioning, of Thomas Starr King's predilection for viewscapes that conform to exacting aesthetic guidelines; to achieve "landscape beauty," writes King, "there must be meadow, river, and . . . distance from the hills" (5–6). In his 1891 book of essays, *The Land of the Lingering Snow*, Bolles narrates his entry into a vacation world during an April trip north from Boston to Chocorua. Bolles's narrative of his trip is very much a process by which he moves from the working world of northern New Hampshire into the idealized world of his vacation retreat. Upon his arrival at the train station near Tamworth Iron Works Village, he sees a "tower of smoke" to the east of Chocorua, stops for a while in the village inn to listen to "tales of winter hardship and spring sickness" recounted by several assembled year-round residents, before walking past "dull masses of firelight" on the smoky horizon and a fisherman fishing by torchlight (151). As the reader follows Bolles through this picturesque narrative, he dramatically rounds a corner to confront Chocorua: "stars burned near it like altar candles. The smoke of fires rose around it like incense . . . the whispering of the wind in the pines was like the moving of many lips in prayer" (151).

By creating of the mountain an altar to the exurban, Bolles in effect repositions the village, its industry, and its residents on the periphery of his "Ultima Thule" ("Three Days" 1). The irony of his suggestion that the very mountains where he tries to catalog and explore the intricacies of nature are in some way distant from the "centres of life" underscores how Bolles defines margin and center. His positioning of Chocorua at the periphery of some urban civilized center does much to import a romantic aesthetic into the center. As Dona Brown argues, it is nature that is the center; thus, the rural village becomes doubly marginalized and thus almost effaced. Although Bolles disparages the trainloads of tourists who visit the region each summer and leave "few nooks left . . . where one can be certain of solitude" because "during the summer months the White Mountains are almost suburban in their seeming nearness to the centres of life" ("Three Days" 1), his community-building enterprises show his own need to bring the urban along. By laying a pastoral veneer across the Tamworth area, Bolles underscores a prevailing aesthetic — and thus necessarily economic — conversion to a pastoral vision of the mountain landscape, a move away from the sublime rhetoric of earlier decades.

In many ways, the very number of tourists visiting the White Mountains each summer made the quest for a sublime experience difficult if not impossible. By 1860 the mountains were visited by more than ten thousand tourists each summer, roughly half of whom reached the summit of Mount Washington (Brown 70). Rather than seek out sublime experiences in the wilderness as their antebellum predecessors had done, late-century tourists were "content with easier forms of conspicuous consumption" available in the region's well-appointed hotels (Brown 72). This late-century gravitation toward the sumptuous rather than the sublime had multiple implications. Since 1850, writers had complained about the annual increase in summer visitors, but by the 1880s, this overcrowding of popular destinations began to impel writers, artists, and outdoor enthusiasts to visit lesser-known regions. In his 1891 Land of Lingering Snow, for instance, Bolles describes his indignation at climbing to the top of Mount Wachusett only to find "a large and commonplace hotel, several barns and ugly sheds, and a bowling alley, billiard room, and tintype gallery." This is decidedly not the picturesque landscape of his adopted Tamworth: "when I seek Nature on a mountain top and find her fettered by civilization," he complains, "I have a right to feel aggrieved" (193).

As I discussed in chapter 3, the mountains appealed to writers like Samuel Drake and Benjamin Willey as the embodiment of a free and independent spirit, a place to market Turner's "new product that is American." By the last decades of the nineteenth century, however, it became clear that the White Mountains could no longer be defined as a frontier in Turner's terms. In 1890 many of the New Hampshire towns that had been losing residents to more fertile western farmlands had become home to a booming tourist industry. Towns in the White Mountain region could boast one hundred thirty-four hotels with accommodations for more than fifty guests each, for a total between sixteen and eighteen thousand overnight rooms available on any given summer night.[7] In this transition from an economy based on subsistence agriculture and resource extraction to one centered on seasonal tourism, rural New Hampshire towns underwent a significant social and political change, drawing in summer residents and seasonal boarders who had significant influence on local social and environmental policies. Upper-middle-class refuges from the urban workaday world often found, rather than a respite from the social stratifications of the city, echoes of society along the northern exurban frontier. Indeed, many critics of Frederick Jackson Turner's frontier hypothesis rejected its "agrarian myth" and suggest that the wilderness frontier simply perpetuated existing social norms and "preserved older ethnic and class distinctions" (Barron 2).

The post–Civil War rural New Hampshire village did not represent everything that Henry Ward Beecher and William Murray, vocal advocates of a rural respite from the rigors of urban life, claimed; it was not a place outside the traditional urban social landscape, but simply a place where urban norms could play themselves out in a romantic locale. The rural town in effect blurs the boundaries between pastoral village image and urban model. What becomes apparent in the work of Bolles and his contemporaries Bradford Torrey and Annie Trumbull Slosson is that their literary vision of these towns has little place for the residents, and focuses, rather, on village inhabitants as part of a constructed place that fits their romantic preconceptions of the ideal rural retreat. Locals inhabit Bolles's text principally as informants like Nat Berry and as workers, often employed by Bolles as drivers and builders. This marginalization of Tamworth residents typifies the author's disengagement from the *work* of the place.

Perhaps best illustrated in his quest to remove the industrial heritage from the town's name, Bolles's separation from the quotidian struggle with the "historical record of agricultural defeat and failure" (James 21) can also be read in his refashioning of a newly purchased farmstead from a working to an experimental farm. Bolles purchased the farm from the Doe family in 1886, and, after having it made more suitable for his family, moved in and continued to visit quite frequently during the remaining eight years of his life. Bolles did not spend his summers in the White Mountains farming in earnest, however; he planted potatoes, buckwheat, flax, and millet more experimentally than for sustenance.[8] In June 1886, shortly after moving to the farm, he wrote his mother,

"I am steeped in the flavor of a horse, a cow, two pigs, two puppies, 11 hens and a rooster," adding "this place is all that fancy painted it" (Bolles, *Life* 1). The romanticism of being "steeped in the flavor" of farming but not dependent upon it is best illustrated by Bolles's decision to rename his newly purchased farm. In a region where farmsteads often retain the names of their original owners for generations, Bolles's choice to rename the Doe Farm Crowlands, and to have the roof of his barn crowned with a weathervane in the likeness of a crow in profile demonstrates a shift in purpose as well as ownership. The crow remains perched atop the well-maintained barn to this day, signifying an invitation to its corvine kin in the place of a traditional scarecrow.

By recovering a "lost trail," refashioning his newly purchased farmstead to suit his idea of a gentleman's farm, and finally by renaming his adopted town to suit his romantic ideas, Bolles continually underscored his desire not merely to write about the landscape, but to write the land itself into his vision of an idyllic pastoral valley. Bolles was in effect mediating between the urban desires for recovering a romantic rural landscape and the realities of the working residents of Tamworth, on whose small farms Henry James would later conclude a "stout human experiment [that] had been tried, had broken down" (21). James argues that the turn-of-the-century White Mountains represent an inversion of traditional relationships between the human and nonhuman worlds; people are no longer of a place, rather, the place exists for the people. It is in tourism's encroachment into the wild margins of the civilized that this transposition becomes most apparent: "the great straddling, bellowing railway, the high, heavy, dominant American train that so reverses the relation of the parties concerned, suggesting somehow that the country exists for the 'cars,' which overhang it like a conquering army, and not the cars for the country" (James 27). Celebrating a landscape that marginalized local residents by positioning them within the landscape of the "*delicately* Arcadian" mountain village (James 14), Bolles, like guidebook authors of the prior quarter-century, helped to perpetuate a vision of the White Mountains that "projected nature as immutable and separate from human activity" (R. Judd 197). The resultant "new landscape mosaic" of the fin-de-siècle Northeast constructs a "dialogue between the locality and the desires and inventions of the urban tourists who apprehended it" (R. Judd 200). Indeed, it was the post-outmigration North Country that drew summer visitors like Bolles. The loss of families and often entire towns to the more fertile West saw an increasing homogeneity among northern New England communities, leading to a social landscape that was "increasingly staid, uniform, and uneventful. . . . Those who lived in the older rural North were not searching for order in the late nineteenth century — they had found it" (Barron 135).

Guidebook writers after the middle of the nineteenth century looked to remote (though well-appointed and comfortable) regions like the White Mountains as potential panaceas for the nation's social ills. Benjamin Willey asserted in 1856 that "no oppression . . . can ever exist around the White Mountains" (295). In 1863, in the midst of the Civil War, Albert Bierstadt interwove his White Mountain landscapes with allegories of hope. After the war, the guidebook writer Samuel Drake narrated his tour through the mountains with a former Confederate colonel and described the region as embodying "a delightful sense of freedom!" (5). This sense of liberation, be it from the desperate conditions of war or the demands of a newly industrialized urban environment, pervaded middle- and upper-class perceptions about the rural landscape. Ideas of freedom and escape from the everyday saddled farming villages with symbolic import they often found difficult to bear.

The idea of the rural vacation as respite from the "flaccid state of inanition" caused by city life was enthusiastically promoted by Henry Ward Beecher and William "Adirondack" Murray (Strauss 275). Murray's emphasis in his 1869 *Adventures in the Wilderness* on wilderness as the ideal antidote to the city advocated an active engagement with the outdoors that involved tramping, camping, and mountain climbing.[9] Flowing in the same vein as William Hazlitt's 1822 assertion that pedestrians "go out of town in order to forget the town and all that is in it" (73), the recreation proposed by Beecher and Murray was a natural extension of the call to farming that echoed across New England throughout the mid-nineteenth century. In one of many examples of this "back to the land" movement, in an 1849 address in Chelsea, Vermont, Waldo Spear advocated farm life for moral and physical fitness:

> Would you be strong? Go follow the plow.
> Would you be thoughtful? Study the fields and flowers.
> Would you be wise? Take on yourself a vow
> To go to school in Nature's sunny bowers.
> Fly from the city; nothing there can charm:
> Seek wisdom, strength and virtue on a farm.
> (Quoted in Barron 36)

This midcentury Jeffersonian sentimentality found its way into the discourse of tourism as wealthier urbanites began to visit rural communities in search of the rural way of life espoused by Beecher and Murray. Missing from Murray's call to a new rural aestheticism (and athleticism) are members of the urban working class and residents of the rural communities who were being gradually driven out.[10] Murray's enthusiasm for the outdoors as a cure for urban life was promoted, at least initially, to more affluent visitors of rural and wild regions. Indeed, as Guy and Laura Waterman tell us, Murray himself disdained climbing mountains. "Tramping is something I never admired," intones Murray, "I can get along very well tramping down hill, but when the path begins to run upward, I always get in and ride" (Waterman and Waterman 162). Despite his own shortcomings and his effacing of undesirable parts of the wilderness, like the realities of visiting an actively logged forest and the forest's very residents, Murray's book sent countless tourists to the Adirondacks and to forests throughout the Northeast, looking for "lovely woods untouched by ax," and leaving behind a landscape that was "never the same unspoiled wilderness again" (Waterman and Waterman 163).

Bolles's creation of a romantic rural experience from an authentic working agricultural landscape effectively crafts an idealized sphere separate from the realities of the area's agricultural and industrial economic history. Tourism critic Dean MacCannell argues that such a "tourist bubble" eventually replaces the aesthetic (as well as economic, cultural, and environmental) identity of an actual place as the "principal signifier of a locality" (quoted in MacCannell, "Tourist Agency" 26).[11] By refashioning the farm from a place of work to a place of observation, Bolles participates in what Lawrence Buell calls a discursive "emptying" and "filling" of landscape iconology that can be traced from seventeenth-century settler culture's importation of Old World ideologies (see chapter 1) through Thoreau's integration of the imported sublime within his rhetoric of the American wilderness (Buell, *Environmental* 70). This aesthetic and environmental history has its parallel in the economics of settlement, tourism, and land speculation that helped to form the late-nineteenth-century White Mountain landscape. We can read this history in the report of the mountains' potential wealth by Darby Field in 1642 (Winthrop), in Lucy Crawford's narrative of her family's eventual failure as hotel proprietors in the face of rampant land speculation in the 1830s, and in the growing tension between the aesthetics of the sublime and the construction of countless hotels throughout the mountains to capitalize on the mountains' scenic currency. Bolles's selective marginalization of local residents and his preoccupation with what he perceives as the area's romantic history in effect rewrite the landscape itself to fit within these existing aesthetic and economic frameworks. Like many of his predecessors, Bolles came to the mountains, as Gretel Ehrlich observes about earlier explorers, "not simply to know, but to change; not just to visit, but to possess" (18).

It is tempting either to indict Bolles for running roughshod over both the inhabited and wild landscapes around Chocorua by changing them to suit his own pastoral ideal, or, conversely, to temper the hyperbole of Bolles's early reviewers, and write him firmly into a Thoreauvian tradition of environmental writing. In fact, he can be situated in both camps. The essays in *Land of Lingering Snow* and *At the North of Bearcamp Water* illustrate Bolles's ability to negotiate between the discourse of romantic pastoralism and the exact, measured language of the naturalist-explorer. This rhetorical facility can be clearly seen developing in Bolles's relationship with the poet James Russell Lowell. Bolles wrote to Lowell in 1891 to point out that the millpond in Lowell's poem "Beaver Brook" was placed a quarter-mile south from its "actual" location, prompting a response of "you are right" from the poet (Bolles, *Life* 152). Furthermore, Bolles was chided by some early readers for his tendency to enumerate at length his ornithological observations; "it must be conceded that only a very limited number of persons can care to know that on the 11th of January a young man climbing the hills of Arlington saw thirty-six robins fly into an oak tree" (*New Orleans Times Democrat*, 10 January 1892). Similarly, Bolles took the substantial effort of running a 66-foot surveying chain around Chocorua Lake for a distance of two and three-quarter miles to calculate the lake's acreage.[12]

This near obsession with providing his readers a factual account of nature complicates a reading of Bolles as a romantic regional writer. The mimetic landscape aesthetic that pervades his journals, letters, and essays reveals his participation in the environmental realism of his contemporary, the nature essayist John Burroughs. Both Bolles and Burroughs were drawn to the "extreme literalism" of exacting nonfictional representation partly for the sake of making "facticity regulate poetic license," and not the other way around (Buell, *Environmental* 89). As is apparent in his letter to Lowell, Bolles was interested in preserving details of the actual landscape in the face of less precise romantic language. In reading the details of the forested slopes of Chocorua north of his Tamworth farm, Bolles revealed an ability to temper the romanticism with which he painted his adopted village and focus on the intricacies of the mountain landscape. By importing the resulting realistic pastoral narratives into the homes of *Boston Post* readers, Bolles's pseudonymous letters to the editor retail the experience of a landscape layered with a diverse inhabitation history to his more urban readership. Thus, while remaking the farms and inns of the Chocorua region as an exurban retreat, Bolles's writing, to borrow from Kinereth

Meyer's discussion of William Carlos Williams's poetry, at the same time "performs, rather than merely thematizes, the interaction in American literature between aesthetics and an ideology of power" (155). The precise language with which Bolles describes the southern White Mountains implicates him in a prevailing movement away from generic expressions of grandeur from well-known mountaintop vistas and makes the nature of the mountains' inner landscape more accessible to potential visitors. While his writing involves Bolles in a late-century appeal to wildness and rural living as potential antidotes to the urban society, his actions also reveal his desire to maintain and even resurrect a rural culture on the decline.

"Intellectually," Bolles wrote in an unpublished essay, "Deserted Homes," "the 'back-towns' which form the great area of the state, rank very low" (7). As an antidote to what he perceived as this intellectual backwardness, Bolles founded public libraries in both Rumney, New Hampshire, and Tamworth Iron Works, which, as he asserts about the library in Rumney, he was afraid to place in the public trust, lest "the poorer and more ignorant citizens [would] in a few years vote to sell it" (7). Notwithstanding the disparaging nature of Bolles's remarks, his concern for the increasing number of deserted homes in New Hampshire was justified. Farmers faced with the prospect of scratching a subsistence living from the hardscrabble terrain of northern New Hampshire were drawn away by the promise of more fertile lands in the West. Bolles's sentiments are echoed in Sam Walter Foss's 1899 poem "Deserted Farms," which laments the loss of a new generation to a better future:

> our boys hez traveled off to where the millions go
> To dig a golden harvesting without a spade or hoe;
> An' down the railroad, through the gulch, be'end their father's sight,
> They went an' left us ol' men to the shadders of the night.
> . . .
> our farms is all deserted; there is no one here to see
> But just a few ol' women an' a few ol' men like me;
> But we still cling, like ol' gray moss, a little totterin' band —
> We cling like ol' gray moss aroun' the ruins of the land.

Written in the vernacular of an old Yankee farmer, Foss's poem underscores the bond between farmer and land that not even the economic realities of New Hampshire agriculture could shake. The abandonment of northern New England farmsteads, and often whole villages, because of a promise of prosperity left behind traces of an inhabited landscape that Robert Frost would later describe in "Directive" as "a farm that is no more a farm / . . . in a town that is no more a town" (377). Tom Wessels notes that in Orford, New Hampshire, the outmigration of farmers to the "rich and unglaciated soils" near the Ohio River contributed to a decrease in the town's population from 1,829 in 1830 to 916 in 1890 (60). The forests of central New England, and often the woodlands at the periphery of the White Mountains, illustrate what Henry James called the "hard little historical record of agricultural failure and defeat" (21). The stone walls that weave through New England's woodlands, occasionally punctuated with long abandoned cellar holes or other detritus of an inhabited landscape, help to enrich the layers of landscape that Bolles was searching for in the rural woodlands south of Chocorua. He was looking to reclaim the historical record layered in sediment from old logging mills and in the old stories that shaped the land at the height of its industrial and agricultural history.

Bolles's literary and aesthetic revision of the northern New Hampshire landscape had its parallel in the region's economic transformation. The late 1880s and 1890s saw the proliferation of state-sponsored programs to reclaim an increasing number of abandoned farmsteads; in 1883, for instance, the Vermont State Board of Agriculture published the *List of Desirable Vermont Farms* to draw out-of-state interest in the properties for summer vacation homes or businesses (Rebek 26–27). Of course, as with Bolles's refashioning of Tamworth Iron Works, the movement of middle- and upper-class tourists into rural agricultural communities was not entirely without conflict. "In the artfully chaotic landscape constructed by the summer visitor," writes Sylvester Judd, there "could be found the nexus of a growing tension between urbanite and native." Judd demonstrates that at the end of the nineteenth century, the summer visitor's "infatuation with 'rustic' scenery incorporated exactly what the farmer saw as scarcity and decay" (205).

William Henry Bishop crafted a part-time vocation out of scouring northern New England for a rural farmhouse where he could enjoy "the pleasant country life" ("Hunting" 34). He described his land in a pair of articles published in *Century Magazine* in 1894 and 1901. When he finally made a purchase and began refurbishing his "bargain," he found to his surprise that his "fellow-villagers . . . do not greatly admire our taste for the quaint and old-fashioned" ("Abandoned" 890). Bishop's praise of the land's aesthetic over its agricultural value prompted a series of impertinent remarks about his rural neighbors that make it quite clear why they might look askance at his arrival: "it is city people who are precisely the best fitted for the country," he writes, since the "average denizen of the country has no appreciation of natural scenery, never raises his eyes to notice it, scarce knows that it exists" ("Hunting" 42). Echoing the sentiments of William Murray and Henry Ward Beecher, Bishop sees in the abandoned farm a rejuvenating potential for "lesser businessmen," members of the middle class who, though they have the opportunity to take vacations, do not possess the leisure time to travel far from home.

A number of other late-century White Mountain writers, including Bradford Torrey, Annie Trumbull Slosson, Slosson's brother-in-law William C. Prime, Lucy Larcom, and John Greenleaf Whittier, came to the White Mountains to experience a rural vision of New England through the lens of a fin-de-siècle romance with regionalism. Perhaps Torrey and Slosson, who were frequent summer boarders at the lavishly appointed Profile House in Franconia Notch, best exemplified the experience of the genteel summer tourist. Bolles and his fellow Tamworth visitors, Larcom and Whittier, also illustrate the duality of the seasonal experience by, in effect, overlapping two distinct social spheres — their affluent, cosmopolitan home lives and the rural "playground for the urban elite" (Wallace 29) they built among the mountains. The wilding social impulse that these writers, among thousands of outdoor enthusiasts and amateur naturalists, brought to the White Mountains helped to refashion rural locales on the edges of the mountains into summer destinations and gateways to the forest interior. Locales throughout the rural Northeast were transformed into sites of play for urban elite and middle classes. The same decades during which these writers were narrating their forays into the New Hampshire woods also saw the founding of the Audubon Society in 1886, the establishment of the first summer camp for children in New Hampshire in 1881, the designation of the Adirondacks and Catskills as forest preserves in 1885; and the formation of Boston's Metropolitan Park Commission in 1892. Also, thanks in some part to the work these writers produced, the Society for the Protection of New Hampshire Forests was founded in 1901.

The economic conditions that made available the deserted farms that Bishop coveted (and that helped entice Bolles to the mountains) very often created complicated and strained relationships between year-round and seasonal residents. Though writing from within the tourist experience — staying at the lavish Profile House in Franconia and visiting decidedly touristic attractions — Bradford Torrey was able to successfully tread a path between tourist and resident perspectives. It is in the works of Torrey, who edited fourteen volumes of Thoreau's journal for the 1906 Houghton Mifflin edition, that we can read the most apparent extension of Thoreauvian ideology into the late-nineteenth-century White Mountain landscape. Torrey's 1889 *Rambler's Lease*, the first of two books of nature writing, draws significantly from Thoreau's essay "Walking" in its approach both to land ownership and to the act of walking itself as a kind of immersion in a specific landscape. Many of the essays in *A Rambler's Lease* are examples of what Kent Ryden calls the peripatetic "essay of place," which he defines as a "sort of imaginative wandering over the local terrain" (*Mapping* 211). It is Torrey's very walking that enables him to break free of his largely sedentary carriage- and train-bound fellow tourists. Torrey prefaces *A Rambler's Lease* with an Emersonian apologia for both his literal and literary trespasses: "The writer of this little book has found so much pleasure in other men's woods and fields that he has come to look upon himself as in some sort the owner of them. Their lawful possessors will not begrudge him this feeling, he believes, nor take it amiss if he assumes, even in this public way, to hold *a rambler's lease* of their property" (iii).

As he traverses property boundaries, Torrey works to bring together the patches of what Thoreau called a "leopard-spotted land" of forests and fields (Howarth, *Thoreau* 273) into a coherent landscape that includes him as a participant-observer. In his second book of New Hampshire essays, *Footing It in Franconia*, Torrey devotes considerable time to a visit to the observatory atop Mount Agassiz in Bethlehem. While there, he speaks irreverently of the throng of assembled tourists (from whom he takes pains to separate himself) who occupy themselves by trying to elicit an echo using a horn mounted on the observatory, and by trying to spot cars descending the Mount Washington cog railway, some dozen miles distant. Not wont to participate in this popular pastime of trying to see other built landmarks in the landscape, Torrey's "eye wanders over the landscape, but not uneasily; nay, it can hardly be said to wander at all; it rests here and there, not trying to see," like his companions, "but seeing" (243).

Elsewhere in *Footing It in Franconia*, Torrey looks out from the top of Bald "Mountain" (Torrey quotes the word in his text ironically to denote its diminutive stature) in Franconia Notch and describes the localities he sees in the distance but then adds that "longer than at anything else, I look at the mountain forest just below me. So soft and bright this world of treetops all newly green!"(142). Rather than perceiving the landscape as composed of a multitude of human aesthetic or technological touchstones like the Mount Washington Railway, hotels, and the summits of named peaks, Torrey chooses to look at, and to describe for his readers, the landscape as an integrated whole. There is perhaps a certain comfort in being able to identify parts of a vast landscape from an observation deck as Torrey describes above, and, indeed, this remains a popular pastime among today's tourists. The "ego-mimetic tourism" (Mac-Cannell, "Tourist Agency" 27) of this observatory culture helps viewers situate themselves with respect to other evidence of the human in what appears to be a trackless wilderness. Torrey makes clear, however, that by creating a virtual catalog of visible artifacts one cannot see the larger ecosystem of which the mountains, trees, and the Mount Washington Railway are all constituent parts.

Torrey's ability to integrate the fragments of the landscape before him reveals an active participation in the formation of that landscape. Leslie Marmon Silko believes that, throughout the landscape of her native Southwest, "viewers are as much a part of the landscape as the boulders they stand on. . . . There is no high mesa edge or mountain peak where one can stand and not immediately be part of all that surrounds" (27 – 28). The separation of Torrey's tourist companions from the "mountain forest just below" underscores a disconnect between visitor and environment that can (and often does) lead to a precarious division between human and nonhuman. The very idea of an observatory, like the one on Mount Agassiz visited by Torrey, or the Mount Washington Observatory (a scientific research station and visitor center atop Mount Washington), suggests that the principal reason for visiting is to look out on some distant viewscape. By positioning himself within the frame and as part of what is being seen, Torrey inhabits a middle ground between the observer and "the seen." It is worthwhile to quote at length from *A Rambler's Lease* to help outline Torrey's perspective on place.

I fall in with persons, now and then, who profess to care nothing for a path when walking in the woods. They do not choose to travel in other people's footsteps — nay, nor even in their own — but count it their mission to lay out a new road every time they go afield. They are welcome to their freak. . . . In my eyes, it is nothing against a hill that other men have climbed it before me; and if their feet have worn a trail, so much the better. I not only reach the summit more easily, but have company on the way — company none the less to my mind, perhaps, for being silent and invisible. It is well enough to strike into the trackless forest once in a while; to wander you know not whither, and come out you know not where; to lie down in a strange place, and for an hour imagine yourself the explorer of a new continent: but if the mind be awake (as, alas, too often it is not), you may walk where you will, in never so well known a corner, and you will see new things, and think new thoughts, and return to your house a new man, which, I venture to believe, is after all the main consideration. (45 – 46)

Mapping the rhetorical functions of travel narratives, Bruce Greenfield distinguishes between the journal as a linear, chronological device and the narrative that both tells a story and establishes a correspondence among the events it depicts. "By means of his journal," Greenfield argues, "the traveler writes himself into and out of the unknown country; by means of his narrative, he makes his journey a significant event" (19). If the "essay of place," as Ryden defines it, is itself a trespass through a deeply layered landscape that fosters "direct engagement with facts and dispassionate contemplation of those facts" (*Mapping* 218), Torrey's accounts of transgressing property boundaries indicate his ability to see the intricacies of a place despite (and perhaps because of) its status as "humanized landscape" (Mitchell and Diamant 216).[13] Either walking the railway lines that are used to ferry tourists to and from the Profile House, or hiking along well-worn trails, or "seeing" and "not trying to see" the view from the Mount Agassiz Observatory, Torrey effectively mediates between the existing tourist apparatus and the remaining wilderness in which it is embedded. Although he clearly participates in tourist excursions and is content to stay at the comfortable Profile House, Torrey's rhetoric distinguishes his perception of the landscape from the passive gaze of his fellow tourists. Like Frank Bolles, Torrey foregrounds the significance of engaging with the landscape as a whole and of seeing the layers of tourism, inhabitation, and environment by occasionally stepping off the mountains' well-worn routes and into the forest.

As I have noted about the work of Frank Bolles and about guidebooks written between 1850 and the 1870s, local residents, whether farmers, hotel employees, drivers, or guides, are often on the margins of tourist discourse. From the vantage of an observatory culture, the landscape is principally populated by large, visible, built landmarks and topographic features, not with individuals. During Torrey's visit to the Mount Agassiz Observatory, he remarks that "the men who live in such houses [as one finds beneath Mt. Agassiz], the keeper [of the observatory] tells me, are very wide-awake and well informed, reading their weekly newspaper with thoroughness, and always ready for rational talk on current topics. They are not rich, of course, in the down-country sense of the word . . . but they are better fed, and really live in more comfort, than a great part of the folks who live in cities" (*Footing* 245).

Torrey's inclusion of local voices in his narrative contrasts with the more common marginalization of local residents often seen in Bolles's writing and further codified in fictional representations of White Mountain rural village life. Local residents were frequently written into stories that either perpetuated class stereotypes or depicted locals as members of a declining culture. Torrey's contemporary and occasional companion Annie Trumbull Slosson, who also regularly visited the Franconia region in the 1880s, wrote a number of brief and often didactically Christian tales based on her summers there. One such story, sold as a thirty-page bound monograph, recounts the adventures of James Whitcher, better known as Fishin' Jimmy, a Franconia resident who, upon inadvertently hearing a sermon in town, devoted his life to fishing, though his ultimate desire was to become a fisher of men. Slosson describes Fishin' Jimmy as one of the forest's last noble denizens, who "had not cared for books, or school, and all efforts to tie him down to study were unavailing. But he knew well the books of running brooks. No dry botanical text-book or manual could have taught him all he now knew of plants and flowers and trees" (6).

Fishin' Jimmy, as an example of the mountain region's older settler culture, remains outside the conventions of the author's own upper-class culture and plays the role of informant and interpreter of the natural world. Indeed, much like earlier representations of locals by artists and newspaper and guidebook writers, Fishin' Jimmy is depicted as natural and untarnished by the influence of civilization. When Fishin' Jimmy eventually loses his life high on Mount Lafayette while trying to rescue a lost dog, however, Slosson's story suggests that such loss is inevitable and that White Mountain residents will no doubt succumb to a fate similar to that of their Native American predecessors, as I have noted earlier. Where Slosson and Bolles saw a declining local culture, Bradford Torrey took pains to include the voices of local residents as part of a larger White Mountain culture that included tourists, residents, and the natural ecosystem of which they were both a part.

Despite Torrey's ability to read the multiple layers of the White Mountains' cultural, economic, and environmental topography, local residents were often implicated in the very tourist apparatus that, in many instances, pushed them to the margins of the tourist-centered economy. Local White Mountain newspapers, published daily at the region's larger hotels, often incorporated the language of landscape and its "native" inhabitants in their advertising agendas. These papers, including *The White Mountain Echo and Tourist's Register* (Bethlehem) and *Among the Clouds* (published on Mount Washington's summit), were established in the 1870s to serve both as souvenirs of the mountain experience and as advertisements for White Mountain events and establishments. In their role as advertising agents, the newspapers' editors often looked to the promotional power of the landscape itself and reported on the color and extent of a particular evening's sunset and on specific natural features in order to attract readers.

The newspapers similarly included stories about White Mountain residents, who were presented as living exemplars of John Spaulding's "historical relics." One recurring illustration of such reporting can be seen in the *White Mountain Echo*'s frequent stories about Allen Thompson, "White Mountain Guide, Hunter, and Trapper — A Veritable Nimrod of the Hills."[14] Embodying the romantic mythos of the pioneer, Thompson was served up as a local, "authentic" informant on the landscape, offering perspectives on tracking, tramping, and fishing for the paper's readers. Though Thompson is not the author of the anecdotes, he is liberally quoted by the reporter as one of the "wild denizens of the forest" whom "the whirr and hum of the busy world had driven . . . deeper into the wilderness" (*Echo,* 9 July 1879, 1). While the article foregrounds Thompson's exploits in the White Mountain backcountry, it also celebrates his marginalization "into the wilderness," as though this makes his comments more genuine.

Furthermore, the newspaper's role was, of course, to perpetuate the very "whirr and hum" that continued to drive residents like Thompson away from more populated tourist centers. In the 9 July 1879 issue of the *White Mountain Echo,* an anonymous writer presents Thompson as a real-life version of Slosson's Fishin' Jimmy and records the guide's perspectives on fishing in White Mountain streams. He quotes Thompson as if Thompson were addressing the readers, informing them that

> "throughout the entire mountain district there is good trouting. . . . But I have no doubt you are surprised that so little trout are to be seen on the tables of the hotels and boarding-houses here. Ah!" said Allen, sadly, and a tear seemed gathering in his eye at the piscatorial vandalism he was about to describe, "no wonder the fish are scarce here in the Summer. Would you believe it, the people along the sides of the brooks and lakes where the trout prevail, break the ice in the winter and fish through the holes, taking thousands of fish and sending them to New York and Boston."

Thompson's voice implicates the very readers of the *Echo,* frequently New York or Boston residents themselves, in the consumption of the landscape he relies upon for economic survival, though, of course, his authority is used to entice still more visitors to draw fish from his familiar streams. This passage also points to the more complicated economic situation brought about by readily accessible commerce with larger southern cities. It is interesting that Thompson allies himself with summer tourists as he charges his fellow "wild denizens" with depleting the same trout streams and lakes for export. Fishing thus becomes symbolic of the tension between resource preservation for both subsistence and recreation on one hand and resource extraction to support the local economy on the other.

In a telling juxtaposition of perspectives, the *White Mountain Echo* interweaves "native" perspectives with hotel and summit "arrivals," "mountain news," train schedules, and advertisements, thereby foregrounding the interconnectedness of local residents and the apparatus of tourism. We can read in the voice of locals like Thompson the economic conflict between an emergent call for preserving the mountains' natural resources and the short-term profitability of resource extraction. The distinctions between tourists and local residents apparent in journalistic accounts like Thompson's, as well as in Bradford Torrey's essays and Annie Trumbull Slosson's stories, reveal a social topography in the process of redefining itself to suit a continually changing economy. White Mountain tourist newspapers, much like the essays of Frank Bolles (who initially wrote them to be printed in newspapers as well), were interested in recovering, or at least preserving, an image of a bucolic, simple past that tourists of the 1870s and 1880s were coming to the mountains to experience.

By retailing this idyllic vision of a "pressure-free and uncomplicated American past" (Tolles 109) to an urban readership, newspaper editors, much like Bolles, Torrey, and Slosson, inevitably promoted the diminishment of that very vision. The influx of tourists each summer, perpetuated largely by an expansion of railways into the heart of the White Mountains and a resulting surge in hotel development, appeared to bring about precisely what Slosson and Thompson had predicted.[15] In an environment that valued observation over participation, the vast majority of summer tourists were content to visit only a handful of mountains, many of which were easily accessible from hotels by bridle path, carriage road, or, on Mount Washington, by cog railway. Although most late-century visitors were satisfied to look on things from afar, as Bolles and Torrey suggest, an increasing number of visitors, impelled by the overcrowding of popular sites, began to take part in sojourns into the wilderness beyond the observatories and *into* the viewscape.

One of the important contributions to the upsurge in hiking in the late 1800s was Charles Hitchcock's publication of *The Geology of New Hampshire* in 1874. Hitchcock's subsequent membership in the newly formed Appalachian Mountain Club also helped to stimulate interest in further exploration of regions not yet overrun by the mountains' well-to-do visitors. Whereas antebellum tourists lingered near the ever-growing resort hotels and ascended the principal peaks of Lafayette, Washington, and Willard, a new class of visitors was keen on exploring the further reaches of the White Mountain range. Guy and

Laura Waterman suggest the new generation of explorers and scientists visiting the mountains had "a burning desire to climb . . . ill-concealed under motives of science" (*Forest* 170). This "love of adventure" was a recent interest among mountain tourists who, in the years before the Civil War, were content to climb only a handful of peaks and otherwise gaze up at the mountains from the comfort of roadside hotels. The railway expansion that helped to stimulate the development of grand resort hotels in the 1870s and 1880s also led to a proliferation of more modest hotels and inns that catered to a less affluent middle class. Frequently situated on the margins of the mountains, either in Woodstock, Campton, Warren, or even Plymouth to the southwest, or in Randolph and Shelburne to the northeast, these smaller hotels were also located on the margins of the tourist culture. The boarders at these hotels were thus often less concerned with participating in bowling, billiards, lavish carriage parades, and other "nonparticipant entertainment" (Bulkley quoted in Tolles 144) and more interested in amusing themselves in the mountains surrounding their hotels.

Charles Hitchcock gave a clarion call to inveterate mountain trampers, decrying that "the great conveniences" of the cog railway and carriage road on Mount Washington "are causing the charming drives in other directions to be forgotten." He suggests that those who are able should seek out the less traveled roads "as they will then best catch the spirit of the hills, especially if they should leave all travelled routes behind, and clamber over the rocks to the summits of the rarely visited peaks" (613). Much like the trampers who followed him, Hitchcock took pains to differentiate his survey expeditions between 1869 and 1871 from the excursions of genteel tourists, noting that

> some have imagined [our] party as enjoying the luxuries of the season in cushioned seats of the well appointed hotels about the mountains, with every want eagerly anticipated by dutiful attendants. On the contrary, our houses were hastily extemporized sheds; our beds, a few boughs or ferns placed upon boards; our food consisted of stale crackers and preserved meats . . . and we were our own servants. (32)

Although Hitchcock's expeditions were, by their very nature, outside the experiential realm of most well-heeled tourists, his own language belies his attempts to separate himself from tourist culture entirely. By elsewhere integrating the aesthetic rhetoric common in midcentury guidebooks, Hitchcock illustrates that, as much as he might espouse backcountry exploration, he remains very much a part of the tourist apparatus.

The tension between scientific and tourist discourses apparent in the interpenetration of science and the sublime in the late eighteenth century (see chapter 1) continued to manifest itself in guidebooks and science writing in the later part of the nineteenth century. The chapters of Thomas Starr King's much reprinted *White Hills* devoted to describing the vegetation and exploration history of the White Mountains find a corollary in Charles Hitchcock's engagement of the region's "Scenographical Geography." Of a vista north of Mount Washington, Hitchcock writes, "this was one of the favorite points of view with Starr King," adding that "it is of easy access, either by a carriage-drive of a dozen miles from Gorham, or a walk of a mile or two from the Milan station on the Grand Trunk Railway. There is a country inn at Milan, where travellers are always welcome" (608). In a later chapter of Hitchcock's *Geology*, "The Scenery of Coos County," Hitchcock's assistant Joshua Huntington further complicates this generic interpenetration in his attempt to refashion scenic destinations in the mountains in scientific terms in the chapter he contributes to Hitchcock's book. His description of Sabbaday Falls below the north slopes of Mount Chocorua is a good example:

> Great is the commotion produced by the direct fall of so great a body of water, and out of the basin, almost at right angles with the fall, it goes in whirls and eddies. The chasm extends perhaps a hundred feet below where the water first strikes. Its width is from ten to fifteen feet, and the height of the wall is from fifty to sixty. The water has worn out the granite on either side of the trap, so that, as the clear, limpid stream flows through the chasm, the entire breadth of the dyke is seen. . . . The fall of water, the whirls and eddies of the basin, the flow of the limpid stream over a dark band of trap set in the bright, polished granite, the high, overhanging wall of rock, all combine to form a picture of beauty, which once fixed in the mind, is a joy forever. (647) [16]

The layering of scenic description and scientific treatise in Huntington's account underscores the close relationship between nineteenth-century scientific exploration and tourism. Huntington's depiction of the cataract as a very "picture of beauty" further demonstrates indebtedness to King's often overstated descriptive rhetoric. As part of a discipline that "represented," as Eric Purchase suggests, "one facet of nineteenth-century tourist culture" (139), Huntington borrows extensively from a lexicon more appropriate for tourists than for visiting geologists. Neither Huntington nor Hitchcock was ignorant of his participation in a larger tourist apparatus, however. Far from oblivious to the mountains' economic potential as a tourist destination, Hitchcock considered trying his own hand at entrepreneurship on the slopes of Maine's Mount Katahdin in

1861 when he envisioned the mountain's Chimney Pond to be "the most romantic spot for a dwelling-house in the whole state." Fortunately for the sanctity of Thoreau's unhandselled wilderness, "as a hotel man, Hitchcock was a great geologist" (Waterman and Waterman, *Forest* 148).

Although the work of late-nineteenth-century scientists and explorers like Hitchcock and Huntington illustrates a permeability between scientific and tourist discourses, the enthusiasm of later amateur botanists, geologists, and cartographers illustrates that while "scientists learn the most about nature when they sightsee and act like tourists" (Purchase 147), tourists also learn more when they act like scientists. The often uncomfortable relationship between scientific, exploratory, and guidebook writing has been apparent since before John Josselyn described what he thought would be "good help to the climbing Discoverer" after his visit to the White Mountains in the late seventeenth century (*New England* 3). The "wonder" that Mary Campbell cherishes in her study of early modern scientific and travel writing, much like the wonder that David Abram has reintroduced to what he sees as a culture detached from its world by scientific empiricism, is the fertile soil in which the new explorers plant their roots at the fin de siècle.[17] A late-nineteenth-century Thoreauvian emphasis on perceptive immersion can also be seen in John Muir's longing to embrace the intimate woods of another post–Civil War wilderness, a forest wherein, as Abram writes, "as we touch the bark of a tree, we feel the tree touching us" (268). When Muir reached Florida during his 1867 walk from Indianapolis (a trip narrated in the posthumously published *Thousand-Mile Walk to the Gulf*), he lamented how he "endeavored repeatedly to force a way through the tough vine-tangles, but seldom succeeded in getting farther than a few hundred yards. . . . feeling sad to think that I was only walking on the edge of the vast wood" (52–53). Members of the new group of amateur mountain explorers that installed itself largely on the periphery of the more affluent resort hotel culture advocated, like Muir in the Southeast and like Bolles and Torrey in the White Mountains, penetrating the edge of the woods and exploring the forest's interior.

Much as these later explorers situated themselves on the edges of tourist culture, the narratives of their adventures in the mountains existed on the margins of tourist discourse. Whereas earlier explorers like Jeremy Belknap and Manasseh Cutler argued that the empirical and the sublime were mutually exclusive ways of looking at the landscape, writers like Huntington, Hitchcock, and the amateur mountain climbers who followed them attempted to merge Belknap's precise language with the more contemporary rhetoric of observation. Thoreau, who argued for an immersion in the environment over a disinterested scientific perspective — "go where we will on the *surface* of things, men have been there before us" (248) — was an apt model for this new generation of explorers and scientists who strove to counteract the frequently overstated rhetoric of the sublime that persisted throughout antebellum guidebooks. The new scientific rigor of the 1880s and 1890s tempered overwrought descriptive language with the tools of late-nineteenth-century science. The Appalachian Mountain Club members, or Appalachians, as they called themselves, well armed with chronograph, compass, thermometer, aneroid altimeter, and heliotrope, ranged widely over largely unexplored terrain.

Tramping, sauntering — being placeless, or *sans terre*, as Thoreau would have it — indeed, simply walking for pleasure was (as it remains today) complicated by issues of class and privilege. Rebecca Solnit articulates these issues clearly when she writes, "to play at tramp or gypsy is one way of demonstrating that you are not one" (123 – 24). A number of late-century mountain visitors passionately asserted that they "did not 'hike.' A bull might hike you over a fence; you might hike yourself up over the tailboard of a wagon . . . but the word applied in no way to foot-travel. We walked or climbed, or scrambled or rock-climbed" (quoted in Koop 142 – 45). Though partly a means of distinguishing themselves from other groups of mountain amblers, as Jennifer Koop suggests, such an ardent declaration concerning how one travels through the woods reveals that this leisure pastime was no less rhetorical than it was physical. These walkers, climbers, and scramblers frequently made efforts to differentiate themselves from tourists who contented themselves with "nonparticipant entertainment." In language typical of her fellow Appalachians, M. F. Whitman casually remarked in her 1877 *Appalachia* article how her group stopped for lunch "on the precipice above [Crystal Cascade], just out of reach of the guide book tourist" (132).

In addition to the upper-class tourists who had been frequenting the ever-growing resort hotels since the midcentury, as I have noted, by the 1870s the White Mountains were becoming host to a new middle class of tourists, "moderately well-off vacationers with summer-time leisure" (Waterman and Waterman 149).[18] Choosing more modest overnight houses often located in towns on the outskirts of the mountains proper like the Ravine House in Randolph, the Russell House in North Woodstock, or the Philbrook Farm Inn or the Merrill House in Warren as residences for a large part of the summer season, this new class of tourists would be topographically confined to a comparatively small region of the mountains, and their climbing exploits would necessarily focus on exploring nearby features. They were also the first participants in the dialogue between tourism and logging and other resource-based economies in the

White Mountains. The letters collected in Peter Rowan and June Hammond Rowan's *Mountain Summers* reveal much about the complicated position occupied by the men and women of the newly founded Appalachian Mountain Club. Compiling a nine-year correspondence between Marian Pychowska, her mother Lucia, her aunt and uncle Edith and Eugene Beauharnais Cook, and their mutual friend Isabella Stone, the book details the group's tramps in the White Mountains, most of which were done under the auspices of the Appalachian Mountain Club's Department of Exploration.

In the 1880s the White Mountains were part of an ecosystem increasingly strained by a hotel industry at its peak as well as by large-scale and essentially unregulated logging. The unchecked clear-cutting by loggers like the J. E. Henry Company in Lincoln led to massive, almost constant fires and smoke that obscured the mountains' scenic vistas for many days each summer. Hotels contributed to the region's environmental degradation as a result of poor waste-processing facilities, and railroads added their own "noise, steam engine soot, smoke and refuse" (Tolles 144). Although it was partly the economic boom that generated these environmental problems that incited many late-century visitors to seek their recreation in lesser-known parts of the White Mountains, these newly arrived outdoor enthusiasts nonetheless brought with them into the wilderness a decidedly nonenvironmental tourist ethic. For instance, in an 1881 letter to her friend Isabella Stone, Marian Pychowska, an annual summer boarder in the White Mountains, describes how, upon climbing to the summit of Mount Kineo (about 3,300 feet high), she was disappointed to find that "the clearing of the top has not been done as thoroughly as I hope it will be one day (not [yet] by fire), but still the view obtained by dodging trees is very fine" (Rowan and Rowan 63). Throughout their correspondence, Stone and Pychowska describe their climbs of various peaks in the White Mountains, narrating their climbs with a wealth of detail about topography, about trail conditions, and what is perhaps most prominent, about vistas afforded along the way. Their position at the intersection of discussions about land use also illustrates a rift between tourist and year-round resident, where the tourist's concern is principally with the view.

When smoke from forest fires and farmers clearing arable lands obscures vistas, climbers like Stone and Pychowska appear less concerned with the underlying environmental transformation of the landscape than with the prevalence of smoke in the mountains (as though it were a phenomenon of weather). In a slightly earlier 1881 letter, Pychowska hopes to have the problem of smoke addressed soon: "the [Boston-based] Appalachian Mountain Club has had the smoke pest brought painfully to its notice, and I hope the members were duly impressed by it" (61). The irony of Pychowska's apparent ignorance of the potential effects of burning Mount Kineo's summit for the sake of creating a view juxtaposed with her justifiable concern for the pervasiveness of smoke and fire in the region points to the difficulties inherent in germinating the seeds of an inchoate environmental awareness in the face of a vast tourist apparatus. Like the essays of Frank Bolles and Bradford Torrey, as well as the voices of Allan Thompson and Annie Trumbull Slosson's Fishin' Jimmy, Pychowska and Stone's correspondence foregrounds the complex relationships among the region's seasonal and year-round residents and the land itself.

Notwithstanding the as-yet-unrefined environmental ethics of Pychowska, Stone, and other members of this new generation of mountain explorers, they were nevertheless encouraged by the work of Charles Hitchcock, and they took to the untraveled hills to explore the interstices between lines on existing maps and reports. The useful but sparsely detailed map of the White Mountains sketched by J. B. Henck Jr. on the basis of a survey by H. F. Walling was published in the first issue of *Appalachia* in 1876 and served principally as a starting point for explorations by Appalachians and other inveterate mountain trampers. Given their almost obsessive attention to details of measurement and observation, the new explorers might well have taken with them into the woods Thoreau's exclamation, "how little there is on an ordinary map!" (quoted in Ryden, *Landscape* 105).[19] Some more prolific members like Stone set out to create extraordinary maps of their own that looked beyond the empty landscapes at the centers of earlier regional maps. Marian Pychowska ("Evans Notch" 265) describes her cadre's "long cherished desire to take possession of the unknown land by actual measure of sole leather." Perceiving themselves as latter-day explorers, who, like their predecessors entered the mountains with a "desire to take possession," Pychowska, Stone, and Edith Cook frequently reveal an adherence to what they held to be "true Appalachian principles." "We did not," Pychowska declares about a partial exploration of Mount Wildcat, "give ourselves up to the enjoyment of the grand prospect until we had first noted its topographical features" ("Partial Exploration" 272). Their attention was focused, like that of Jeremy Belknap during his visit to the White Mountains a century earlier, on exploring the spaces between the contour lines on existing maps, these writers attempted to separate themselves from the more passive "possession" of the land in which their more affluent counterparts found enjoyment. By focusing their physical and literary energies on the descriptive work of exploration, however, the Appalachian Mountain Club walkers and their contemporaries were at times criticized for, as Samuel Clemens lamented in *Life on the Mississippi*, the loss of the landscape's poetry as a price paid for learning the letters of its alphabet — a loss that "could never be restored" (quoted in Sanders 189).

Despite the Watermans' assertion that late-century mountain climbers sought lodging that was "smaller, intimate, [and] moderately comfortable but not ostentatiously luxurious" (149), it is apparent that some of the era's visitors were trying to find a middle ground between the extravagant and the everyday — somewhere between Hazlitt's antipodes of going "to watering-places . . . carry[ing] the metropolis with them" and finding space for "more elbow-room and fewer incumbrances." As part of her attempt to determine the level of comfort in these smaller boardinghouses, Isabella Stone corresponded with numerous hotel proprietors to ask about such details as the orientation of the windows, the frequency with which fresh produce is delivered, and the content of the mattresses. A letter Stone received from Amos Merrill (of the Merrill House in the out-of-the-way town of Warren) points to the disconnect between her expectations and the reality of modest overnight houses in 1880: "I wish to explain a little about my house, as I think by your letter that your idea of it is a fashionable boardinghouse or Hotel which it is not so. I am a farmer and this house was built for that purpose fifty years ago. Since travel commenced to the mountains it has been built over with additions" to accommodate a number of boarders each summer (Rowan and Rowan 30). Stone's reluctance to make a commitment to a boardinghouse without amenities that proprietors of more modest means saw as extravagant reveals that, although Stone and her mountain-climbing contemporaries were content to separate themselves from the often overbearing moneyed culture of the upper classes, they were nonetheless accustomed to a certain level of luxury that their proprietors could not always provide. Stone's canvassing boarding houses on the periphery of the White Mountain region exemplifies the changing economic landscape of the 1880s and 1890s during which middle-class tourists were beginning to visit the mountains more frequently at the same time as local residents of more modest means were trying to better their own financial situations in the climate of the region's late-century economic prosperity.

The hardscrabble land of northern New Hampshire from the surface of which farmers had scratched their living required them to interweave a diversity of industries in order to get by. As Stuart Wallace indicates, in the unforgiving nature of the northern farm, farmers "had to turn to hunting in the fall, lumbering in the winter, and maple sugaring in the spring" (20). To further augment their incomes, many farming families also took in boarders during the summer months. Although putting up summer boarders, as Ethan and Lucy Crawford did as early as the 1820s, began simply as an additional source of revenue, by the late 1800s, it had reinvented the family farm itself as spectacle. Advocates of country living like William Murray and Henry Ward Beecher promoted rural destinations for urban residents as an antidote to the confines of a growing industrial society. The resulting influx of visitors to rural villages helped to perpetuate the notion of the farmstead, or even the entire village, as an attraction. By literarily and literally refashioning the terrain of these villages, adoptive residents like Frank Bolles worked to transform rural New Hampshire to suit their own ideas of what this rural spectacle ought to look like.

As I discussed earlier, the development that resulted from the region's promotion as a resort destination by hotel and railway proprietors significantly affected the White Mountains' natural environment and threatened the region's wild nature. Environmentally minded tourists, such as the members of the Appalachian Mountain Club, were eager to save parts of the mountains from the development that had despoiled more popular places like the Crawford and Franconia Notches and Mount Washington, and they often used the meetings and publications of the club to garner interest in their preservationist causes. In a letter to Marian Pychowska, Isabella Stone exclaims, "have you heard the dreary news that a railroad up Mt. Lafayette has been determined upon and surveys will be commenced this summer? Alas! Can we hope it is a false rumor? Can nothing be done to prevent it?" (Rowan and Rowan 55). Marian Pychowska replies that this "is not the only enormity being planned" and presents her own rumor about a new road through Franconia Notch, writing "I can already imagine how its embankment will scar the green meadows and wooded shores of our quiet stream" as "all-pervading rapid transit takes possession" (56 – 57).

It was of course not only the tourist industry that drew the growing ire of the region's summer visitors; the logging industry, which reached its zenith virtually simultaneously with the proliferation of resort hotels at the end of the nineteenth century, operated under the observant eye of outdoor enthusiasts like Stone, Pychowska, and other club members. For instance, in 1883 Marian Pychowska writes "what a pity the loggers and barkers are always upsetting our paths" (157). Though the denuded hillsides were a strong impetus to consider a conservation ethic, the smoke from forest fires that burned throughout the summer was a much more consistent reminder of the industry at work, often only on the other side of the mountain ridge from some of the most expansive resort hotels. Throughout their correspondence, Marian and Lucia Pychowska and Isabella Stone complained about the proliferation of the "rising smoke of pestiferous brush fires" (150) responsible for "sulphurous dark day[s]" (61), of smoke that "forbade distant views" (243), and of summits "bathed in summer heat and smoke"(246). The "obscuration of the atmosphere" caused by logging and agricultural fires (16) became more than a nuisance as outdoor enthusiasts brought the smoke to the attention of organizations like the Appalachian Mountain Club, which helped advocate fire prevention measures like spark screens on locomotive smokestacks. Sylvester Judd asserts that "tourists and recreationists from across the region joined the call for regulation as the slopes of the White Mountains, including the Presidential Range itself, were stripped of coniferous growth. The remaining thin hardwood forest had a 'bedraggled appearance'" (101). This nascent tourist-based conservation movement was spurred by a contention over aesthetics rather than over the health of the forest ecosystem. Judd adds that resort proprietors "grew concerned about the visual impact of forest destruction" and its potential negative impact on their own industry.[20]

Like her contemporaries Bolles and Slosson, Isabella Stone envisions White Mountain residents principally as parts of the landscape she gazes upon from various mountain roads and summits. The "scarcity and decay" (S. Judd 205) that came to represent human inhabitation as farmers abandoned their houses for the promise of more fertile fields in the American West became, for late nineteenth-century tourists, a piece of the pastoral vision they came to the mountains to find. For Stone, the farmer's struggle for sustainability itself becomes picturesque; the "old disused road . . . is interesting for its wild pastures and woody dells, and deserted houses fallen to ruins not yet picturesque though hinting at the pathos of a vain struggle for livelihood and a home" (Rowan and Rowan 85). Marian Pychowska replies to Stone, agreeing that, indeed, "those old roads high up among the hills are usually very fine places for views, as well as lovely in their immediate surroundings" (86). Robert Frost would trace the continuation of this transformation when he bought his own northern New Hampshire farm less than thirty-five years later and tramped through the same woods, often finding a "house that is no more a house, / But only a belilaced cellar hole, / Now closing like a dent in dough" (45–47). In the 1880s and 1890s, the house, though "no more a house," came to represent something between the decay decried by Bolles in "Deserted Homes" and a touchstone of the middle landscape.

Friction between users of bridle paths and carriage roads and the new pedestrian enthusiasts was inevitable, both as a result of class disparities and very real issues of access and development. The walkers "never used the word 'trail,'" eschewing it in favor of "path" to differentiate their exploits from those of less adventuresome genteel tourists (Koop 145). Mountain climbers were similarly disparaged as elitist; in 1882, a reader of the *Boston Traveller* wrote to the magazine's editor complaining about a new class of visitor to the White Mountains:

> We are disgusted with the arrogant claims of educated tramps and "culchowed" [cultured] pedestrians who have set up a sole-leather aristocracy, insisting that nobody can "do" the mountains except under the aegis of the Appalachian Club, or on foot, alone with scribe and staff, wallet, hammer and impaling needles. (Rowan and Rowan 75)

The Appalachians' position on the periphery of the White Mountains' upper-class resort hotel culture, while still clearly sufficiently affluent to spend each summer furthering the mission of the club did locate them awkwardly between an affluent elite intent on preserving their cosmopolitan mores in the region's hotels and local residents, for whom a mountain was more often a resource or an obstacle than an end in itself.

The privileged status, of which some of the club's women members were quite conscious, actually enabled them to explore some of the mountains' less traveled paths in an attempt to recover the remnants of a region's wild frontier. The "'wilderness' taboo" that, Dawn Lander writes, "denies feminine wanderlust" (quoted in LaBastille 19), did not limit the adventurous nature of Pychowska, Stone, Cook, and their contemporaries, partly as a result of their economic separation from the lower-class domestic duties that often kept other women occupied with more traditional gender roles. The privileged status of these tourists sometimes, in fact, enabled a reversal of traditional roles and allowed women like Marian Pychowska and her mother, Lucia, to maintain hiking trails and sketch new maps while Lucia's husband remained behind at their boardinghouse to write and play music (Rowan and Rowan 4). The summers that Stone, Pychowska, and their families spent among the mountains, often tramping and climbing without male chaperones or guides, allowed them to participate in a simulated frontier wilderness experience that, although very different from the experiences of Lucy Crawford and Dolly Copp earlier in the century, effectively "restructured and reshaped" their roles as "women in the American wilderness" (Rowan and Rowan 21).

Nearly two decades after first visiting the White Mountains at age thirteen, Isabella Stone begins to articulate her own position as privileged tourist, while at the same time trying to locate herself in the gender landscape of the fin de siècle, writing about a vista in the mountains in 1882, "the view reminds me of

'Aurora Leigh's' sight of Italy" (Rowan and Rowan 83). Stone goes on to quote from Elizabeth Barrett Browning's description of the Italian coast near Genoa from Aurora Leigh's shipboard prospect as

> The old miraculous mountains heaved in sight,
> One straining past another along the shore,
>
> . . .
>
> Peak pushing peak
> They stood. (7:489–94)

While Stone's self-fashioning as the White Mountains' Aurora Leigh may appear wistfully romantic, by incorporating Browning's revolutionary poem into her own writing, she is able to declare what would otherwise remain unstated; Stone successfully retails her knowledge of (and abilities among) the mountains to create a position for herself among the region's mountaineering elite. Where Lucy Crawford and other writers of the settlement experience frequently used their writing as currency with the hope of recovering a lost experience, the writers of the Appalachian Mountain Club possessed a privilege of class and of distance from the economic realities of year-round life in northern New Hampshire that enabled them to write only for one another, either in a coherent epistolary narrative or in the exclusive club journal *Appalachia*. Stone and her contemporaries, Marian and Lucia Pychowska and Edith Cook, saw themselves at the forefront of their field, following the trail set for them in the 1820s by the pioneering Austin sisters (see chapter 2) and joining established pedestrians like M. F. Whitman and Mrs. William Murray.

Taking full advantage of the club's decision at its second meeting in 1876 to include women members, the White Mountains' summer residents rose to create and maintain voices for themselves in public discourse. Much as Stone, Whitman, and Marian and Lucia Pychowska wrote *about* the landscape, these late-century explorers wrote *upon* it as well. Isabella Stone, for instance, was instrumental in planning and building trails near Woodstock and in "straighten[ing] out the topography" of the western White Mountains (Rowan and Rowan 4; Waterman and Waterman, *Forest*).[21] Whitman's trailblazing in the largely unexplored area known today as the Pemigewassett Wilderness and Edith Cook's exploratory tramps with her husband, recorded in personal letters and sketches as well as in the club's journal, are testaments to the quantity of exploration undertaken by this new generation of outdoor enthusiasts. Marian Pychowska's own map of the Northern Presidential Range persisted as the most detailed map of the region for fifteen years. The extensive journals and letters (and sketches made by Edith Cook, Marian Pychowska's aunt) that the group sent back and forth and the entries they presented and had published in the early volumes of *Appalachia* empowered them to write (and reconstruct) the mountains through their own eyes. The layering of text and terrain in these writings reveals the ability of this new generation of explorers to transform the White Mountains from a distant tableau of anonymous forested peaks into a landscape that, like trails themselves, encouraged interaction between the human and wild.

BY THE LAST DECADES of the nineteenth century, the White Mountains were increasingly layered with often conflicting rhetorical and economic landscapes of promotion, industry, inhabitation, and preservation. It is within this contested terrain that the writings of Stone, Pychowska, Whitman, and Cook, like the works of Frank Bolles and Bradford Torrey, helped the public to envision a mountain landscape that was simultaneously economically, recreationally, and environmentally sustainable. Whereas a desire for wildness among late-century outdoor enthusiasts helped to incite interest in environmental issues, the move toward preserving forests in the White Mountains was also prompted by public outcry against the destruction of wild lands by the competing industries of tourism and logging. Writers like Torrey explicitly appealed to the public for the preservation of his adopted summer residence. We can read in Torrey's essays the beginnings of the conservation movement that led to the passage of the 1911 Weeks Act and the founding of the White Mountain National Forest. Questioning the necessity of the annual Christmas tree harvest in 1889, for instance, Torrey intones, "the unhappy trees had a hard shift to live, so broken down were they with each recurring December." "But who," he asks, "thinks of sympathizing with a tree?" (*Rambler's Lease* 66 – 67). Sentiments like these lay the groundwork for cooperation among citizens, societies like the Appalachian Mountain Club and the Society for the Protection of New Hampshire Forests, and state and federal legislators to construct a cohesive forest out of a patchwork of private and unorganized land holdings.

The conservation movement gained momentum by the late 1870s largely as a result of rhetorical and political interplay between tourist sentiment and scientific treatise. In 1885 the State of New York designated a 715,000-acre "forever wild" forest preserve in the Adirondack Mountains. The establishment of the Adirondack preserve was significantly assisted both by George Perkins Marsh's advocacy of forest conservation and by William "Adirondack" Murray's promotion of the region and his publication of *Adventures in the Wilderness* in

1869. Echoing this interweaving of economic and recreational issues, legislation to preserve America's wild lands similarly depended upon economic motivations, such as preserving New York's water supply by forestalling large-scale logging in the Adirondack Mountains. Yellowstone was similarly designated America's first national park in 1872 principally to "prevent private acquisition and exploitation" of its natural features (Nash 108). As in the Northeast, railroad entrepreneurs were interested in developing the unique landscape of Yellowstone into a "national vacation mecca like Niagara Falls or Saratoga Springs. . . . A wilderness was the last thing they wanted" (Nash 111).

Proponents of forest conservation were profoundly influenced by George Perkins Marsh's 1864 *Man and Nature* and by his articulation of the connection between the condition of a forest and the health of its watershed. Franklin B. Hough, for instance, argued as early as 1873 for "laws to regulate, promote and protect the growth of wood" and for provisions that would set aside forests to maintain the nation's navigable rivers (6). Joseph P. Walker's declaration in 1872 that with regard to forest management, "We are doing less than our forefathers did, more than two hundred years ago" ("An Address" 6) led him to connect Marsh's idea of an ecosystem with the more contemporary vision of the forests as scenic resources. "In the first place we want to preserve our forests so far as we can and preserve the scenery," said Walker in an 1891 address before the New Hampshire Board of Agriculture, adding that forests also temper the seasonal fluctuation of downstate rivers, "and we have as a result the reliable Merrimack, which at all times of the year provides our manufactories with water and yet never becomes a fierce destroyer" ("Our New Hampshire Forests" 29).

In 1891 the United States Congress passed the Forest Reserve Act, which in effect allowed the creation of forest preserves, later known as national forests, and made provisions for their management under the newly formed Department of Agriculture. Two decades later, in March 1911, Congress passed the Weeks Act, directing the secretary of agriculture to "examine, locate, and purchase such forested, cut-over, or denuded lands within the watersheds of navigable streams as in his judgment may be necessary to the regulation of the flow of navigable streams or the production of timber" (16 USC 515§17). As a culmination of public outcry against the misuse of natural lands and evidence of unchecked growth of resource-based industries into wild areas, the Weeks Act codified environmental interrelationships that Jeremy Belknap had begun to articulate more than a century earlier. The activity of White Mountains writers throughout the nineteenth century helped to build the ideological soil from which, for visitors and residents alike, a sustainable future might emerge.

Reading and Teaching Region

IN THE PREDAWN morning of a day when spring seems poised to slip suddenly into summer, I wake early and head out for a short bike ride before my wife and son begin to stir. As I turn the bicycle downhill toward the Franconia Valley just north of the White Mountain National Forest, the sky in the east is painted with broad vivid stokes the color of roadside clusters of hawkweed — orange, vermillion, and yellow — while to the west, mist rises slowly from the surface of Streeter Pond, just as the sun crests the high ridge between Mounts Garfield and Lafayette. I pass the iron furnace, a striking reminder of the early nineteenth-century mining industry in the now quiet rural village of Franconia, and turn right past the farmhouse, which, in 1915, Robert Frost "had to take by force rather than buy" (163), straight past several country inns built before tourism's heyday in the middle and late 1800s — one of which, first established in 1784, hosted Thoreau and his brother John during their 1839 trip recounted in "A Week on the Concord and Merrimack" (Sayre). Turning back north and uphill toward home, I squint against the now bright eastern sky and think about returns and cycles, and coming back home to ground myself.

As I have worked to finish this book over the last few months, I have often found myself reflecting on the historical depth, what John Elder calls the "natural, historical, and aesthetic *thickness*" (*Reading* 112) of the landscape, in the woods and on the mountainsides near our home. In the past year, I have spent many days in the field with students, drawing them into dialogue with the rich varied stories that the landscape has to offer. Whether from the perspective of literary studies, history, sustainability, environmental policy, media, or regional studies, our forays into the north woods resonate with the stories of place, and with the voices from the land.

New England, and in particular the White Mountains that are at the center of this book, is woven through with stories of residents, visitors, settlers, farmers, explorers, hunters, traders, developers, loggers, all of which add their voices to the layers of last autumn's leaves littering the forest floor. We inhabit a landscape written over by inhabitation history, evidence of resource-based industries, the needs of a contemporary tourist economy, and a diversity of ecological systems — all interconnected within and around the borders of a federally managed national forest. My work with numerous lesser-known histories, guidebooks, essays, and works of poetry and fiction in writing this book has itself begun to reveal the region as one layered with many different and often competing voices of residents, tourists, business owners, environmentalists, and land managers.

Thickets of meaning — both figurative and literal — abound in the New England woods; there are stories everywhere in the mountains, forests, and farms of the Northeast. It isn't possible to walk far in the steadily rewilding woods without stumbling on some artifact of farming, or of the logging, mining, or tourist industries. This is exactly what has become more and more central to my teaching — the notion that one need not go far at all to find a landscape rich with stories; one just needs to know how to look.

Northern New England's mixed hardwood forests present a rich history for the willing reader; any amble across the landscape is inevitably a movement through its layered record of many cycles of inhabitation, abandonment, logging, and regrowth. The very local, intimate "facts" of the woods help us define the landscape of New England's northern forest, a disputed topographical and rhetorical landscape, one that has long been defined as a zone of transition, a place where the southern hardwood forests merge with the expansive boreal forests of the north, where tourism and wildness test one another's limits, both because of the region's easy accessibility and its recovering wilderness.

I took my second trip to Frank Bolles's backyard woods in Tamworth this spring with my students for the last day of a graduate course in heritage studies. It is the work of Bolles, one of the writers whose work contributed to the emerging conservationism that led to the creation of the White Mountain National Forest early in the twentieth century (see chapter 4), that brings together the disparate threads of literature, history, and environment. If my work on this book has itself been a process of developing an understanding of the many-layered terrain of the White Mountains, Bolles's work as a writer, seasonal resident, amateur naturalist, and mountain explorer in the 1880s and 1890s perhaps best illustrates the culmination of a century of cultural and environmental history. Although still rooted in the discourse and apparatus of tourism, fin-de-siècle writers like Bolles (and his contemporaries Bradford Torrey and Annie Trumbull Slosson) cultivated the seeds of environmental concern sown earlier in the nineteenth century, effectively introducing the language of conservation into the White Mountains' often contested rhetorical and physical terrain.

By drawing students into moments like Bolles's rediscovery of an old sawmill site, or into the December woods with saws and peaveys to buck up a fallen spruce into four-foot lengths of pulpwood, or into the backyard woods to read black bear claw marks on beech tree bark, or across seldom-traveled trails and rivers in the far northern reaches of the state to add our own footprints to those of writers and explorers who passed there before — all these moments in the field empower students to recognize the significance not only of how the landscape has shaped the cultural and literary history of the region, but also how their own thinking and writing can contribute to the still developing identity of both this place and other places they might call home. The intimate connection with the land that the northern forest demands, the same one that frustrated the region's early visitors and trail builders, cannot help but build connections between students, teachers, and the larger world beyond this region of the Northeast.

During a fall semester exploring the ties between literature, culture, and environment, our class spent an afternoon first touring the nearby iron furnace, making clear the relationship between economic prosperity and environmental impact from the extensive clear-cutting of forests in the area to support the furnace's growing need for charcoal as fuel at the beginning of the nineteenth century. The now mostly forested surrounding area, with its quiet, rural, recreation- and vacation-centered economy, belies this dramatically different ecological topography, which I hoped my students would begin to see simply by making the connections between the furnace and the comments of early visitors to the area, including Thoreau, who in 1858 called this area to the north of Mount Lafayette a "leopard-spotted land" of clear-cut, farm, and forest. We then drove to the foot of that same peak, and, within the class period's time constraints, were able to climb a spur of the mountain, which offered views similar to Thoreau's. The students were then asked to write a pair of journal entries, one as they looked upon Mount Lafayette, the other as they turned around and looked to the north, in effect, through Thoreau's eyes, toward what has once again become a leopard-spotted land. This journaling sparked conversations — and, later, more writing — about cleared fields and farming, ridgeline construction, recent development, and, certainly, about the ski area immediately to our south. By seeing various kinds of development as cyclical, the students were able to point to similarities between early 1800s industrial logging and the second home construction boom two hundred years later. In addition, the ability to see early cultural and economic impacts on the forest resonate in current land-use decisions depended on our reading nineteenth-century writers such as Thoreau, Timothy Dwight, Edward Kendall, and Nathaniel Hawthorne, as well as more regionally known writers like Bolles, Torrey, and Lucy Crawford, as a lens through which to better understand (and become sensitive to) the region's complex, layered landscape.

Whereas Thoreau's trips into New Hampshire in the 1830s and 1850s illustrate cyclical changes in the land, the interplay of nature and culture (and the effect of writing on the environment itself) becomes perhaps more apparent in the proliferation of environmental writing of the late nineteenth century. Writers who followed Thoreau, as well as the conservation-minded George Perkins Marsh, turned their attention to an inhabited wild landscape — the wildness of "big trees and backyards" (Ryden, *Landscape* 1). Such writing helped to bring the rhetoric of preservation into the public forum. My current approach to the study of the Northeast bioregion as discursive community takes seriously its goal to "ground environmental thought in the real circumstances of everyday life. It demands that people connect their livelihood to their sense of place" (Thomashow 63). If, as David Orr has written, "locality has no standing in the modern curriculum," and "locality" has been subsumed by the "abstractions, generalized knowledge, and technology" (*Earth* 129) of a homogeneous global culture, then it becomes an educational imperative to refocus a displaced student population with place-based pedagogy.

On an earlier trip with another class, as my students explore the remains of hundred-year-old mountain logging camps, we assemble an impressive array of evidence of the area's many different uses. The springiness of a persistent sawdust pile was a welcome island of sun in a forest that still retained most of its autumn leaves — and provided an ideal venue to reread descriptions of earlier tramps along the same path. Our guides there, nineteenth-century writers Frank Bolles, Brooks Atkinson, and the prolific writer and mountaineer Charles Fay, among others, enabled us to see that we are part of a process of development in these mountains; that the third-growth forest that surrounds, the trail we follow, and of course the sawdust into which we sink our heels are less historical relics than layers onto which we continue to add our own story. We began to realize that the terrain we were traversing had seen many cycles of logging and regrowth and had been seen through many frames: as inhospitable wilderness, as raw material, as the sublime, as a recreational playground, or as a federally designated wilderness.

If students, as readers and as writers, become inhabitants of a particular region, they become invested in that particular landscape — residents of the textual and topographic terrain. John Elder's thoughtful inducement to teachers and students "to experience personally the images and rhythms we meet . . . on the page" (Elder, "Poetry" 320), for instance, is paramount to cultivating a sensitivity to a text's connection to nature. In our region, which is often affected as much by cultural as by natural forces, the text can similarly inform our relationship to an understanding of the nonhuman world. As one of my students in an environmental literature class commented, "When we take time to interact with our surroundings, we grow as people who are part of the landscape." If students are taught to be members of an ecological community — to develop, in Wendell Berry's words, an "ecological intelligence" (111) and have an awareness of their environment, then it serves them, too, to be conscious of the cultural terrain that is interwoven in that environment — both to be aware of a region's literary and cultural history and also to be sensitive to the cycles of use, growth, and development that shape our region.

For now, I put away the backpack and camping equipment until the next trip, and I turn to other work. Looking out my window across the greening lawn and toward the new dark green spears of undergrowth just emerging from beneath the mat of last year's leaves, I reflect on a growing record of moments of understanding between human and wild, between student, teacher, and place. If the history of northern New Hampshire, and northern New England as a whole, is written into the layers of leaves on the forest floor and plowed into fields — both fertile and fallow — of local farms and in the many voices that shape the land, then perhaps the future of what has been a frequently contested landscape lies in continuing to dig through these layers so we might better understand the long and profound relationship between people and place in the forests of northern New England.

1. Texts and Terrain

1. Paul Lindholt traces source material in Josselyn's *Two Voyages to New England* and notes Josselyn's evident debt to John Smith's *Description of New England* (1616), William Wood's *New England's Prospect* (1634), Thomas Morton's *New English Canaan* (1637), Roger Williams's *Key into the Language of America* (1643), and Edward Johnson's *Wonder-Working Providence* (1654).

2. For a detailed account of seventeenth- and eighteenth-century White Mountain explorers, see Russell Lawson, *Passaconaway's Realm*.

3. Guy and Laura Waterman explain that "the Belknap-Cutler expedition . . . was a landmark event in northeastern mountain climbing history. . . . Popular reports of this trip, mostly by Belknap, were widely circulated, and created considerable interest in the White Mountains" ("Reverends, Soldiers, Scientists" 42). Jeremy Belknap published a number of accounts of the trip in his lifetime, including an address before the American Philosophical Society on 15 October 1784 ("Description" 42–49) and a chapter in the third volume of his *History of New Hampshire*. His published correspondence with Ebenezer Hazard includes a number of descriptions of the trip, included in letters dated 16 and 19 August.

4. Belknap offers the following table compiled by Rev. Haven of Rochester, New Hampshire, "whose house is in plain view of the south side of the mountain, distant about sixty miles."

> Sept. 17 and 18. A N.E. storm of rain.
> 20, Mountain appeared white.
> 22, Of a pale blue.
> Oct. 3 and 4. Rain, succeeded by frost.
> 5, Mountain white.
> 8, Of a pale blue.
> 10, White in the morning, most part blue P.M.
> 22 and 24, Blue.
> 28, White at the west end, the rest blue.
> Nov. 2, A spot of white at the west end.
> 4, Uniformly white.
> 5, Very white.

5. Experiments with color as a relationship among distance, season, and time of day on Mount Washington can be seen in a number of Benjamin Champney paintings, including *Mount Washington from Sunset Hill* (1858), *Tuckerman's Ravine and Lion's Head* (1877), *White Mountains from Conway, Early Autumn* (1879). Comparable works

include Sylvester Hodgdon, *Mount Washington and Tuckerman's Ravine* (undated); John Kensett, *Mount Washington from the Valley of Conway* (1851); Thomas Cole, *View of the White Mountains* (1827); George Inness, *Mount Washington* (1875).

6. The range's eight other prominent peaks were not named until 1820. See chapter 2.

7. While Belknap did not return to the White Mountains, Manasseh Cutler was able to visit and reascend Mount Washington in 1804 (Lawson, *Passaconaway* 129 – 30).

8. Michel de Certeau suggests in *The Practice of Everyday Life* that one's elevation above the surrounding landscape "transfigures him into a voyeur. It puts him at a distance. It transforms the bewitching world by which one was 'possessed' into a text that lies before one's eyes. It allows one to read it, to be a solar Eye, looking down like a god" (92).

9. See Lawson, *Passaconaway* 135 – 39. For further discussion of place and space, see Yi-Fu Tuan, *Space and Place: The Perspective of Experience*, and several essays in Wayne Franklin and Michael Steiner, eds., *Mapping American Culture*.

10. In her glossary of "Landscape Poetics," Anne Whiston Spirn offers that in "euphony landscape patterns are perceived as harmonious, in cacophony as discordant" (*Language of Landscape* 236).

11. For readings that engage the interplay of text and topography in early discovery and exploration narratives, see for instance Mary Baine Campbell, *The Witness and the Other World*; Stephen Greenblatt, *Marvelous Possessions*; Mary Louise Pratt, *Imperial Eyes*; and Wayne Franklin, *Discoverers, Explorers, Settlers*.

12. Tracing a parallel situation in human geography, in *Ideology, Science, and Human Geography*, Derek Gregory offers that "Spatial structure is not, therefore, merely the arena within which class conflicts express themselves . . . but also the domain within which — and, in part, through which — class relations are constituted, and its concepts must have a place in the construction of the concepts of determinate social formations. . . . [S]patial structures cannot be *theorized* without social structures, *and vice versa*, and . . . social structures cannot be *practised* without spatial structures, *and vice versa*." (120 – 21).

13. For a detailed discussion, see Casey, 3 – 19.

2. Economic Topographies

1. While hunting for moose in 1771, Timothy Nash spied the gap between mountain ranges that would become the Notch of the White Mountains. After traversing the Notch and following the valley to the south, he appealed to Governor John Wentworth to lay claim to the land. In a story difficult to separate from fiction, Nash was told that if he were able to convey a horse laden with a barrel of rum from Lancaster, New Hampshire, to the south through the Notch, the state would grant him a tract of land. With the help of his friend Benjamin Sawyer, Nash successfully got the horse (and most of the rum) through the Notch, though with prodigious use of ropes and pulleys on the craggy northern end of the trip. Nash and Sawyer's Location, comprising several square miles of forest to the north of the Notch, still bears the names of Timothy Nash and Benjamin Sawyer today. See Waterman and Waterman, *Forest* 37 – 38.

2. Shortly before his death, Eleazer Rosebrook convinced his grandson, Abel Craw-

ford's son Ethan, to care for him. Ethan was ably assisted by his cousin, Lucy, and after Rosebrook's death, Lucy Howe and Ethan Allen Crawford were married on 1 November 1817. See Waterman and Waterman, *Forest* 39–41.

3. Wilson draws on examples of built and altered natural landscapes to argue that Western culture reveals an "increasing production of natural attractions. For a long time now, our culture of nature has typed certain topographies and climates — mountains, coastlines, islands, exotic or fragile ecosystems — as special places. But inevitably . . . certain elements have to be rearranged to meet tourist expectations" (49).

4. Crawford writes that Colonel Amos Binney of Boston, accompanied by two other men, was the first visitor whose sole intent was to climb Mount Washington. Binney and his companions "never reached the summit, but managed to get along on some of the hills" (*History* 31).

5. Crawford, *History* 39.

6. Charles Hitchcock devotes a chapter of his *Geology of New Hampshire* to "scenographical geology," in which he argues for the importance of a working knowledge of geology in order to effectively appreciate and re-present the landscape. He asserts that "the artist, who represents a mountain correctly upon a canvas, has discovered the fundamental type of its structure, whether he uses geological phrases or not — otherwise his painting will not be recognizable" (589).

7. For an extended discussion of Philip Carrigain's map of New Hampshire, see Mevers and Stark. In addition to more than a dozen incidental references in histories and travel narratives, Hanrahan lists four scientifically oriented magazine articles derived from visits to the White Mountains in the thirty-five years after Belknap's 1784 expedition: B. S. Barton, "Notice of the Botany of the White Mountains"; George Shattuck, "Some Account of an Excursion to the White Hills of New Hampshire in the Year 1807"; Jacob Bigelow, "Some Account of the White Mountains of New Hampshire"; and Alden Partridge, "The Altitude of Moose-Hillock in New Hampshire Ascertained Barometrically."

8. See Dona Brown, *Inventing New England*, 52–56.

9. John Hayward's 1849 *Gazetteer of New Hampshire* records the town of Carroll as being granted in 1772 to "Sir Thomas Wentworth, Rev. Samuel Langdon, and eighty-one others" (43) and the town's population as follows: 108 in 1830, 218 in 1840. Hayward notes that Bethlehem's population grew from 40 settlers in 1798 to 171 residents in 1800, 422 in 1810, 467 in 1820, 665 in 1830, and 779 in 1840. Jefferson, north of Carroll, settled in 1773 by Col. Joseph Whipple and Samuel Hart, incorporated in 1796, records a population increase from 112 in 1800 to 575 in 1840. Hamilton Child's 1886 *Gazetteer* adds that Bethlehem's population expanded to 1,400 by 1880.

10. See Brown 35–36 for an extended discussion.

11. See Brown 59 for further discussion.

12. Hanrahan lists only four books and twenty-nine magazine and journal articles published before 1846. The two decades after the publication of Crawford's *History* saw the publication of twenty book-length White Mountain histories and guidebooks.

13. For a discussion of paintings of inhabited nature, see Novak, *Nature and Culture*, 157–200 and McGrath, *Gods in Granite*, 147–62.

14. With the closure of many of the grand resort hotels and the concurrent decline

in White Mountain tourism at the beginning of the twentieth century came a decline in readers of White Mountain literature, and the *History of the White Mountains* was not reprinted again until 1966 by Stearns Morse at Dartmouth College.

15. A letter from Charles L. Turner dated 19 March 1847 apologizes that "I am under the necessity of returning those books 'History of the White Mountains' that I received from you last fall to sell. I made some effort to sell them before I went to Boston. . . . I should have been very glad to have sold them for you, but the price seems to be the greatest obstacle" (Crawford papers, Dartmouth College Library).

16. The notice that precedes Lucy Crawford's manuscript reads, in its entirety:

> In 1846 the author of the following pages published a small work entitled "The History of the White Mountains" but through the carelessness of the printer and the Crawford family leaving the mountains about that time a second edition was never issued.
>
> Since the above period other works relative to the "White Hills" have been presented to the public, but the connection by marriage of the author of this work to one of the earliest settlers and her long residence at the mountains gives her advantage for narrating facts concerning the hardships of the first emigrants to this romantic spot.
>
> The great slide of 1826 as well as the biography of the Crawford family [are described] more correctly than can be given by any other person.
>
> Her knowledge of the above facts and the great changes that have taken place about those regions since 1846 has induced her to revise and enlarge her former work not only that the public may be correctly informed of the hardships and privations to which those hardy mountaineers were subjected, but also to aid the writer in her declining years to regain her old homestead.
>
> Literary fame is no part of our intention. We leave that to those, whose imagination serves them as a guide rather than facts, while we speak of circumstances coming under our own observation, and from early history.
>
> Considerable expense has attended this book in furnishing plates representing some of the most noted localities, as well as some of the feats of the mountain giant. (ii – iii)

17. Mid-nineteenth-century guidebook and travel writers looked to the White Mountains for literary and historical associations with which to embellish their descriptions and to attract tourists. Spaulding's "Indian Prophesy on Giant's Grave," was concretized as legend in later histories, including Thomas Starr King's 1859 *White Hills*, Merrill's 1888 *History of Coos County*, and as late as Earnest Poole's 1946 *Great White Hills of New Hampshire*. In *The White Hills*, King acknowledges Spaulding's "Indian Prophesy on Giant's Grave" only in passing, suggesting, rather, that "we are happy that we can leave this [tradition] with those of our readers who love the atmosphere of wild traditions . . . better than the evening light that glows on their tops, or the rare flowers and plants that climb their ravines" (229).

18. David Miller defines iconology as "the rhetoric of images." Drawing on the work of W. T. J. Mitchell (*Iconology*), he further describes iconology as "the study of both 'what images say' and 'what to say about images'" (2).

19. Chapter 14 is bound with the manuscript's other chapters, though it is clearly written in a different hand. While doing research for the 1966 Dartmouth edition of the *History*, Stearns Morse corresponded with Helen Crawford Wells, who provided

him with a final chapter that had been missing from the original materials. When submitting the manuscript for sale in 1951, Lucy Howe Crawford Merrill, Lucy Crawford's great-granddaughter, wrote, "most of the book was written by Lucy — I do not know who wrote the rest of it, probably one of her children. The spicier passages cut out by her daughter, Lucy, who was an ardent member of the WCTU [Women's Christian Temperance Movement], and intended to see that no mention was made of Ethan's occasional lapses from virtue" (qtd. in Morse xvi). Therefore, despite the chapter's continuation of Lucy's first-person narrative, its origins are somewhat suspect. It would be inappropriate, however, to discount the significance of the final chapter, as its origins are most likely a collaboration between Lucy and her daughter (possibly Ellen Wile Howard, in whose possession the manuscript remained after Lucy Crawford's death). As the original *History* is itself a "communo-bio-oratory" and presents a pastiche of Lucy and Ethan's voices combined with transcribed guest-book entries, an additional authorial voice functions to further complicate, rather than cast suspicion upon, the narrative as a whole.

20. The party of seven consisted of Adino N. Brackett, John W. Weeks, General John Wilson, Charles J. Stuart, N. S. Dennison, and Samuel A. Pearsons, all of Lancaster, and Philip Carrigain, whose meticulously detailed map of New Hampshire had been published only four years earlier (1860 ms. 6).

21. The northern summits were first ascended by three Lancastrians, who returned a month later for a six-day survey of the newly christened peaks (Waterman and Waterman, "Reverends" 44).

22. Since the Lancastrians' 1820 visit, there has been debate over which peak north of Mount Washington they intended to name after Jefferson and which after Adams. Nineteenth-century descriptions often confuse the two, but in the twentieth century, Mount Adams has persevered as the name of the taller northern peak.

23. Henry Ward Beecher, Harriet Beecher Stowe's brother, was a vocal advocate for the mountains' contribution to visitors' physical and spiritual well-being, and he stayed at the Crawford House during a visit to the White Mountains in 1856. It is possible that Lucy Crawford's appeal to Stowe for assistance resulted from an interaction with, or at least an awareness of, Beecher.

24. For further discussion, see Mott and Zuckerman.

25. Sweetser, *White Mountains* 35. For an extended discussion of women hikers in the White Mountains, see Waterman and Waterman, *Forest*.

3. The Sublime and the Sumptuous

1. Charles H. Hitchcock's 1874 *Geology of New Hampshire* estimates that in 1858, 5,000 people visited the summit of Mount Washington. In 1870 the number had increased to 7,000.

2. See Waterman and Waterman 83 – 87 for a detailed discussion of the mountaintop phenomenon.

3. See for instance the "Guide from New York and Boston to the White Mountains" by Nathaniel Noyes, published as an appendix to Benjamin Willey's *Incidents in White Mountain History*, 309 – 22.

4. King Ravine on Mount Adams and Mount Starr King in the Pliny Range north of Jefferson, New Hampshire, are two examples of King's own name finding its way onto prominent White Mountain landmarks. King's eventual move to San Francisco and his exploration of mountains in California's Sierra Nevada Range prompted his admirers on the West Coast to name a peak in Yosemite after him as well.

5. Native to Western Europe, the gorse is prevalent on both the East and West Coasts of the United States, from Virginia to Massachusetts and California to Washington. Originally imported as an ornamental and for hedges, gorse is listed as an invasive pioneer species, whose habitat consists of logged areas, abandoned fields, cleared areas, and sandy coastal areas according to the U.S. government database ‹http://plants .usda.gov›, accessed 8 June 2005.

6. Ripley was editor of two reprints of Lucy Crawford's *History* in 1883 and 1886. In 1876 Moses Sweetser suggested that the "old fisherman" who informed Ripley and Porter was Abel Crawford, who had discovered the falls "while out on snowshoes, hunting sable" (Julyan and Julyan 130). It is unlikely that Ripley's informant was Abel Crawford, as the mountain patriarch had died in 1851.

7. For further discussion of representations of absent and present Native cultures, see Fiedler; Tompkins, *West of Everything,* esp. 7–10; Robtoy, Brightstar, Obomsawin, and Moody; Vizenor.

8. For discussion of Champney and the White Mountain school, also see *Beauty Caught and Kept* and McGrath and MacAdam.

9. Judd argues elsewhere that Marsh's perspectives were not wholly original but were significantly influenced by a growing popular sentiment. See Judd 99–111 for a discussion of forest conservation in the White Mountains.

10. In a thorough examination of the 1853–1854 visitor's register from Mount Washington's Tip-Top House Hotel, Peter B. Bulkley notes a change from the genteel, elite tourists who toured the White Mountains in the 1820s and 1830s to the larger number of tourists who visited the mountains in the 1850s. He identifies four discrete groups of tourists in this later group. An upper-class group, comprised of merchants, proprietors, managers, officials, professionals, gentlemen, and students composed 52 percent of the Tip-Top House register's entries. "Lesser White Collar Occupations' (119), an emergent middle class made up of semiprofessional clerks and salesmen, contributed just less than 14 percent of the entries. Farmers (who where on average "more affluent than most laborers, clerks, and even some small businessmen" [130]) made up 10 percent, and laborers another 20 percent (only about a quarter to a third of whom were paying guests). Four percent of visitors are designated as having "no occupation." From Bulkley's reading of the register, it is apparent that, although 1850s tourists represented a greater diversity of occupations and economic classes than their predecessors, they were nonetheless predominantly members of the upper and middle classes.

11. Tolles notes that "Resort architecture of the late 1860s and 1870s . . . often emphasized the unusual, the cosmopolitan, the exotic and the picturesque" (19).

12. I am grateful for Jane Zanger's insight into Chocorua's rich and complex history. Her unpublished 1992 thesis, "A Greek-Like Tragedy in New Hampshire: Literary and Artistic Manifestations of Chocorua," was invaluable.

13. For Henry James's perspective on the White Mountains and their inhabitants, I am indebted to William Stowe's unpublished essay on Henry James's visit to the White Mountains, "'Oh, the land's all right!': Henry James and American Nature in Chocorua, New Hampshire." Child's story enjoyed continued popularity throughout the nineteenth century, and it was reprinted in *The Lady's Cabinet Album* in 1832, 1834, 1837, and 1838. It was also published (often unattributed) in various guidebooks and in Child's own 1831 collection *The Coronal: a Collection of Miscellaneous Pieces, Written at Various Times.*

14. Francis Parkman remarks of his visit to the Willey House in 1841 only that he "walked down the Notch to the Willey House and, out of curiosity, began to ascend in the pathway of the avalanche" (Wade 13).

15. See McGrath, *Gods,* 11–13.

16. For further discussion, see Nash 96–107.

17. *Among the Clouds,* the *Littleton* [N.H.] *Journal,* the *Littleton White Mountain Republic,* and the *White Mountain Echo* all carried news of the event. The *Republic,* quoting extensively from the tourist paper *Among the Clouds,* was among the first to note that "the fact is, there is no comparison between this and the Willey slide. . . . It is none the less a marvelous display of the program of nature, though entirely unlike the former catastrophe in amount and in result" (18 Aug. 1885: 1).

18. It is interesting to note that the New Hampshire State Historical Marker describing the slide follows the same itinerary as the original 1885 *Echo* article. The article reads: "On July 10, 1885, at 6 A.M., a slide from Cherry Mountain's northern peak left a deep gash from Owl's Head to the Valley. A million tons of boulders, trees and mud loosed by a cloudburst rolled and tumbled a tortuous two miles, destroying Oscar Stanley's new home and his cattle, barn and crops. Farm hand Don Walker, rescued from debris of the barn, died four days later; but Stanley's family was not there and was spared. Excursion trains and carriages brought people from far and wide to view the tragic sight, which has now almost disappeared through nature's healing process."

19. For early twentieth-century descriptions of tourism, see Anderson and Morse, Kilbourne, and Poole.

20. For further discussion, see McAvoy and Tolles. Additional markers of tourism's sudden growth in the 1860s and 1870s can be found in daily newspaper publication records; the two most prominent White Mountain tourist dailies began their run in the mid–late 1870s: *White Mountain Echo* (1878), published in Bethlehem, and *Among the Clouds* (1877), published on the Mount Washington summit. The opening of the Mount Washington Carriage Road in 1861 and the Mount Washington Cog Railway in 1869 both heralded a significant influx of tourists in the years immediately after the Civil War.

4. Alone with Scribe and Staff

1. Paugus was the Sokosis chief killed (along with about sixty Sokosis and eighteen Euroamericans) in Lovewell's Massacre, an attack by Captain John Lovewell on a Sokosis village near present-day Fryeburg on 8 May 1725. Mount Paugus has also been

called Bald, Barry, Middle, Deer, Frog, and Hunchback (the latter two presumably for its profile).

2. For further discussion of rewilding, see Klyza.

3. Also a member of the faculty at Tufts University, Charles E. Fay held the following positions in the AMC during his membership: president (in 1878 and 1893), vice-president, councilor of art, councilor of explorations, corresponding secretary, trustee of real estate and editor of the AMC's journal, *Appalachia*, for almost forty years (Rowan and Rowan 17).

4. Hanrahan's edition of Bent's bibliography identifies thirty book-length guides and histories and more than one hundred magazine articles (not including the dozens of articles published in the Appalachian Mountain Club's journal *Appalachia* and the countless others printed in local newspapers) published between 1875 and 1900.

5. The brief period of Bolles's and Torrey's canonization is further illustrated by the 1909 publication of Thoreau and others, *In American Fields and Forests*.

6. Bolles was also interested in changing the name of Pequaket (near what is now Conway) to the name of his beloved Chocorua.

7. Bryant Tolles Jr. has cataloged White Mountain hotels with a capacity of at least fifty guests built before 1930. According to Tolles's table (239–46), in the summer of 1890, there were rooms for between 16,670 and 18,020 guests distributed among the following White Mountain towns (number of guest accommodations in parentheses): Albany (60–70), Bartlett (475–680), Bethlehem (3,015–3,170), Carroll (1,050–1,200), Colebrook (275), Conway (75–125), Crawford Notch (470–520), Dalton (75), Dixville Notch (400+), Franconia (1,072–1,137), Gorham (250–75), Holderness (380), Jackson (1,005–75), Jefferson (1,175–1,275), Lancaster (300), Lincoln (300), Lisbon (175–210), Littleton (425), Mount Moosilauke (60), Mount Washington (280–330), North Conway (1,725–1,915), North Woodstock (460–550), Pinkham Notch (500), Plymouth (250–300), Randolph (185–210), Sandwich (50), Shelburne (125–50), Stratford (50), Sugar Hill (925–75), Tamworth (225), Warren (210), Waterville Valley (175–200), Whitefield (420–70).

8. Alan Phenix, Frank Bolles's great grandson, believes Bolles's principal intention in planting grains was to attract birds to the property (personal interview, 2 April 2002).

9. For more information on Murray, see Strauss and Waterman and Waterman 161–66.

10. David Strauss makes the point that Murray's vacations "mentioned only ministers, businessmen, lawyers, and bankers. Farmers and city workers were conspicuously absent" (275).

11. For further discussion, see Judd and Fainstein and Urry.

12. In a 15 October 1891 note to his Chocorua neighbor, C. P. Bowditch, Bolles states that he "ran a chain around Chocorua Pond (the larger one)" to calculate the lake's size to be 235 acres. "As I did not follow all the undulations," Bolles adds, "a few acres can be added." Tamworth Historical Society, Wiesner Bolles Collection, No. 58.

13. Mitchell and Diamant define the "humanized landscape" as "the ecotone where civilization and wilderness meet. These are lands that have long had a human imprint,

areas traditionally used for agriculture or forestry or developed as town and cities" (216).

14. Allen Thompson was occasionally employed as an "axe-man," or guide, for tramps into less-explored regions of the forest. For instance, he was the senior guide on the notable seven-day traverse of much of the Twin Range north of the Pemigewassett wilderness led by A. E. Scott in 1882. See *Echo* of 9 July 1879 for one such article.

15. See Tolles 109–10 for an overview of the expansion of railways in the White Mountains between 1869 and 1882.

16. The overlap between scientific and guidebook writing was substantial. For instance, Joshua Huntington, a member of Charles Hitchcock's surveying team in 1869–1871, was also a guide for Moses Sweetser when he was collecting notes for his guidebook *The White Mountains,* originally published only two years after Hitchcock's *Geology.*

17. Mary Campbell considers the both/and symbiosis of wonder and science in her book and questions the marginalization of wonder in contemporary scientific discourse: "Its status in the last stages of modern Western culture in its dominant form is ambivalent — it is eschewed but also craved, wildly popular and markedly absent as a value, in discourses of power such as those of business, government, the sciences, and 'rigorous' scholarship" (4). David Abram, in a study of wonder in our relationships with the nonhuman world, critiques the role of the "Western industrial society" in separating itself from the diversity of multicultural human and nonhuman "voices, to continue by our lifestyles to condemn these other sensibilities to the oblivion of extinction, is to rob our own senses of their integrity, and to rob our minds of their coherence. We are human only in contact, and conviviality, with what is not human" (22).

18. George McAvoy reports that by 1882, four grand hotels in the town accommodated more than a thousand guests nightly (McAvoy 71–72). Bryant Tolles Jr. writes that the Second Glen House, built between 1884 and 1887 on Mount Washington's east side, could house 500 guests each night (193). By the early 1900s, the newly completed Mount Washington Hotel could accommodate more than 400 guests nightly (Tolles 221). In contrast, the smaller, family-run establishment of Philbrook Farm Inn was set somewhat apart from the mountains and grew to accommodate only 75 guests as late as 1934 (Tolles 164).

19. Specific inadequacies of the Walling map are noted by Marian Pychowska in letters to Isabella Stone (Rowan and Rowan 78 and 123).

20. Fore more examples of nineteenth-century conservation attitudes, see Walker's addresses. Also see *New England Homestead* (esp. 19 January 1901) on resort owners' responses to growing logging practices.

21. Rowan and Rowan detail Stone's accomplishments near North Woodstock, noting that she "was responsible for the trails to Georgiana and Bridal Veil Falls, obtaining rights of way from property owners and urging the Appalachian Mountain Club . . . to hire local woodsmen to work on improving those trails" (4).

Abram, David. *The Spell of the Sensuous: Perception and Language in a More-Than-Human World.* New York: Vintage Books, 1996.

Allen, Ethan. *The Legend of the Curse of Chocorua.* Ashland, New Hampshire: Grafton Independent Order of Odd Fellows Lodge No. 62, 1931.

"Allen Thompson: White Mountain Guide, Hunter and Trapper. — A Veritable Nimrod of the Hills." *The White Mountain Echo and Tourist Register,* 9 July 1879: 1.

Anderson, John, and Stearns Morse. *The Book of the White Mountains.* New York: Minton, Balch, 1930.

Atkinson, Brooks, and W. Kent Olson. *New England's White Mountains: At Home in the Wild.* Boston: Appalachian Mountain Club, 1978. [Originally published as *Of Skyline Promenades: A Potpourri,* 1925.]

Bacon, William. "Unenclosed Lands." *Cultivator* 5 (1848): 58 – 59.

Ball, Benjamin L. *Three Days on the White Mountains: Being the Perilous Adventure of Dr. B. L. Ball on Mount Washington, during Oct. 25, 26, and 27, 1855, Written by Himself.* Boston: Lockwood, Brooks, 1877.

Bancroft, George. *History of the United States from the Discovery of the American Continent.* Vol. 2. Boston: Charles Bowen, 1837.

Barron, Hal S. *Those Who Stayed Behind: Rural Society in Nineteenth Century New England.* Cambridge, U.K.: Cambridge University Press, 1984.

Barstow, George. *The History of New Hampshire from Its Discovery in 1614, to the Passage of the Toleration Act, in 1819.* Concord, New Hampshire: I. S. Boyd, 1842.

Barton, B. S. "Notice of the Botany of the White Mountains." *Philadelphia Medical and Physical Journal* 2 (1806): 57 – 58.

Bartram, William. *The Travels of William Bartram.* Athens: University of Georgia Press, 1998.

Belcher, Francis C. *Logging Railroads of the White Mountains.* Boston: Appalachian Mountain Club, 1990.

Belknap, Jeremy. *The Belknap Papers.* Ser. 5, vols. 2 and 3. Boston: Massachusetts Historical Society, 1877 – 1891.

———. *The Belknap Papers.* Ser. 6, vol. 3. Boston: Massachusetts Historical Society, 1877 – 1891.

———. "Description of the White Mountains in New Hampshire." *Transactions of the American Philosophical Society* 2 (1786): 42 – 49.

———. *History of New Hampshire.* 3 vols. Boston: Lockwood, Brooks, 1877.

———. *Journal of a Tour of the White Mountains in July 1784.* Boston: Historical Society, 1876.

Bennett, Dean B. *The Forgotten Nature of New England.* Camden, Maine: Down East Books, 1996.

Berry, Wendell. *The Unsettling of America: Culture and Agriculture.* San Francisco: Sierra Club, 1977.

Bidwell, Percy Wells. "Rural Economy in New England at the Beginning of the Nineteenth Century." *Transactions of the Connecticut Academy of Arts and Sciences* 20 (April 1916): 241–399.

Bigelow, Jacob. "Some Account of the White Mountains of New Hampshire." *New England Journal of Medicine and Surgery* (October 1816): 321–38.

Bishop, William Henry. "The Abandoned Farm Found, or the Country Home and the New Means of Transportation." *Century Magazine* 40 (1901): 884–92.

———. "Hunting an Abandoned Farm in Upper New England." *Century Magazine* 26 (1894): 30–43.

Boardman, Julie. *When Women and Mountains Meet: Adventures in the White Mountains.* Etna, New Hampshire: Durand Press, 2001.

Bolles, Frank. *At the North of Bearcamp Water: Chronicles of a Stroller in New England from July to December.* Boston: Houghton Mifflin, 1899.

———. "Deserted Homes." Typescript. Wiesner Collection No. 69. Tamworth, New Hampshire, Historical Society.

———. *Land of the Lingering Snow: Chronicles of a Stroller in New England from January to June.* Boston: Houghton Mifflin, 1891.

———. "Three Days in the Snow." Wiesner Collection. Tamworth, New Hampshire, Historical Society.

Brackett, Adino Nye. "Sketches of the White Mountains." In *Collections, Historical and Miscellaneous,* edited by J. Farmer and J. B. Moore, 97–107. Concord, New Hampshire: Hill and Moore, 1822.

Bradford, William. *Of Plymouth Plantation, 1620–1647.* New York: Modern Library, 1981.

Branch, Michael. "Indexing American Possibilities: The Natural History Writing of Bartram, Wilson, and Audubon." In *The Ecocriticism Reader: Landmarks in Literary Ecology,* edited by Cheryl Glotfelty and Harold Fromm, 282–302. Athens: University of Georgia Press, 1996.

Branch, Michael, Rochelle Johnson, Daniel Patterson, and Scott Slovic, eds. *Reading the Earth: New Directions in the Study of Literature and the Environment.* Moscow: University of Idaho Press, 1998.

Brown, Alice. *Meadow Grass: Tales of New England Life.* Boston: Geo. H. Walker, 1895.

Brown, Dona. *Inventing New England: Regional Tourism in the Nineteenth Century.* Washington, D.C.: Smithsonian Institution Press, 1995.

Bryant, William Cullen. *Picturesque American; or, The Land We Live In.* 2 vols. New York: D. Appleton, 1872–1874.

Buell, Lawrence. *The Environmental Imagination: Thoreau, Nature Writing, and the Formation of American Culture.* Cambridge, Massachusetts: Belknap Press, 1995.

———. *New England Literary Culture: From Revolution through Renaissance.* Cambridge, U.K.: Cambridge University Press, 1986.

———. *Writing for an Endangered World: Literature, Culture and Environment in the U.S. and Beyond.* Cambridge, Massachusetts: Belknap Press, 2001.

Bulkley, Peter B. "Identifying the White Mountain Tourist, 1853–54: Origin, Occupation, and Wealth as a Definition of the Early Hotel Trade." *Historical New Hampshire* 35.2 (1980): 107–62.

Burke, Edmund. *A Philosophical Enquiry into the Origin of Our Ideas of the Sublime and Beautiful.* Edited by James T. Boulton. London, U.K.: Routledge, 1958.

Byerly, Alison. "The Uses of Landscape: The Picturesque Aesthetic and the National Park System." In *The Ecocriticism Reader: Landmarks in Literary Ecology*, edited by Cheryl Glotfelty and Harold Fromm, 52–68. Athens: University of Georgia Press, 1996.

Campbell, Catherine H., Donald D. Keyes, Robert L. McGrath, and R. Stuart Wallace. *The White Mountains: Place and Perceptions.* Hanover, New Hampshire: University Press of New England, 1980.

Campbell, Mary Baine. *The Witness and the Other World: Exotic European Travel Writing, 400–1600.* Ithaca, New York: Cornell University Press, 1988.

———. *Wonder and Science: Imagining Worlds in Early Modern Europe.* Ithaca, New York: Cornell University Press, 1999.

Carroll, Aileen M. *The Latchstring Was Always Out: A History of Lodging Hospitality and Tourism in Bartlett, New Hampshire.* Portsmouth, New Hampshire: Peter Randall, 1994.

Carter, Erica, James Donald, and Judith Squires. *Space and Place: Theories of Identity and Location.* London, U.K.: Lawrence and Wishart, 1993.

Casarotto, Joan. "Frank Bolles." Unpublished essay, 1999. Remick Country Doctor Museum and Farm, Tamworth, New Hampshire.

Casey, Edward S. *Representing Place: Landscape Painting and Maps.* Minneapolis: University of Minnesota Press, 2002.

Champney, Benjamin. *Sixty Years' Memories of Art and Artists.* Woburn, Massachusetts: Wallace and Andrews, 1900.

Chaney, Michael P. *Beauty Caught and Kept: Benjamin Champney in the White Mountains.* Spec. issue of *Historical New Hampshire* 51.3–4 (1996): 67–135.

Chastellux, Marquis de. *Travels in North America in the Years 1780, 1781, and 1782.* Edited by Howard Rice. Chapel Hill: University of North Carolina Press, 1963.

Child, Hamilton. *Gazetteer of Grafton County, N.H., 1709–1886.* Syracuse, New York: Syracuse Journal Company, 1886.

Child, Lydia Maria. *The Coronal: A Collection of Miscellaneous Pieces, Written at Various Times.* Boston: Carter and Hendee, 1831.

———. *Hobomok and Other Writings on Indians.* New Brunswick, New Jersey: Rutgers University Press, 1992.

Clark, Charles E. *The Eastern Frontier: The Settlement of Northern New England, 1610–1763.* New York: Knopf, 1970.

Clifford, James. Introduction to *Writing Culture: The Poetics and Politics of Ethnography*, edited by James Clifford and George E. Marcus. Berkeley: University of California Press, 1986.

Cole, Thomas. "Essay on American Scenery." In *American Art, 1700–1960*, edited by John W. McCoubrey, 98–109. Englewood Cliffs, N.J.: Prentice-Hall, 1965.

———. "Sketch of My Tour to the White Mountains with Mr. Pratt." *Bulletin of the Detroit Institute of Arts* 66.1 (1990): 27–33.

Conzen, Michael P., ed. *The Making of American Landscape.* Boston: Unwin Hyman, 1990.

Cooper, Susan Fenimore. *Rural Hours.* Edited by Rochelle Jackson and Daniel Patterson. Atlanta: University of Georgia Press, 1998.

Cosgrove, Denis E., and Stephen Daniels, eds. *The Iconography of Landscape: Essays on the Symbolic Representation, Design, and Use of Past Environments.* New York: Cambridge University Press, 1988.

Cox, T., R. Maxwell, P. Thomas, and J. Malone. *This Well-Wooded Land: Americans and Their Forests from Colonial Times to the Present.* Lincoln: University of Nebraska Press, 1985.

Crawford, Lucy. *The History of the White Mountains.* Portland, Maine: F. A. and A. F. Gerrish, 1846.

———. *History of the White Mountains.* Edited by John T. B. Mudge. Etna, New Hampshire: Durand Press, 1999.

———. *The History of the White Mountains, from the First Settlement of Upper Coos and Pequaket.* Edited by Henry Wheelock Ripley. Portland, Maine: B. Thurston, 1886. [Cited as Crawford 1886 in text.]

———. "The History of the White Mountains, with the Life of Ethan Allen Crawford. From the First Settlement of Upper Coos and Pequaket." Unpublished ms., 1860. Crawford Papers. [Cited as 1860 ms. in text.]

Crawford Papers. Ms. no. 626. Rauner Special Collections, Dartmouth College Library, Hanover, New Hampshire.

Crèvecoeur, Hector St. John de. *Letters from an American Farmer and Sketches of Eighteenth-Century America.* New York: Penguin Books, 1981.

Cronon, William. *Changes in the Land: Indians, Colonists, and the Ecology of New England.* New York: Hill and Wang, 1983.

———. "The Trouble with Wilderness; or, Getting Back to the Wrong Nature." In *Uncommon Ground: Rethinking the Human Place in Nature,* edited by William Cronon, 69–90. New York: W. W. Norton, 1996.

Cutler, William Parker, and Julia Perkins Cutler. *Life, Journals and Correspondence of Rev. Manasseh Cutler, LL.D.* 2 vols. Cincinnati: Robert Clarke, 1888.

De Certeau, Michel. *The Practice of Everyday Life.* Trans. Steven Rendall. Berkeley: University of California Press, 1984.

Dickerman, Mike. *Why I'll Never Hike the Appalachian Trail: More Writings from a White Mountains Tramper.* Littleton, New Hampshire: Bondcliff Books, 1997.

———, ed. *Mount Washington: Narratives and Perspectives.* Littleton, New Hampshire: Bondcliff Books, 1999.

Dobbs, David, and Richard Ober. *The Northern Forest.* White River Junction, Vermont: Chelsea Green, 1995.

Drake, Samuel Adams. *The Heart of the White Mountains: Their Legend and Scenery.* New York: Harper and Brothers, 1882.

Dwight, Theodore. *The Northern Traveler; Containing the Routes to Niagara, Que-*

bec, and the Springs; with Descriptions of the Principal Scenes, and Useful Hints to Strangers. New York: Wilder and Campbell, 1825.

Dwight, Timothy. "Greenfield Hill." In *Early American Poetry*, edited by Jane Donahue Eberwein, 139–89. Madison: University of Wisconsin Press, 1978.

———. *Travels in New-England and New-York, 1821–1822.* Vol. 2. Cambridge, Massachusetts: Harvard University Press, 1969.

Eastman, Samuel C. *The White Mountain Guide Book.* Concord, New Hampshire: E. C. Eastman, 1858.

Ehrlich, Gretel. "Landscape." In *Legacy of Light*, edited by Constance Sullivan, 17–21. New York: Knopf, 1987.

Elder, John. "The Poetry of Experience." In *Beyond Nature Writing: Expanding the Boundaries of Ecocriticism*, edited by Karla Armbruster and Kathleen R. Wallace, 213–24. Charlottesville: University of Virginia Press, 2001.

———. *Reading the Mountains of Home.* Cambridge, Massachusetts: Harvard University Press, 1998.

Emerson, Ralph Waldo. *Essays and Lectures.* Compiled by Joel Porte. New York: Library of America, 1983.

Entrikin, J. Nicholas. *The Betweenness of Place: Towards a Geography of Modernity.* Baltimore: Johns Hopkins University Press, 1991.

Erdrich, Louise. *Love Medicine.* New York: Harper Perennial, 1993.

Evernden, Neil. *The Social Creation of Nature.* Baltimore: Johns Hopkins University Press, 1992.

Farmer, John, and Jacob Moore. *A Gazetteer of the State of New Hampshire.* Concord, New Hampshire: Jacob B. Moore, 1823.

Fay, Charles E. "Mount Passaconaway." *Appalachia* 16 (1892): 302–18.

Fiedler, Leslie A. *The Return of the Vanishing American.* New York: Stein and Day, 1968.

Fields, Annie, ed. *Letters of Sarah Orne Jewett.* Boston: Houghton Mifflin, 1911.

Fisher, Philip. "Democratic Social Space: Whitman, Melville, and the Promise of American Transparency." *Representations* 24 (1988): 60–101.

Forman, Richard, and Michael Gordon. *Landscape Ecology.* New York: John Wiley and Sons, 1986.

Foss, Sam Walter. "Deserted Farms." In *New Hampshire Literature*, edited by Robert C. Gilmore, 200. Hanover, New Hampshire: University Press of New England, 1981.

Franklin, Wayne. *Discoverers, Explorers, Settlers: The Diligent Writers of Early America.* Chicago: University of Chicago Press, 1979.

———, and Michael Steiner, eds. *Mapping American Culture.* Iowa City: University of Iowa Press, 1992.

Frost, Robert. *The Poetry of Robert Frost.* Edited by Edward Connery Lathem. New York: Henry Holt, 1975.

Fuller, Margaret. *A Summer on the Lakes, in 1843.* Urbana: University of Illinois Press, 1991.

Gilmore, William. *Reading Becomes a Necessity of Life: Material and Cultural Life in Rural New England, 1780–1835.* Knoxville: University of Tennessee Press, 1989.

———, ed. *New Hampshire Literature: A Sampler*. Hanover, New Hampshire: 1981.

Glotfelty, Cheryl, and Harold Fromm. *The Ecocriticism Reader: Landmarks in Literary Ecology*. Athens: University of Georgia Press, 1996.

Gorges, Thomas. *The Letters of Thomas Gorges*. Edited by Robert E. Moody. Portland, Maine: Portland Historical Society, 1978.

Gove, Bill. *J. E. Henry's Logging Railroads: The History of the East Branch and Lincoln and Zealand Valley Railroads*. Littleton, New Hampshire: Bondcliff Books, 1998.

Greenblatt, Stephen. *Marvelous Possessions: The Wonder of the New World*. Chicago: University of Chicago Press, 1991.

Greenfield, Bruce. *The Romantic Explorer in American Literature, 1790–1855*. New York: Columbia University Press, 1992.

Gregory, Derek. *Ideology, Science, and Human Geography*. London, U.K.: Hutchinson, 1978.

Hale, Sarah Joseph. *Northwood; or, Life North and South*. Freeport, New York: Books for Libraries Press, 1972.

———. *Traits of American Life*. Philadelphia: Carey and Lea, 1835.

Hall, Basil. *Travels in North America in the Years 1827–1828*. Edinburgh, U.K.: Cadell, 1830.

Hall, Joseph Fred. *The Legend of Chocorua: A Story of the Hills of New Hampshire*. Norwood, Massachusetts: Ambrose Brothers, 1915.

Hancock, Ann Johnson. *Saving the Great Stone Face: The Chronicle of the Old Man of the Mountain*. Canaan, New Hampshire: Phoenix, 1984.

Hanrahan, E. J., ed. *Bent's Bibliography of the White Mountains*. Somersworth, New Hampshire: New Hampshire Publishing, 1971.

Harkness, Marjory Gene. *The Tamworth Narrative*. Freeport, Maine: Bond Wheelwright, 1958.

Harrington, Karl. *Walks and Climbs in the White Mountains*. New Haven, Connecticut: Yale University Press, 1926.

Hathaway, Richard D. *Sylvester Judd's New England*. University Park: Pennsylvania State University Press, 1981.

Hawthorne, Nathaniel. "The Ambitious Guest." *New-England Magazine,* June 1835: 425–31.

———. *The Great Stone Face and Other Tales of the White Mountains*. Boston: Houghton Mifflin, 1935.

———. *Hawthorne's American Travel Sketches*. Edited by Alfred Weber, Beth Lueck, and Dennis Berthold. Hanover, New Hampshire: University of New England Press, 1989.

Haycox, Stephen Walter. *Jeremy Belknap and Early American Nationalism: A Study in the Political and Theological Foundations of American Liberty*. Ann Arbor, Michigan: University Microfilms, 1974.

Hayward, John. *A Gazetteer of New Hampshire* [1849]. Reprinted, Bowie, Maryland: Heritage Books, 1993.

Hazlitt, William. "On Going a Journey." *New Monthly Magazine and Literary Journal,* January 1822: 73–79.

Heffernan, Nancy Coffey, and Ann Page Stecker. *New Hampshire: Crosscurrents in Its Development*. Grantham, New Hampshire: Tompson and Rutter, 1986.

Henck, J. B., Jr. "A New Map of the White Mountains." *Appalachia* 1.1 (1876): 26–29.

Henderson, John J. *Incomparable Scenery: Comparable Views in the White Mountains*. Glenn, New Hampshire: Glenn-Bartlett, 1999.

Hitchcock, Charles H. *The Geology of New Hampshire*. Concord, New Hampshire: Edward A. Jenks, 1874.

Hough, Franklin B. "On the Duty of Governments in the Preservation of Forests." In *Proceedings of the American Association for the Advancement of Science,* edited by F. W. Putnam, 1–10. Salem, New Hampshire: Salem Press, 1873.

Howarth, William. "Some Principles of Ecocriticism." In *The Ecocriticism Reader: Landmarks in Literary Ecology*, edited by Cheryl Glotfelty and Harold Fromm, 69–91. Athens: University of Georgia Press, 1996.

———. *Thoreau in the Mountains*. New York: Farrar, Straus and Giroux, 1982.

Irving, Washington. *A Tour on the Prairies* [1835]. Reprinted, Norman: University of Oklahoma Press, 1956.

Jackson, Charles T. *Final Report on the Geology and Mineralogy of the State of New Hampshire*. Concord, New Hampshire: Carrol and Baker, 1844.

James, Henry. *The American Scene*. Bloomington: Indiana University Press, 1969.

Jefferson, Thomas. *Notes on the State of Virginia*. New York: Penguin Books, 1999.

Jewett, Sarah Orne. *The Country of the Pointed Firs*. Boston: Houghton Mifflin, 1896.

———. *Deephaven*. Boston: James R. Osgood, 1877.

Johnson, Clifton. *Highways and By-Ways of New England*. New York: Macmillan, 1915.

Josselyn, John. *John Josselyn, Colonial Traveler: A Critical Edition of Two Voyages to New-England*, edited by Paul J. Lindholdt. Hanover, New Hampshire: University Press of New England, 1988.

———. *New England Rarities Discovered*. London, U.K.: G. Widdowes, 1672.

Judd, D. R., and S. S. Fainstein, eds. *The Tourist City*. New Haven, Connecticut: Yale University Press, 1999.

Judd, Richard W. *Common Lands, Common People: The Origins of Conservation in Northern New England*. Cambridge, Massachusetts: Harvard University Press, 1997.

Judd, Sylvester. *Margaret: A Tale of the Real and the Ideal, Blight and Bloom*. Boston: Roberts Brothers, 1871.

Julyan, Robert, and Mary Julyan. *Place Names of the White Mountains*. Hanover, New Hampshire: University Press of New England, 1993.

Kawashima, Yasuhide. "Forest Conservation Policy in Early New England." *Historical Journal of Massachusetts* 20 (1992): 1–15.

Kendall, Edward Augustus. *Travels throughout the Northern Parts of the United States in the Years 1807 and 1808*. Vol. 3. New York: I. Riley, 1809.

Keyes, Donald. "Harmony of Man and Nature in the Valley of Conway." *A Suburb of Paradise: The White Mountains and the Visual Arts*. Special issue of *Historical New Hampshire* 54.3–4 (1999): 71–172.

Kieth, Michael, and Steve Pile, eds. *Place and the Politics of Identity*. New York: Routledge, 1993.

Kilbourne, Frederick W. *Chronicles of the White Mountains*. Boston: Houghton Mifflin, 1916.

King, Thomas Starr. *The White Hills: Their Legends, Landscape, and Poetry* [1859]. New York: Hurd and Houghton, 1870.

Klyza, Christopher McGrory, ed. *Wilderness Comes Home: Rewilding the Northeast*. Hanover, New Hampshire: Middlebury Press, 2001.

Knox, M. V. B. "Notes on the Slide at Jefferson." *Appalachia* 4 (March 1886): 254–56.

Kolodny, Annette. *The Land before Her: Fantasy and Experience of the American Frontiers, 1630–1860*. Chapel Hill: University of North Carolina Press, 1984.

Koop, Jennifer. "Randolph, New Hampshire, a Special Community: Founded by Farmers, Transformed by Trailmakers." *Historical New Hampshire* 49.3 (1994): 133–56.

Krupat, Arnold. *For Those Who Come After: A Study of Native American Autobiography*. Berkeley: University of California Press, 1985.

LaBastille, Anne. *Women and Wilderness*. San Francisco: Sierra Club Books, 1980.

Lawson, Russell. "Elder Scripture: Jeremy Belknap's Journey to the White Mountains in 1784." *Historical New Hampshire* 49.4 (1994): 201–27.

———. *Passaconaway's Realm: Captain John Evans and the Exploration of Mount Washington*. Hanover, New Hampshire: University Press of New England, 2002.

Lawson-Peebles, Robert. *Landscape and Written Expression in Revolutionary America*. New York: Cambridge University Press, 1988.

The Life of Frank Bolles as Told in His Letters and Journals. Ms. 66. Wiesner Collection. Tamworth, New Hampshire, Historical Society.

Little, Daniel. "Journals of Reverend Daniel Little." Unpublished ms., Brick Store Museum, Kennebunk, Maine.

Lopez, Barry. *About This Life: Journeys on the Threshold of Memory*. Toronto: Random House, 1998.

MacCannell, Dean. *The Tourist: A New Theory of the Leisure Class*. Berkeley: University of California Press, 1999.

———. "Tourist Agency." *Tourist Studies* 1.1 (2001): 23–38.

Maclean, Norman. *Young Men and Fire*. Chicago: University of Chicago Press, 1992.

Maclear, Anne Bush. *Early New England Towns: A Comparative Study of Their Development*. New York: Columbia University Press, 1908.

Marchand, Peter J. *North Woods: An Inside Look at the Nature of Forests in the Northeast*. Boston: Appalachian Mountain Club, 1987.

Marsh, George Perkins. *Man and Nature: Physical Geography as Modified by Human Action*. Cambridge, Massachusetts: Harvard University Press, 1965.

Marshall, David, ed. *The New Hampshire Book, Being Specimens of the Literature of the Granite State*. Boston: James Munrose, 1842.

Marshall, Ian. *Story Line: Exploring the Literature of the Appalachian Trail*. Charlottesville: University of Virginia Press, 1998.

Marx, Leo. *The Machine in the Garden: Technology and the Pastoral Ideal in America*. New York: Oxford University Press, 1964.

McAvoy, George E. *And Then There Was One: A History of the Hotels of the Summit and the West Side of Mt. Washington*. Littleton, New Hampshire: Crawford Press, 1988.

McDowell, Michael J. "The Bakhtinian Road to Ecological Insight." In *The Eco-criticism Reader: Landmarks in Literary Ecology*, edited by Cheryl Glotfelty and Harold Fromm, 371–91. Athens: University of Georgia Press, 1996.

McGrath, Robert. *Gods in Granite: The Art of the White Mountains of New Hampshire*. Syracuse, New York: Syracuse University Press, 2001.

———. "The Real and the Ideal: Popular Images of the White Mountains." In *The White Mountains: Place and Perceptions*, edited by Catherine H. Campbell, Donald D. Keyes, Robert L. McGrath, and R. Stuart Wallace, 59–69. Durham, New Hampshire: University Press of New England, 1980.

McGrath, Robert, and Barbara MacAdam. *"A Sweet Foretaste of Heaven": Artists in the White Mountains, 1830–1930*. Hanover, New Hampshire: University Press of New England, 1988.

McKibben, Bill. *Hope, Human and Wild: True Stories of Living Lightly on the Earth*. Saint Paul, Minnesota: Hungry Mind Press, 1995.

McNulty, J. Bard, ed. *Correspondence of Thomas Cole and Daniel Wadsworth*. Hartford: Connecticut Historical Society, 1983.

Melish, John. *Travels through the United States of America in the Years 1806 and 1807, and 1809, 1810, and 1811*. London, U.K.: George Cowie, 1813.

Merchant, Carolyn. *Ecological Revolutions: Nature, Gender, and Science in New England*. Chapel Hill: University of North Carolina Press, 1989.

———, ed. *Major Problems in American Environmental History*. Lexington, Massachusetts: D. C. Heath, 1993.

Merrill, Georgia Drew, comp. *History of Coos County* [1888]. Reprinted, Somersworth, New Hampshire: New Hampshire Publishing, 1972.

Mevers, Frank C., and Mica B. Stark. "The Making of the Carrigain Map of New Hampshire, 1803–1816." *Historical New Hampshire* 54.3–4 (1997): 79–95.

Meyer, Kinereth. "Possessing America: William Carlos Williams's *Paterson* and the Poetics of Appropriation." In *Mapping American Culture*, edited by Wayne Franklin and Michael Steiner, 152–70. Iowa City: University of Iowa Press, 1992.

Miller, Angela. "The Mechanisms of the Market and the Invention of Western Regionalism: The Example of George Caleb Bingham." In *American Iconology: New Approaches to Nineteenth-Century Art and Literature*, edited by David C. Miller, 112–34. New Haven, Connecticut: Yale University Press, 1993.

Miller, David C. Introduction to *American Iconology: New Approaches to Nineteenth-Century Art and Literature*. New Haven, Connecticut: Yale University Press, 1993.

Mitchell, John Hanson. *Ceremonial Time: Fifteen Thousand Years on One Square Mile*. Reading, Massachusetts: Addison-Wesley, 1984.

Mitchell, Nora, and Rolf Diamant. "Stewardship and Sustainability: Lessons from the 'Middle Landscape' of Vermont." In *Wilderness Comes Home: Rewilding the Northeast*, edited by Christopher McGrory Klyza, 213–33. Hanover, New Hampshire: Middlebury Press, 2001.

Mitchell, W. J. T. *Iconology: Image, Text, Ideology*. Chicago: University of Chicago Press, 1986.

———, ed. *Landscape and Power*. Chicago: University of Chicago Press, 1994.

Monmonier, Mark. *Mapping It Out: Expository Cartography for the Humanities and Social Sciences.* Chicago: University of Chicago Press, 1993.

Morse, Stearns. *Lucy Crawford's History of the White Mountains.* Boston: Appalachian Mountain Club, 1978.

Mott, Frank Luther. *A History of American Magazines: 1850 – 1865.* Cambridge, Massachusetts: Belknap Press, 1967.

Mudge, John T. B. *The Old Man's Reader: History and Legends of Franconia Notch.* Etna, New Hampshire: Durand Press, 1995.

Mugerauer, Robert. *Interpreting Environments: Tradition, Deconstruction, Hermeneutics.* Austin: University of Texas Press, 1995.

Muir, John. *A Thousand-Mile Walk to the Gulf.* San Francisco: Sierra Club, 1991.

Murray, William Henry Harrison. *Adventures in the Wilderness; or, Camp-Life in the Adirondacks.* Boston: Field and Osgood, 1869.

Musgrove, Eugene R., ed. *The White Hills in Poetry: An Anthology.* Boston: Houghton Mifflin, 1912.

Myers, Kenneth John. "On the Cultural Construction of Landscape Experience: Contact to 1830." In *American Iconology: New Approaches to Nineteenth-Century Art and Literature,* edited by David C. Miller, 58 – 79. New Haven, Connecticut: Yale University Press, 1993.

Nash, Roderick Frazier. *Wilderness and the American Mind.* New Haven, Connecticut: Yale University Press, 1967.

Novak, Barbara. *American Painting of the Late Nineteenth Century: Realism, Idealism, and the American Experience.* New York: Harper and Row, 1979.

———. *Nature and Culture: American Landscape Painting, 1825 – 1875.* New York: Oxford University Press, 1995.

Nowell, W. G. "A Mountain Suite for Women." *Appalachia* 1 (1877): 181 – 83.

Oakes, William. *Scenery of the White Mountains.* Boston: Little, Brown, 1848.

O'Grady, John P. "Bodega Head: An Excursion in Nuclear Shamanism." *Reading the Earth: New Directions in the Study of Literature and the Environment,* edited by Michael Branch, Rochelle Johnson, Daniel Patterson, and Scott Slovic, 41 – 51. Moscow: University of Idaho Press, 1998.

Orr, David W. *Earth in Mind: On Education, Environment, and the Human Prospect.* Washington, D.C.: Island Books, 1994.

———. *Pilgrims to the Wild.* Salt Lake City: University of Utah Press, 1993.

Parsons, Thomas William. *The Willey House and Sonnets.* Cambridge, Massachusetts: John Wilson, 1875.

Partridge, Alden. "The Altitude of Moose-Hillock in New Hampshire Ascertained Barometrically." *American Monthly Magazine* 2 (1817): 51 – 52.

Poole, Earnest. *The Great White Hills of New Hampshire.* New York: Doubleday, 1946.

Pratt, Mary Louise. *Imperial Eyes: Travel Writing and Transculturation.* New York: Routledge, 1992.

Purchase, Eric. *Out of Nowhere: Disaster and Tourism in the White Mountains.* Baltimore: Johns Hopkins University Press, 1999.

Pychowska, Marian. "Evans Notch, Royce, and Baldface." *Appalachia* 3 (December 1883): 264–71.

———. "A Partial Exploration of Mt. Wildcat." *Appalachia* 3 (December 1883): 271–74.

Raymo, Chet. *Written in Stone: A Geological and Natural History of the Northeastern United States.* Chester, Connecticut: Globe Pequot Press, 1991.

Rebek, Andrea. "The Selling of Vermont: From Agriculture to Tourism, 1860–1910." *Vermont History* 44.1 (1976): 14–27.

Regis, Pamela. *Describing Early America: Bartram, Jefferson, Crèvecoeur, and the Rhetoric of Natural History.* DeKalb: Northern Illinois University Press, 1992.

Robtoy, Hilda, Dee Brightstar, Tom Obomsawin, and John Moody. "The Abenaki and the Northern Forest." In *The Future of the Northern Forest,* edited by Christopher McGrory Klyza and Stephen C. Trombulak, 27–35. Hanover, New Hampshire: University Press of New England, 1994.

Rogers, Sherbrooke. *Sarah Josepha Hale: A New England Pioneer, 1788–1879.* Grantham, New Hampshire: Tompson and Rutter, 1985.

Rorty, Richard. *Philosophy and the Mirror of Nature.* Princeton, New Jersey: Princeton University Press, 1979.

Rowan, Peter, and June Hammond Rowan, eds. *Mountain Summers: Tales of Hiking and Exploration in the White Mountains from 1878 to 1886 as Seen through the Eyes of Women.* Gorham, New Hampshire: Gulfside Press, 1995.

Ruskin, Judith A. "Thomas Cole and the White Mountains: The Picturesque, the Sublime, and the Magnificent." *Bulletin of the Detroit Institute of Arts* 66.1 (1990): 19–25.

Ryden, Kent C. *Landscape with Figures: Nature and Culture in New England.* Iowa City: University of Iowa Press, 2001.

———. *Mapping the Invisible Landscape: Folklore, Writing, and the Sense of Place.* Iowa City: University of Iowa Press, 1993.

Said, Edward W. "Identity, Authority, and Freedom: The Potentate and the Traveler." *Boundary* 2.21 (1994): 1–18.

Sanborn, Edwin D. *History of New Hampshire, from Its First Discovery to the Year 1830.* Manchester, New Hampshire: John B. Clarke, 1875.

Sanders, Scott Russell. "Speaking a Word for Nature." In *The Ecocriticism Reader: Landmarks in Literary Ecology,* edited by Cheryl Glotfelty and Harold Fromm, 182–95. Athens: University of Georgia Press, 1996.

Sayre, Robert F., ed. *Henry David Thoreau.* New York: Library of America, 1985.

Schama, Simon. *Landscape and Memory.* New York: Knopf, 1995.

Scheese, Don. *Nature Writing: The Pastoral Impulse in America.* New York: Twayne, 1996.

Sears, John F. *Sacred Places: American Tourist Attractions in the Nineteenth Century.* New York: Oxford University Press, 1989.

Sedgwick, Catherine Maria. *Hope Leslie; or, Early Times in Massachusetts.* New York: White, Gallaher, and White, 1827.

———. *A New-England Tale; or, Sketches of New-England Character and Manners.* New York: E. Bliss and E. White, 1822.

Shattuck, George. "Some Account of an Excursion to the White Hills of New Hampshire in the Year 1807." *Philadelphia Medical and Physical Journal* 3 (1806): 26–35.

Shields, Rob. *Places on the Margin: Alternative Geographies of Modernity.* New York: Routledge, 1991.

Silko, Leslie Marmon. *Yellow Woman and a Beauty of Spirit: Essays on Native American Life Today.* New York: Simon and Schuster, 1996.

Simon, Janice. "'Naked Wastes . . . Glorious Woods': The Forest View of the White Mountains." *Historical New Hampshire* 54.3–4 (1999): 93–106.

Slosson, Annie Trumbull. *Fishin' Jimmy.* New York: C. Scribner's Sons, 1898.

Solnit, Rebecca. *Wanderlust: A History of Walking.* New York: Viking, 2000.

Spaulding, John H. *Historical Relics of the White Mountains* [1855]. Reprinted, Littleton, New Hampshire: Bondcliff Books, 1998.

Spirn, Anne Whiston. *The Language of Landscape.* New Haven, Connecticut: Yale University Press, 1998.

Stowe, William. "'Oh, the Land's All Right!': Henry James and American Nature in Chocorua, New Hampshire." Unpublished ms., 2001.

Strauss, David. "Toward a Consumer Culture: 'Adirondack Murray' and the Wilderness Vacation." *American Quarterly* 39.2 (1987): 270–86.

Sweetser, Moses Foster. *Views in the White Mountains.* Portland, Maine: Chisolm Brothers, 1879.

———. *The White Mountains: A Handbook for Travellers* [1876]. Reprinted, Boston: Ticknor, 1888.

Taylor, Alan. *Liberty Men and Great Proprietors: The Revolutionary Settlement on the Maine Frontier, 1760–1820.* Chapel Hill: University of North Carolina Press, 1990.

Thomas, Mary Jane. "Reminiscences of the White Mountains." Edited by Harriet S. Lacy. *Historical New Hampshire* 28.1 (1973): 37–52.

Thomashow, Mitchell. *Ecological Identity: Becoming a Reflective Environmentalist.* Cambridge, Massachusetts: MIT Press, 1995.

Thoreau, Henry David, John Burroughs, John Muir, Bradford Torrey, Dallas Lore Sharp, and Olive Thorne Miller. *In American Fields and Forests.* Boston: Houghton Mifflin, 1909.

Tichi, Cecelia. *New World, New Earth: Environmental Reform in American Literature from Puritans through Whitman.* New Haven, Connecticut: Yale University Press, 1979.

Tocqueville, Alexis de. *Democracy in America.* New York: Vintage Books, 1945.

Tolles, Bryant F., Jr. *The Grand Resort Hotels of the White Mountains: A Vanishing Architectural Legacy.* Boston: David R. Godine, 1998.

Tompkins, Jane. *Sensational Designs: The Cultural Work of American Fiction, 1790–1860.* New York: Oxford University Press, 1985.

———. *West of Everything: The Inner Life of Westerns.* New York: Oxford University Press, 1992.

Torrey, Bradford. *Footing It in Franconia.* Boston: Houghton Mifflin: 1901.

———. *A Rambler's Lease.* Boston: Houghton Mifflin, 1889.

Tuan, Yi-Fu. *Space and Place: The Perspective of Experience.* Minneapolis: University of Minnesota Press, 1977.

Tuckerman, Frederick. "Gleanings from the Visitors' Albums of Ethan Allen Crawford." *Appalachia* 14 (1919): 377–82.

Turner, Frederick. *Spirit of Place: The Making of an American Literary Landscape.* San Francisco: Sierra Club Books, 1989.

Turner, Frederick Jackson. *The Frontier in American History.* New York: Henry Holt, 1920.

Urry, John. *The Tourist Gaze: Leisure and Travel in Contemporary Societies.* London, U.K.: Sage Publications, 1990.

Vance, James E., Jr. "Democratic Utopia and the American Landscape." In *The Making of the American Landscape,* edited by Michael P. Conzen, 204–20. Boston: Unwin Hyman, 1990.

Varney, Marion L. *Hart's Location in Crawford Notch: New Hampshire's Smallest Town.* Portsmouth, New Hampshire: Peter E. Randall, 1997.

Vizenor, Gerald. *Manifest Manners: Postindian Warriors of Survivance.* Hanover, New Hampshire: University Press of New England, 1994.

Wade, Mason, ed. *The Journals of Francis Parkman.* New York: Harper and Brothers, 1947.

Walker, Joseph B. *An Address upon the Forests of New Hampshire Delivered before Several Meetings Held under the Auspices of the Board of Agriculture, during the Winter of 1871–72.* Manchester, New Hampshire: Campbell and Hanscom, 1872.

———. *Our New Hampshire Forests: An Address Delivered at a Meeting of the New Hampshire Board of Agriculture Holden at Concord, on the 11th and 12th of February 1891.* Concord, New Hampshire: Ira C. Evans, 1891.

Wallace, R. Stuart. "A Social History of the White Mountains." In *The White Mountains: Place and Perceptions,* edited by Catherine H. Campbell, Donald D. Keyes, Robert L. McGrath, and R. Stuart Wallace, 17–38. Durham, New Hampshire: University Press of New England, 1980.

Wallach, Alan. "Making a Picture from Mount Holyoke." In *American Iconology: New Approaches to Nineteenth-Century Art and Literature,* edited by David C. Miller, 80–91. New Haven, Connecticut: Yale University Press, 1993.

Ward, Julius H. *The White Mountains: A Guide to Their Interpretation.* Boston: Houghton Mifflin, 1896.

Waterman, Guy, and Laura Waterman. *Forest and Crag: A History of Hiking, Trail Blazing, and Adventure in the Northeast Mountains.* Boston: Appalachian Mountain Club, 1989.

———. "Reverends, Soldiers, Scientists: The Belknap-Cutler Ascent of Mount Washington, 1784." *Appalachia* 45 (Summer 1984): 41–52.

Watters, David H. "'Build Soil': Language, Literature, and Landscape in New Hampshire." In *At What Cost? Shaping the Land We Call New Hampshire: A Land Use History,* edited by Richard Ober, 61–73. Concord, New Hampshire: New Hampshire Historical Society, 1992.

Weinstein, Cindy. *The Literature of Labor and the Labors of Literature: Allegory in Nineteenth-Century American Fiction.* Cambridge, U.K.: Cambridge University Press, 1995.

Weld, Isaac, Jr. *Travels through the States of North America, and the Provinces of*

Lower Canada, during the Years 1795, 1796, and 1797. 2 vols. London, U.K.: John Stockdale, 1807.

Wessels, Tom. *Reading the Forested Landscape: A Natural History of New England.* Woodstock, Vermont: Countryman Press, 1997.

Westbrook, Perry D. *A Literary History of New England.* Bethlehem, Pennsylvania: Lehigh University Press, 1988.

White, Richard. *The Organic Machine: The Remaking of the Columbia River.* New York: Hill and Wang, 1995.

Whitman, Cedric. *Chocorua and Other Poems.* Dublin, New Hampshire: William L. Bauhan, 1983.

Whitman, M. F. "A Climb through Tuckerman's Ravine." *Appalachia* 1.3 (1877): 132–37.

Willey, Benjamin G. *Incidents in White Mountain History.* Boston: Nathaniel Noyes, 1856.

Willis, Nathaniel P. *American Scenery; or, Land, Lake, and River: Illustrations of Transatlantic Nature.* London, U.K.: George Virtue, 1840.

Wilson, Alexander. *The Culture of Nature: North American Landscape from Disney to the "Exxon Valdez."* Cambridge, U.K.: Blackwell, 1992.

Wilson, Harold Fisher. *The Hill Country of Northern New England: Its Social and Economic History, 1790–1930.* New York: Columbia University Press, 1936.

Winthrop, John. *The History of New England from 1630 to 1649.* Boston: Little, Brown, 1853.

Wong, Hertha Dawn. *Sending My Heart Back across the Years: Traditions and Innovation in Native American Autobiography.* New York: Oxford University Press, 1992.

Worster, Donald. *Nature's Economy: A History of Ecological Ideas.* New York: Cambridge University Press, 1977.

Zanger, Jane. "A Greek-like Tragedy in New Hampshire: Literary and Artistic Manifestations of Chocorua." M.A. thesis, Dartmouth College, 1992.

Zuckerman, Mary Ellen. *A History of Popular Women's Magazines in the United States, 1792–1995.* Westport, Connecticut: Greenwood Press, 1998.

Abenaki Indians, 1, 12, 71
Abram, David, xx, 131, 157n17
Adirondacks, 118, 122, 140
Agiocochook. *See* Mount Washington
agrarianism. *See* farming
Allen, Ethan, 85
Anderson, John, 69, 87, 94
Appalachia (journal), 53, 93, 105, 134, 139,
    140, 156n3
Appalachian Mountain Club, xxii, xxv,
    93, 105, 107–8, 132–34, 136–40, 156n3
Appalachian Trail, 108
Atkinson, Brooks, 103, 146
Audubon, John James, 91
Austin, Nicholas, 4

Bartlett, William Henry, xvii
Barton, Nancy, 31, 49–50, 68
Bartram, William, xxiii, 4–5, 14–16, 20
Beecher, Henry Ward, 57, 112, 115, 117–
    18, 122, 136, 153n23
Belknap, Jeremy, xvi, xxi, 149n4;
    Belknap-Cutler Expedition, xxiii, 1–
    25, 28, 80, 149n3; ecological aware-
    ness, 8, 15–16, 18, 24, 77, 134, 141; em-
    piricism, 5, 8, 131; *The Foresters*, 5; as
    proto-tourist, 57; and sublime, 4, 12,
    21, 90, 131
Berry, Nathaniel, 104, 110–11, 115
Berry, Wendell, 147
Bierstadt, Albert, xvii, 19, 73–76, 80, 117
Binney, Amos, 151n4
biophilia, xxi
Bishop, William Henry, 121–22
Bolles, Frank, xxii, xxv, 109–16, 118–21,
    131; Crowlands, 115–16; "Deserted
    Homes," 120, 137; environmentalism,

76, 107, 140, 144, 146; "A Lost Trail,"
    104, 110–11; tourist-resident relation-
    ship, 107, 134, 136–37
Brazer, John, 26–30, 47
Brown, Alice, 112
Brown, Dona, 40, 44–46, 65, 67, 86, 91,
    113
Browning, Elizabeth Barrett, 68, 139
Bryant, William Cullen, 39
Buell, Lawrence, xvi, 10, 14, 118
Bulkley, Peter B., 154n10
Burke, Edmund, 4–5, 21, 30
Burroughs, John, 112, 119
Byron, Lord, 30, 39, 40, 68

Campbell, Mary, 131, 157n17
Campton, N.H., 19, 59–60, 129
Carrigain, Philip, 28, 151n7
Catskills, 122
Champney, Benjamin, 8, 99, 113, 149–
    50n5, 154n8; *Mount Washington from
    the Intervale*, 71–74
Cherry Mountain Slide. *See* Stanley
    Slide
Child, Lydia Maria, 84–86, 155n13
Chisolm, Hugh, 98
Church, Frederick, 113
Civil War (U.S.), 74, 82, 117, 131
class relationships: environment and,
    107; tourist and resident, 26, 30, 41–
    45, 132, 137, 154n10; urban and rural,
    56, 115
Clemens, Samuel, 135
Clifford, James, xix
Cole, Thomas, xvii, 90, 113, 150n5; "Essay
    on American Scenery," 29, 34, 39; and
    Hudson River School, 71; and Mount

Chocorua, 83, 85–86; and Mount Washington landscape, 8; role of residents in paintings, 71

conservation, 95–96, 100–1, 140–41, 146, 157n20

Cook, Edith, 107, 133, 134, 138, 140

Cook, Eugene Beauharnais, 133

Cooper, James Fenimore, 91

Cooper, Susan Fenimore, 74

Copp, Dolly, 138

Crawford, Abel, 8–9, 26, 69, 150n2, 154n6

Crawford, Ethan Allen, xxiii, 26, 29, 32, 43–44, 78, 97–98, 136, 151n2

Crawford family, 26, 31–32, 44–45, 48, 69, 78, 86, 90, 118

Crawford, Frederick, 37

Crawford House, 29, 42, 45–46, 64, 68, 78

Crawford, Lucy, xx–xxi, xxiii, 25, 97–98, 136, 138–39, 146, 151n2, 153n23; authority of, 32, 37–38, 42; critique of tourism, 41–42, 98; *History of the White Mountains* (1846), xxiv, 30–32, 35–57; *History of the White Mountains* (1860), 37–42, 47–57, 68, 107; illustrations, 51–52; land speculation, 118; publication history, 36–37, 64

Crawford Notch, 6, 32–36, 96–98, 150n1; descriptions of, 21, 34, 50, 68; as tourist destination, xv, 25–26, 45–46, 136; Willey Slide, 89–92, 95

Crawford Path, 33, 35–36, 109

Crawford, Tom, 46

Crevecoeur, Hector St. John de, 16, 32, 34, 44

Cronon, William, 39

Cutler, Manasseh, 1, 4, 14–16, 18, 20, 28, 77, 131, 150n7

Dawson, George, 26–30, 47

de Certeau, Michel, 10, 17, 150n8

development, 22–23, 57, 70, 76, 136, 145; Crawfords' role in, 30, 32, 45; critique of, 99–100; hotels and, 106, 108, 129; railways and, 64

Dickerman, Mike, 104

Divine Comedy (Dante), 101

Drake, Samuel, xxiv, 71, 76–77, 80–83, 114, 117

Durand, Asher, 74

Dwight, Timothy, xvi, 23, 31, 33–34, 43, 146; and Eleazer Rosebrook, 5–6, 46–47, 73, 106

Eastman, Samuel, 90

ecological awareness, 57, 83, 96, 105, 108, 123–26, 133, 137, 144

Ehrlich, Gretel, 78, 119

Elder, John, 36, 143, 146

Emerson, Ralph Waldo, 9, 39

Erdrich, Louise, 86

Evans, John, 4

Evernden, Neil, 46

exploration, 131, 149n2, 150n11

Fabyan, Horace, 89

farming, 97, 100, 104, 106–7, 110, 133, 135–37, 147; as agrarian enterprise, 6, 23, 31, 33–34, 72–73, 115, 117; hardship and, 32, 46, 92–93, 118, 120–22; romanticized, 89, 115–16

Fay, Charles, xxii, 105, 107–8, 146, 156n3

Field, Darby, 1–2, 3, 14, 25, 118

Fisher, Philip, 5

forest fires, 133–34, 136, 137

Forest Reserve Act, 141

Foss, Sam Walter, 120

Franklin, Wayne, xix

Frost, George Albert, 60

Frost, Robert, 36, 120–21, 137, 143

Garland, Richard, 46

Gerry, Samuel, 60, 61

Gibson, W. Hamilton, 80–81

Goethe, Johann Wolfgang von, 39, 68

Gorges, Ferdinand, 2

Gorges, Thomas, 2

Greenfield, Bruce, 3, 125
Greenleaf, Charles H., 79
Gregory, Derek, 20, 150n12

Hale, Sarah Josepha, 40, 55
Hall, Basil, xvii
Hall, Joseph Fred, 85
Harkness, Marjory Gene, 103
Hawthorne, Nathaniel, xv, xvii, xxii, 9, 25, 29, 44, 87 – 88, 146
Haycox, Stephen, 6
Hazlitt, William, 35, 135
Hazzard, Ebenezer, 10
Henck, J. B., Jr.,134
Henry (J. E.) Logging Company, 100, 133
hiking, 35 – 36, 59, 82, 103 – 5, 125; as antidote to city life, 127, 117 – 18; as middle-class pastime, 132; popularity of, 63, 107 – 10, 128 – 29; women and, 53 – 55, 133 – 40
Hill, Edward, 19, 60
Hill, Thomas, 74, 76
Hitchcock, Charles, xx, 61, 93 – 94, 98, 134; *Geology of New Hampshire*, 128 – 31, 151n6, 153n1; critique of tourism, 129
Hodgdon, Sylvester, 8, 150n5
Homer, Winslow, 76 – 77
hotels, xxii, 63; grand resort hotels, 46, 79 – 80, 106, 114, 122, 132, 154n11, 156n7, 157n18; middle-class inns, 129, 132, 135
Hough, Franklin B., 141
Hudson River School, 31, 71, 78
Huntington, Joshua, 94, 130 – 31

iconology, 152n18
Inness, George, 8, 150n5

Jackson, Charles, 94
James, Henry, 116, 155n13
Jefferson, N.H., 12, 92, 94
Jefferson, Thomas, xxiii, 5, 6, 13 – 14, 16, 44, 117

Jewett, Sarah Orne, 112
Johnson, David, 19, 76
Josselyn, John, xxiv, 1 – 3, 8, 16, 24, 27 – 28, 106, 149n1
Judd, Sylvester, 137, 154n9

Kendall, Edward Augustus, xvi, 8, 22 – 24, 27, 31, 33, 35, 146
Kensett, John Frederick, 8, 72 – 74, 150n5
Kilbourne, Frederick, 47, 94
Kolodny, Annette, 52 – 53, 56
Koop, Jennifer, 132

LaBastille, Anne, 108
Lancastrians, 43, 153n20 – 22
Lander, Dawn, 138
landscape: defined, 17, 23 – 24, 113; in painting, 34, 42 – 43, 71 – 77
Larcom, Lucy, xxii, 76, 122
Little, Daniel, 6, 13, 16, 18, 20
logging, 95 – 97, 100, 103, 109, 133, 136 – 37, 144 – 45
Longfellow, Henry Wadsworth, 39, 85
Lowell, James Russell, 39, 119

magazines, 29, 55, 89, 121, 138
maps, 53, 57, 60 – 61, 153n20; hiking, 108 – 9, 134, 139, 157n19; pretourist, 10 – 12, 27 – 28
Marsh, George Perkins, xxi, 16, 74, 83, 100, 107, 140 – 41, 146; description of Willey Slide, 95 – 97
Marshall, Ian, 108
Marx, Leo, 6
McCannell, Dean, 29, 118
McGrath, Robert, xvii, 41
McKay, Charles, 68
Merrill, Amos, 135
Merrill House, 135
Meyer, Kinereth, 119 – 20
Miller, Angela, 26
Mitchell, John Hanson, xviii, 105
Mitchell, W. J .T., 17
Mont Blanc, 40

Morse, Stearns, 37, 39, 69, 87, 94

Mount Adams, 43

Mount Chocorua, 83, 103, 113, 119, 154n12; "Chocorua's Curse," 84–86

Mount Franklin, 43

Mount Fuji, 108

Mount Garfield, 143

Mount Jefferson, 43, 93

Mount Katahdin, 131

Mount Kineo, 63

Mount Lafayette, 128, 143, 145; bridle path to, 109

Mount Madison, 43

Mount Monadnock, 108

Mount Monroe, 43

Mount Moosilauke, 109

Mount Paugus, 103

Mount Pleasant (Mount Eisenhower), 43

Mount Wachusett, 114

Mount Washington, xxi, xxiii, 1, 12–14, 45; ascents, 26, 53–55, 68, 71–73, 78, 123–24, 128, 136, 155n20; naming of, 14, 16, 18, 25–26, 43, 109; trails of, 26, 35–36, 43, 53–55, 109, 114; Carriage Road, 16, 36, 45, 60, 62–63, 128–29; Cog Railway, 16, 36, 63, 78, 99–100, 123–24, 128–29

Mount Wildcat, 134

Mount Willard, 109, 128

Mudge, John, 49

Muir, John, 18, 20, 82, 105, 131

Murray, William "Adirondack," 55, 112, 115, 117–18, 122, 136, 140

Nash, Roderick, 91, 106

Nash, Timothy, 25, 33, 150n1

National Forest Service, xviii, 104

Native Americans, 38–39, 70–71, 111. See also Abenaki, Sokosis, Pequawket

newspapers, xxii, 55, 79, 92, 126, 155n20

Niagara Falls, 86, 141

Nowell, W. G., 53

Noyes, Nathaniel, 50–51, 153n3

Oakes, William, xxiii, 38

O'Grady, John, 42

Orr, David, 146

painting. See names of specific artists or schools

Park, John, 54–55

Park, Louisa Jane, 54

Parkman, Francis, 91, 155n14

Parsons, Thomas W., xxii, 88–90

pastoral, 20, 23–24, 89, 110, 113–16, 119, 137

Paulding, James K., 29

Pemigewassett Wilderness, 139, 157n14

Pequawket Indians, 85

Pequawket, N.H., 1, 156n6

Phenix, Alan, 156n8

Philbrook Farm, 132

picturesque, 19, 21, 33, 39, 41, 43, 60, 65, 72–74, 89, 110, 113–14, 137

Poole, Ernest, 94

population, 151n9

Pratt, Henry Cheever, 86, 90

Pratt, Mary Louise, 24, 79

preservation, xxi–xxii, xxv, 83, 91, 96–98, 105, 128, 136, 140–41, 146

Presidential Range, 10, 66, 70, 92, 137, 139

Prime, William C., 112, 122

Profile House, 60, 79, 122, 125

Purchase, Eric, 16, 42, 45, 86, 89, 101

Pychowska, Lucia, xxii, 136, 138–39

Pychowska, Marian, xxii, xxv, 76, 93, 107, 133–40

railroads, 93, 98–99, 106, 133, 141

Randolph, N.H., 97, 129, 132

Ravine House, 132

Regis, Pamela, 4

Ripley, Henry Wheelock, 32, 36, 51, 69, 154n6

Rorty, Richard, 22

Rosebrook, Eleazer, xvi, xxiv, 25, 31, 33, 35, 46, 56, 106, 150n2

Rowan, June Hammond, 133

Rowan, Peter, 133
Ruskin, John, 80, 91
Russell House, 132
Ryden, Kent, 123, 125

Sandwich Range, 103
Sawyer, Benjamin, 25, 33, 150n1
scientific writing. *See* Jeremy Belknap, John Josselyn, Charles Hitchcock
Scott, Sir Walter, 39
Sews, John, 86
Shapleigh, Frank, 60
Shattuck, Aaron, 74
Shelley, Percy Bysshe, 30, 39, 40
Shields, Robert, 42
Silko, Leslie Marmon, xviii, 111, 124
Simon, Janice, 74
Slosson, Annie Trumbull, xxii, 78, 107, 112, 115, 122, 128, 134, 144; as entomologist, 78; stories of Fishin' Jimmy, 126
Smith, John, 2
Society for the Protection of New Hampshire Forests, 122, 140
Sokosis Indians, 103, 155n1
Solnit, Rebecca, 132
Spaulding, John, xvii, xxiii, 44, 64, 127; description of Willey Slide, 87, 90; intertextuality and, 38–39, 48, 152n17
Spear, Waldo, 117
Spirn, Anne Whiston, 17, 24, 150n10
Stanley Slide, 92–94, 155n17–18
Steiner, Michael, xix
Stone, Isabella, xxii, xxv, 76, 93, 107, 133–140, 157n21
Stowe, Harriet Beecher, 51
Stowe, William, 155n13
sublime, 37, 39–40, 43, 47, 54, 114, 118; defined, 21, 28; empiricism and, 4, 12; and Willey Slide, 91–92, 95–96
Sweetser, Moses, xvii, xxiii, 55, 64, 71, 76–77; critique of tourism, 98–100

Taft, Richard, 79
Tamworth, N.H., 103, 110, 114, 122, 144

Tennyson, Alfred Lord, 39
Thackery, Emily, 55
Thomas, Mary Jane, 45
Thompson, Allen, 127–28, 134, 157n14
Thoreau, Henry David, xvii, xxi–xxii, 112, 118–19, 131–32, 134, 143–46; environmentalism, 83, 91, 107; use of Belknap, 9, 19; "Walking," 123; and White Mountain landscape, 17–18, 76
Tidd, Marshall M., 51
Torrey, Bradford, xxii, xxv, 76, 107, 112, 115, 122–26, 134; environmentalism, 140, 144
tourism, 116, 151–52n14; Crawfords and, 27–31, 33, 38, 42, 48, 51; growth of, 63, 129; as rural vacation, 117–18; spectacle and, 86, 93–94. *See also specific places and events*
trails, 33, 35–36, 63, 109–10, 137, 157n21
Tuan, Yi-Fu, 9–10
Tuckerman, Edward, 67–69, 95
Turner, Charles L., 152n15
Turner, Frederick Jackson, xxi, 32, 106, 114

Vance, James Jr., 33

Walker, Joseph B., 100, 141
walking, 105, 109, 131–32
Wallace, Stuart, 135
Walling, H. F., 134
Ward, Julius, xvii
Warren, N.H., 135
Washington, George, 14
Waterman, Guy and Laura, 33, 35, 118, 128–29
Weeks Act, xvii, 101, 140–41
Weld, Isaac, 21
Wentworth, John, 3, 150n1
Wessels, Tom, 121
Whipple, Joseph, 12
White Hills (King), xvii, xxi, xxiii, 19, 44, 57, 154n4; Chocorua, 83–85; critique of tourism, xx, 78, 96–98; envi-

ronmental awareness, xxiv, 47–
48, 67, 69, 76, 95, 97, 99; landscape
description, 65–67, 73, 88, 107, 113;
literary associations, 39–40, 67–71,
152n17; marginalization of residents
in, 73; Willey Slide description, 88–
91
White Mountain Echo, 55, 92–93, 126–
28
White Mountain National Forest, 92,
101, 143–44
White Mountain Notch. *See* Crawford
Notch
White Mountain residents, 125, 127
White Mountain School, 31, 71–76,
154n8
Whitman, Cedric, 85
Whitman, M. F., 132, 140
Whittier, John Greenleaf, xxii, 39, 84,
96–97, 122
wilderness, 14, 71, 85, 104–10, 114–18,
124–25, 146; development of, 6, 23,
33, 41–44, 57, 73, 91, 100, 127–28, 133;
ecology of, 15; exploration of, 131, 138–
39; inaccessibility of, 3, 4, 7; protec-
tion of, 141, 144; rhetoric of, 25, 68, 80;
settlers in, 39, 78; sublime and, 47
Will, Thomas, 100
Willey, Benjamin, xxiii, 38, 44, 56, 67, 77,
85, 88–89, 114
Willey family, 69–70
Willey Slide, 31, 48, 69, 70, 86–96
Williams, William Carlos, 120
Willis, Nathaniel, xvii, 29
Wilson, Alexander, 79
Winthrop, John, 1–2, 3
women: climbers and hikers, 53–55,
108, 133, 138; readers, 55–57, 153n25;
writers, 56, 139. *See also* Lucy Craw-
ford, Marian and Lucia Pychowska,
Isabella Stone, M. F. Whitman, Edith
Cook
Wong, Hertha, 32
Wood, William, 2
Wordsworth, William, 30, 39, 40, 68

Yellowstone National Park, 141

Zanger, Jane, 154n12

Bachelor Bess:
The Homesteading Letters of Elizabeth Corey, 1909–1919
Edited by Philip L. Gerber

Botanical Companions:
A Memoir of Plants and Place
By Frieda Knobloch

Circling Back:
Chronicle of a Texas River Valley
By Joe C. Truett

Edge Effects: Notes from an Oregon Forest
By Chris Anderson

Exploring the Beloved Country:
Geographic Forays into American Society and Culture
By Wilbur Zelinsky

Father Nature: Fathers as Guides to the Natural World
Edited by Paul S. Piper and Stan Tag

The Follinglo Dog Book: From Milla to Chip the Third
By Peder Gustav Tjernagel

Great Lakes Lumber on the Great Plains:
The Laird, Norton Lumber Company in South Dakota
By John N. Vogel

Hard Places:
Reading the Landscape of America's Historic Mining Districts
By Richard V. Francaviglia

Landscape with Figures:
Scenes of Nature and Culture in New England
By Kent C. Ryden

Living in the Depot: The Two-Story Railroad Station
By H. Roger Grant

Main Street Revisited:
Time, Space, and Image Building in Small-Town America
By Richard V. Francaviglia

Mapping American Culture
Edited by Wayne Franklin and Michael C. Steiner

Mapping the Invisible Landscape:
Folklore, Writing, and the Sense of Place
By Kent C. Ryden

Mountains of Memory:
A Fire Lookout's Life in the River of No Return Wilderness
By Don Scheese

The People's Forests
By Robert Marshall

Pilots' Directions:
The Transcontinental Airway and Its History
Edited by William M. Leary

Places of Quiet Beauty:
Parks, Preserves, and Environmentalism
By Rebecca Conard

Reflecting a Prairie Town: A Year in Peterson
Text and photographs by Drake Hokanson

Rooted: Seven Midwest Writers of Place
By David R. Pichaske

A Rural Carpenter's World:
The Craft in a Nineteenth-Century New York Township
By Wayne Franklin

Salt Lantern: Traces of an American Family
By William Towner Morgan

Signs in America's Auto Age:
Signatures of Landscape and Place
John A. Jakle and Keith A. Sculle

This Vast Book of Nature:
Writing the Landscape of New Hampshire's
White Mountains, 1784 – 1911
By Pavel Cenkl

Thoreau's Sense of Place:
Essays in American Environmental Writing
Edited by Richard J. Schneider